The Experimental Self

Ad Feminam: Women and Literature
Edited by Sandra M. Gilbert

Christina Rossetti
The Poetry of Endurance
By Dolores Rosenblum

Lunacy of Light
Emily Dickinson and the Experience of Metaphor
By Wendy Barker

The Literary Existence of Germaine de Staël
By Charlotte Hogsett

Margaret Atwood
Vision and Forms
Edited by Kathryn VanSpanckeren and Jan Garden Castro

He Knew She Was Right
The Independent Woman in the Novels of Anthony Trollope
By Jane Nardin

The Woman and the Lyre
Women Writers in Classical Greece and Rome
By Jane McIntosh Snyder

Refiguring the Father
New Feminist Readings of Patriarchy
Edited by Patricia Yaeger and Beth Kowaleski-Wallace

Writing in the Feminine
Feminism and Experimental Writing in Quebec
By Karen Gould

Rape and Writing in the Heptaméron *of Marguerite de Navarre*
By Patricia Francis Cholakian

Writing Love: Letters, Women, and the Novel in France, 1605–1776
By Katharine Ann Jensen

The Body and the Song
Elizabeth Bishop's Poetics
By Marilyn May Lombardi

Millay at 100
A Critical Reappraisal
Edited by Diane P. Freedman

The Experimental Self
Dialogic Subjectivity
in Woolf, Pym, and
Brooke-Rose

Judy Little

Southern Illinois University Press
Carbondale and Edwardsville

Copyright © 1996 by Judy Little
All rights reserved
Printed in the United States of America
Designed by Joyce Kachergis

99 98 97 96   4 3 2 1

Illustrations on title page: *Left to right*, Virginia Woolf, reprinted by permission of The Bettmann Archive; Barbara Pym, courtesy of Hilary Walton; Christine Brooke-Rose, courtesy of Christine Brooke-Rose.

An earlier version of a portion of chapter 2 is reprinted from "Feminizing the Subject: Dialogic Narration in *Jacob's Room*," *LIT* 3 (1992): 241–51, with permission of Gordon and Breach Science Publishers. Earlier versions of portions of chapter 4 are reprinted from "S(t)imulating Origins: Self-Subversion in the Early Brooke-Rose Texts," in *Utterly Other Discourse: The Texts of Christine Brooke-Rose*, edited by Ellen G. Friedman and Richard Martin (Dalkey Archive Press, 1995), 64–75, courtesy of the publisher; and from "*Amalgamemnon* and the Politics of Narrative," *Review of Contemporary Fiction* 9 (fall 1989): 134–37, with permission of the publisher.

Library of Congress Cataloging-in-Publication Data

Little, Judy, 1941–
    The experimental self : dialogic subjectivity in Woolf, Pym, and Brooke-Rose / Judy Little.
        p.   cm. — (Ad feminam)
    Includes bibliographical references and index.
    1. English fiction—20th century—History and criticism.
    2. Experimental fiction—Great Britain—History and criticism.
    3. Women and literature—Great Britain—History—20th century.
    4. English fiction—Women authors—History and criticism. 5. Brooke-Rose, Christine, 1923– —Technique. 6. Woolf, Virginia, 1882–1941—Technique. 7. Authorship—Sex differences. 8. Subjectivity in literature. 9. Pym, Barbara—Technique. 10. Self in literature.
    11. Fiction—Technique. 12. Literary form. I. Title. II. Series.
PR888.W6L58   1996
823'.9109'082—dc20   95-53744
ISBN 0-8093-2061-4   CIP

The paper used in this publication meets the minimum requirements of American National Standard for Information Sciences—Permanence of Paper for Printed Library Materials, ANSI Z39.48-1984. ∞

For Frances Little Gier
origin
and experimental self

Contents

Ad Feminam: Women and Literature   ix
Sandra M. Gilbert

Preface   xi

1   *Subjectivity and Appositional Discourse*   1
2   *Virginia Woolf*   25
      Feminizing the Symbolic
3   *Barbara Pym*   76
      Textualizing the Trivial
4   *Christine Brooke-Rose*   122
      S(t)imulating Origins
5   *Conclusion*   158
      The Implied Critic

Notes   167
Works Cited   187
Index   201

Ad Feminam:
Women and Literature

> Ad Hominem: to the man; appealing to personal interests, prejudices, or emotions rather than to reason; *an argument ad hominem.*
> —*American Heritage Dictionary*

Until quite recently, much literary criticism, like most humanistic studies, has been in some sense constituted out of arguments *ad hominem.* Not only have examinations of literary history tended to address themselves "to the man"—that is, to the identity of what was presumed to be the *man* of letters who created our culture's monuments of unaging intellect—but many aesthetic analyses and evaluations have consciously or unconsciously appealed to the "personal interests, prejudices, or emotions" of male critics and readers. As the title of this series is meant to indicate, the intellectual project called "feminist criticism" has sought to counter the limitations of *ad hominem* thinking about literature by asking a series of questions addressed *ad feminam:* to the woman as both writer and reader of texts.

First, and most crucially, feminist critics ask, What is the relationship between gender and genre, between sexuality and textuality? But in meditating on these issues they raise a number of more specific questions. Does a woman of letters have a literature—a language, a history, a tradition—of her own? Have conventional methods of canon-formation tended to exclude or marginalize female achievements? More generally, do men and women have different modes of literary representation, different definitions of literary production? Do such differences mean that distinctive male- (or female-) authored images of women (or men), as well as distinctly male and female genres, are part of our intellectual heritage? Perhaps most important, are literary differences between men and women essential or accidental, biologically determined or culturally constructed?

Feminist critics have addressed themselves to these problems with increasing sophistication during the last two decades, as they sought to revise, or at times replace, *ad hominem* arguments with *ad feminam* speculations. Whether explicating individual texts, studying the oeuvre of a single author, examining the permutations of a major theme, or charting the contours of a tradition, these theorists and scholars have consistently sought to define literary manifestations of difference and to understand the dynamics that have shaped the accomplishments of literary women.

As a consequence of such work, feminist critics, often employing new modes of analysis, have begun to uncover a neglected female tradition along with a heretofore hidden history of the literary dialogue between men and women. This series is dedicated to publishing books that will use innovative as well as traditional interpretive methods in order to help readers of both sexes achieve a clearer consciousness of that neglected but powerful tradition and a better understanding of that hidden history. Reason tells us, after all, that if, transcending prejudice and special pleading, we speak to, and focus on, the woman as well as the man—if we think *ad feminam* as well as *ad hominem*—we will have a better chance of understanding what constitutes the human.

Sandra M. Gilbert

Preface

In the broadest sense, this book finds its origin in the interpretive community of scholars and teachers who are still responding to recent sea changes in literary theory, especially the invigorating changes that these theories have produced in everything from reading a text to reading politics to reading feminism. I am a convert to the new academic discourse, yet a convert who is concerned less with theology than with the old songs (and the new ones). That is, I will be using theory in this study primarily as a reading strategy, although chapter 1 (and some later notes) will refer readers to discussions of those admittedly important philosophical issues such as Mikhail Bakhtin's relevance (or irrelevance) for feminism and the formidable issue of whether there may be really (and in what sense) a feminine language and a masculine language. These are important issues, but my study of Woolf, Pym, and Brooke-Rose is chiefly concerned with how these and other issues play out textually—and they do play.

This approach means that I have tried to limit my use of recent theory's inkhorn terms and certainly to avoid overuse of those "nyce and straunge" words, which Chaucer feared (in *Troilus and Criseyde*) that future readers might not understand. Yet I am pleased to thank the English Department's "theory group" for our years of lively, even contentious, dialogue about these "straunge" words and theories. I am especially grateful to Mary Lamb, Iris Smith, and Clarisse Zimra for many hours of invigorating challenge and delight. We are still friends, even though I was more interested in learning (and practicing) how to "do things with theory" than in speaking in metatongues. I appreciate the fact that the group did not deny me communion, even when my attitude was less than reverential.

I am also happy to acknowledge a wider circle of colleagues who have contributed more than they realize to the growth and process of this book. Regina Barreca's affirmative response to my analysis of *Jacob's Room* let me know that I was on the right track. I am especially grateful to Richard Martin for including my paper in the special session on Christine Brooke-Rose at the 1987 MLA convention. I wish also to thank Ellen Friedman and Miriam Fuchs for their encouragement with my work on Brooke-Rose's novels.

My more pragmatic acknowledgment goes to Southern Illinois University for granting me a sabbatical and later a part-time leave, both of which gave me extended periods for work. I am also grateful to the University's Office of Research and Development for the funding of two projects that became part of this book. In addition, the College of Liberal Arts generously supplied funds and personnel at a critical moment. Our former department chair, Richard Peterson, and the assistant to the chair, Betty Mitchell, have even more generously treated all my moments as critical. I appreciate their moral support. I wish to thank Pauline Duke for typing the manuscript initially, and I appreciate also the diligent editors at the Southern Illinois University Press, especially Carol Burns, Rebecca Spears Schwartz, and James Simmons. I am particularly grateful to my recent typist, Eileen Glass, whose energy, accuracy, and gracious interface skills have kept her on friendly terms with both the computer and me.

More difficult to thank (because it is impossible to thank them enough) are several quite special people who have understood why I have turned down invitations to visit (and haven't extended any) during vacation after vacation. Friends such as Lois Blotz and Sharon McWilliams have been very understanding about my need for a long-term room of my own when I am working. Sandra Freeman and Kay Kennedy have also been willing to substitute text (phone calls) for presence. Joan O'Brien has not (not always), but my many dialogic walks around the campus lake with her have encouraged me to take the long view concerning any textual gender shifts that might have occurred in Homeric times (feminine to masculine?) and any that might be occurring (masculine to feminine?) in ours. Finally, I am happy to dedicate this book to my mother; her confident and attentive inquiries about "your book" have often been responsible for "hailing" it into identity again.

The Experimental Self

1 *Subjectivity and Appositional Discourse*

People are hard to "sum up," as several of the experimental voices in Virginia Woolf's fiction observe. Other novelists and theorists declare that there is nothing to sum up, since the "self" and the "author" no longer exist; for the radical theorist, as Fredric Jameson notes, the subject never existed in the first place.[1] In twentieth-century fiction, the self and subjectivity have become problematic concepts. D. H. Lawrence rejected in his fiction the "old stable ego" of character, and E. M. Forster acknowledged that psychology had "split and shattered the idea of the 'Person,'" while Woolf declared that human character had changed around December 1910.[2] Putting into experimental practice his distinctive sense of the flexible concept of the self, James Joyce orchestrated the many-voiced *Finnegans Wake* where self slurs into self and the old stable ego dissolves in a salty sea of puns. More recently, Christine Brooke-Rose deconstructs the presumptions of agency and authorship as her puzzled characters in *Thru* try to ward off the comic frustration of having written each other.

Such experimental characters are hard to sum up, partly because they disclaim the "stable ego" of realism; they seem to acknowledge, even indulge in, their nonexistence, their written and flexible quality. They also are hard to sum up because their flexibility turns these unconventional voices into a dense complex of discourses, a mingling of several languages and ideologies. Even the more conventionally narrated "selves" in the novels of Barbara Pym (and other writers as well, such as E. M. Forster) often inscribe a rich dialogic play of discourse. Further, the narrated voices are not usually characterized by a discourse of "difference"—for instance, by a readily identifiable "feminine" language in conflict with a "masculine" one.

In the fiction of Woolf, Pym, and Brooke-Rose, the multiple discourses constituting the narrated self or subjectivity cannot always be described as binary or as polarized inscriptions of difference. Instead, the discourses are usually in *apposition* to each other. Rather than being poised oppositionally or even subversively, the implicit discourses amplify, explain, modify, or subtly transform each other. While there may be an occasional opposition, where one discourse subverts another, the experimental self that is the focus of this study is one constructed by discourses that are placed next to each other; they are in creative and transformative apposition.

The discourses that shape a character or self in the novels of Woolf, Pym, and Brooke-Rose tend to become new, experimental constructions. In a richly narrated work, there are often many more than two identifiable and different discourses. The Bakhtinian concept of "inner speech" (unspoken speech) affirms the variety of discourses available to reflection even if one's outer speech is more strictly directed to social and political expectation; yet inner speech also is socially constructed, being "the product of [one's] entire social life." In the novel especially, the resulting tension "between the external and the internal man," Mikhail Bakhtin notes in *The Dialogic Imagination*, means that "the subjectivity of the individual becomes an object of experimentation and representation," while discourse itself may form dialogic and "hybrid" constructions.[3]

Even though Pym's novels are not experimental in narrative style, they are experimental in their structure—or lack of it. Consistently examining the trivial (something by definition lacking importance, significant structure, or story), Pym's fiction browses through the nonstories, the nonendings—even a few comic nonstarters. Indeed, the popular idiom of these novels is in some ways very close to the richest mines of the dialogic as Bakhtin describes such resources; he focuses on the novel for his examination of the dialogic because the novel, he says, "is associated with the eternally living element of unofficial language and unofficial thought (holiday forms, familiar speech, profanation)" (*DI*,20). Though there is little profanation in Pym's work, there is the occasional carnivalization of church ritual, and her novels virtually consist of unofficial language and unofficial thought (with dialogic parodies of the "official" discourse). The very unofficial people in the novels of Pym are subtle, experimental selves, their dialogic subjectivities exploring more than one ideology or discourse, and these discourses are usually appositional rather than conflictual.

For these reasons, the fiction of Barbara Pym will be examined in this study. Her inclusion allows me to look at the experimental self in three generations of women writers who primarily construct characters or selves dialogically and appositionally rather than from discursive oppositions. In these writers, other textual strategies are related to this mode of characterization. For instance, the fiction of each shows not so much an opposition or (political) difference— between a voice or character and its society—as an apposition to the discourses of the culture. Because the political and discursive habitat of the self is central to my argument and to recent theory, I will develop in this chapter a brief defense of the idea of a subject as a complex of experimental appositions and especially as a dialogic individual.

The Implied Subject

The oppositional subject, or "opposing self," as Lionel Trilling called it, has enjoyed a long and still vigorous history, especially as a paradigm of the heroic male subject's relation to cultural institutions. Although writing before the advent of structuralism into the English-speaking world, Trilling is subtle in his acknowledgement of the intimate links between the imagination and the protested culture that at the same time structures that imagination; in figures like Arnold's Scholar Gypsy, or Keats as a hero-poet, this opposing self has an "intense and adverse imagination of the culture in which it has its being."[4] The rebellious impact of the adverse imagination is not restricted to patriarchal bureaucracies, to religious ideologies, or to the heroic achievements of dead poets; it also asserts an anxious difference from the world of women and especially from women of some achievement. While Harold Bloom has described the "anxiety" of each generation of (male) writers as they seek to distinguish their own voice from the persistent "influence" of older voices in the literary tradition, Sandra Gilbert and Susan Gubar emphasize in *No Man's Land* another manifestation of oppositional anxiety; modernists like T. S. Eliot sought to develop a discourse that would be special to them as men and thus link them to a *patrius sermo*, a patrocentric tradition of manly discourse, one that was apart from the incursions of women's voices into published fiction and poetry.[5]

The masculine opposing self is thus embattled on at least two fronts. It must secure a voice that can be heard above the great male voices of the past, and it must protect itself, by a strategy of "difference," from the voices and culture of women. Jacques Lacan's linguistic revision of Freud's concept of castration anxiety elaborates very well both aspects of an oppositional male subjectivity, a subjectivity that eventually identifies with the initially intrusive father (the Law of the Father) and his symbolic discourse, while establishing or inscribing women as "other," absence, as "lack," or as an "imaginary" pre-oedipal locus or construct of "difference."[6]

Commenting on the oppositional paradigm of male development, Nancy Chodorow offers an explanation for its prevalence. As she describes the developmental process, both boys and girls at first identify strongly with the mother (because she is still the primary caregiver in our society). The boy then must negotiate a major psychological shift by identifying with the father; the ego of the boy (and man) tends as a result to develop around this acknowledgement of difference. Both sexes, however, develop an identity through a process of differentiation, or "separation-individuation." Every child needs to perceive itself as an identity distinct from others; even so, for men the ordinary process of differentiation can sometimes lead to defensiveness, to a sense of "not feeling separate enough," and to difference.[7] Whatever the explanation for the oppositional stages and strategies in the development of men socially and linguistically, the opposing subjectivity, the generational anxiety, and the canonization of a *sermo patrius* are major and important structures in much of Western literature.

Occasionally, oppositional structures emerge in women's writing also, but the oppositional self and its binary political oppositions

Subjectivity and Appositional Discourse 5

are not my primary focus. Since the paradigm of oppositional difference has become the privileged or preferred model for recent literary studies, I do need to indicate briefly the usefulness of these theories and especially to point out their limitations. Theories of difference are prominent in the work of European feminists. Several women theorists have looked at the pre-oedipal linguistic potential implied in Lacan's theories and have claimed it as the site of various disruptive or distinctively feminine discourses. Julia Kristeva redefines Lacan's "imaginary" (the pre-oedipal realm of sound and sight before the Law of the Father intervenes) as the "semiotic," a playful discourse associated with the instinctual and the maternal; such nonpaternally structured "poetic language" Kristeva sees as having a renewing, disruptive, invigorating force. Similarly, Luce Irigaray and Hélène Cixous also emphasize the revolutionary, fluid, playful, disruptive potential of the unconventionally structured *écriture féminine*.[8]

Literary critics have further developed this notion of the feminine imaginary, a semiotic discourse, as a radically experimental language. Susan Friedman perceives a "lyric subversion" of the "masculine" narrative structures in Woolf's *To the Lighthouse*, while Makiko Minow-Pinkney, offering a Lacanian reading of that novel, argues that modernism, feminism, and the experimental were virtually the same concern for Woolf; in their book, on experimental writers, Ellen Friedman and Miriam Fuchs affirm that the experimental prose of Woolf, Richardson, Brooke-Rose, and others undermines certain "patriarchal assumptions" such as plot linearity and closure of action.[9] Yet male writers also use these "experimental" techniques, as Brooke-Rose points out.[10] So it is awkward to designate such strategies as distinctly female, or feminist. Indeed, Alice Jardine focuses on male authors in her study of a stylistically radical "gynesis," or feminine writing, and Woolf is the only female author whom Gabriele Schwab includes (with Joyce, Beckett, Melville, and Pynchon) in *Subjects Without Selves*, an examination of "poetic language" and the unconscious as the sources of modernist subjectivities and texts.[11]

Although theories of a feminine/feminist opposing self do offer some reading strategies that illuminate or privilege certain elements of a text that might otherwise be missed, theories of difference are limited as descriptions of complex modern texts and modern societies where the social structures of gender, ethnicity, and economic status mingle and overlap in many forms and combinations. Even if we isolate a radically unique style as experimental (and one that is either written by a woman or by a man who inscribes a "gynesis"), still the stylistically experimental (the semiotic, nonlinear, disruptive) does not necessarily write or invoke a revolutionary ideology. As Rita Felski argues in *Beyond Feminist Aesthetics*, the ambiguities of a semiotic discourse are not the exclusive medium of women writers or even of most radical political groups, the latter often preferring to attempt clarity and conviction; looking at the implicit politics of narrative, Brooke-Rose emphasizes that many experimental novels "are surprisingly phallocratic," and Marianne DeKoven perceives men giving their own "signature" to the "subversive cultural feminine" while ignoring the experimental work of women authors themselves.[12] An experimental style does not in itself indicate freedom from a conventional ideology that engenders oppositions, an ideology that privileges the male author (while proclaiming also the difference, the oppositional and supposedly feminine gynesis or *écriture*).

Further, theories that affirm an oppositional discourse (a different female subjectivity opposing a patriarchal social structure, or a conflicted single subjectivity constructed of masculine and feminine discourses) are a useful but often limited resource for describing the texts of women writers, especially recent women writers. In *Writing Beyond the Ending*, Rachel Blau DuPlessis argues that in many narratives written by women the "romance plot separates love and quest"; that is, for the major female character the middle-class discourse of the quest is "oppositional" for her gender.[13] Her cultural inscription prevents her from becoming both a woman and, say, an artist—unless the text is written "beyond the ending," beyond the "happy ending" of marriage.

One could argue, however, that the discursive mingling and jostlings in women's fiction are not so much conflicted or even subversive oppositions as they are dialogic appositions. That is, the once severely gendered pattern of quest (as male-only, virtually an archetypal *sermo patrius*) is now often in textual dialogue with the once securely feminine paradigm of romance, love, and relationship. It is after all significant that in the woman's text the quest is even there—juxtaposed appositionally with the discourses of romance. Although a critical theory of oppositional discourses is helpful (and I will occasionally require it), my central concern as I look at the complex, experimental selves in the texts of Woolf, Pym, and Brooke-Rose is with a dialogic mix of appositional discourses— discourses not readily or accurately identifiable in terms of the masculine/feminine opposition.

Nor are these dialogically mingled discourses readily assignable to a (supposedly patrocentric or even phallocratic) symbolic that is radically distinct from a feminine imaginary or semiotic. For several hundred years, women writers certainly have made creative use of literacy and literature; they have been appropriating the symbolic. Although several scholars, such as Patricia Yaeger and Dale Bauer, have found in women's writing much dialogic play *between* the imaginary and the symbolic,[14] there has been little acknowledgment of the dialogic play *within* and *among* the symbolic discourses that women writers are adapting and transforming. In her book on Virginia Woolf and Christa Wolf, Anne Herrmann moves toward a more subtle reading of dialogism when she emphasizes that dialogic discourse implies a subject speaking to a subject (and not to an object or other); Beth Rosenberg looks at Woolf's dialogic "conversation" with her predecessors, especially Samuel Johnson, as she formed her style, and Peter Hitchcock explores various symbolic discourses (working-class, "masculinist," racist, feminist, bourgeois) used by contemporary women authors in their construction of character and agency.[15] Women have begun to appropriate symbolic discourses, and their experimental revision of these languages does not always mean a nonlinear, semiotic play.

The woman novelist's continuing appropriation of the symbolic may mean that women simply have less regard for difference than men do. Margaret Homans emphasizes that Lacan's "myth of childhood" is a narrative of the son's movement into the symbolic order (and his painful concomitant break with the mother); the daughter, on the other hand, certainly does enter the symbolic order, but this entry is not accompanied by a crisis of renouncing the mother. Thus, the daughter "does not enter the symbolic order as wholeheartedly or exclusively as does the son." As a result, the daughter "speaks two languages at once."[16] I would argue that she speaks many more than two, since the symbolic world is multiple in any complex modern society.

If there is a distinctive feminine (semiotic? disruptive?) discourse or writing, that language also is multiple. Woolf said that women writers think back through their mothers—and she added that they think back through their fathers as well.[17] Both traditions are plural. Each offers a complex of languages, and the supposed difference between the two multiplexes is hard to sum up. Arguing that the discourse of nineteenth-century women was more literal and less figurative than male discourse, Homans employs the word *nonsymbolic* to designate this feminine literalness.[18] Obviously, the term *semiotic* would hardly be appropriate for a distinctly bare, literal discourse. Perhaps the paradoxical term *nonsymbolic* can help to describe a woman's distinctive use of representation, that is, of the symbolic (for even the literal is symbolic—a representation).

Most hypotheses that attempt to distinguish between male and female cultures and discourses are successful to the extent that they allow for enormous areas of overlap; that is, they avoid the binary oversimplification of a polarized difference. Developing Edwin Ardener's insight that the women's subculture in any given society tends to be muted, Elaine Showalter has emphasized that women belong to both the dominant (largely male-defined and administered) culture and to the less vocal subculture of women; women learn both cultures and hence speak a "double-voiced" language.[19] Exploring modern American society, psychologist Carol Gilligan's study, *In a Different Voice*, indicates that most women speak and live by a relational ideology and language; they formulate an ethical decision out of a sense of their relationship with others, for instance, while men generally talk about themselves and about ethical principle when faced with a moral dilemma.[20]

Mutedness (or a distinctive, unofficial rhetoric and ideology) and a relational quality are indeed sometimes features of the language and characterization of the experimental selves and voices that speak in modern novels by women. Yet a study—such as Gilligan's—that shows *most* women speaking a relational language does not mean that all women use such a discourse or fashion such a relational self. The categories of male culture/female subculture, or of principle and ego as opposed to "relationality," do not exhaustively define current voices in fiction or even definitively separate male from female discourse. The experimental subjectivity is more than double-voiced and tends to draw upon more than one discourse, or even more than two.

If women do generally employ a more relational discourse, can one affirm that men never use such a discourse? Is the language of endearment, the "little language" of affection, that Bernard speaks of in *The Waves*, exclusively feminine though it is appropriated by a male character? Is gossip exclusively a discourse of a muted, female culture? Patricia Spacks has observed that some forms of gossip help to define identity and community among subordinated groups, such as women; yet the discourse of gossip has also been appropriated by Conrad's Marlow who narrates tales of opinion and hearsay.[21] A binary theory of (linguistic, political, sexual) difference does not allow for *enough* difference, for a multiplicity of overlapping differences.

Among the symbolic discourses in our time, for instance, there are the distinctive discourses of the professions, disciplines in which many women now work, teach, and even publish. Can we any longer assign such discourses confidently to a masculine order? Perhaps, eventually it will be a moot point whether or not these discourses are described as masculine and under the aegis of the Law of the Father. There is some evidence also that the discourses of the workplace and the professions may well evolve into less masculine, more feminine modes. As sociologist Kathy Ferguson's research suggests, women perceive a career as primarily providing personal fulfillment and an opportunity to serve others; men also want these things, but they especially see the career as offering them progressively greater compensation and recognition.[22] Several career ideologies, we might say, are mingling appositionally; the result may be a new experimental professional discourse and identity for women—probably for men as well.

Finally, how are we to classify the discourse and implied ideology of Mary Carmichael, Woolf's invented novelist in *A Room of One's Own*? Mary Carmichael's writing is somewhat experimental, her fiction breaking both "sentence" and "sequence." The characters or selves that she is describing are also experimental; not only do we read that "Chloe liked Olivia," but we learn that these two scientists share a laboratory and that Olivia goes home to her children at a certain time (*Room*, 86–88). Woolf has argued in this feminist text that a woman writer needs a room (and income) of her own. Yet the scientists narrated by her experimental novelist share the professional room. Neither woman is the classic, gothic individualist, the Frankenstein with a sinister lab of his own. Lillian Robinson accuses Woolf of advocating, in *A Room of One's Own*, a privileged, isolationist individualism.[23] Woolf, however, is here implying a new, experimental self. In Mary Carmichael's narrative of the two women scientists, the discourse of motherhood and the discourse of career are in apposition to each other, not opposition. The experimental subjectivity of Olivia is a new mesh, a complex of discourses, some once identified as largely masculine, others as feminine.

The linguistic theories of Mikhail Bakhtin are obviously very helpful as a means of distinguishing and identifying these complexes of language and ideology that construct an experimental subjectivity. Although he did not himself explore any of the distinctions that might be made about gender discourses, Bakhtin's understanding of the interplay of language and of the inevitably inscribed ideology of any discourse provide a rich critical mechanism, which I will use in this study. As Bakhtin emphasizes in *The Dialogic Imagination*, the "word in language is half someone else's"; all living language has an "organic double-voicedness" and a fundamental "heteroglossia" (293, 326–27). In the complex heteroglossia of a good novelist's prose, Bakhtin finds a mix of ideologies as the languages of different generations, professions, and classes merge or conflict, often within the speech of one character (270–72, 311). Bakhtin describes how a character may begin to borrow the phrasing and ideology of another (or of the narrator); the resulting juxtaposition of one speaker's ideology may in effect evaluate or ridicule that of the other; or a dialogic struggle may indicate that one voice is trying to "liberate" itself from the discourse of an imposed authority (41–47, 303–4, 348).

Bakhtin not only identifies various discourses but looks at their political impact. Absolutes are prevented from becoming serious when they are "carnivalized," for instance, as in parody; in *Problems of Dostoevsky's Poetics*, Bakhtin illustrates in the fiction of Dostoevsky the transforming effect of this dialogic carnivalization, and he also emphasizes the impact of dialogic discourse generally: "The point is the *dialogical angle* at which they (the styles, dialects, etc.) are juxtaposed and counterposed in the work"[24] (my emphasis). This angle is also an important feature of the experimental or appositional subjectivity, and Ferguson's distinction between the career discourse of men and women helps to illustrate the difference of angle. Both men and women develop a discourse in their (similar) professions, but the dialogic features of each discourse are distinctive without necessarily being oppositional; hers emphasizes (among other things) service, his achievement.

Further clarification of this concept of the dialogical angle of a discourse can be derived from Michel Foucault's interesting notion of the "technology of the self." In his very elaborate analysis of the strategy by which selves are constructed, Foucault suggests that there is always something that gets "worked over," a substance that is taken into account as the self develops in any given society. He theorizes that the Athenian middle-class male typically considered self-mastery as the substance of identity, while a modern Western person might instead reflect on sexuality as the very substance and core of identity. Foucault also suggests that there is a means or discipline, a mode of practicing and shaping a given subjectivity; he asks further what the person hopes "to gain" by becoming that self.[25] Returning to the example of men and women in the modern workplace, we could say that the substance (of their adult subjectivity) is the same—or very similar, if they are in the same profession. Yet what they hope to gain from adhering to that profession, their expectation or rationale, is distinctive without being oppositional.

The difference is not one of polarity. Further, both versions of the professional discourse (the man's and the woman's) are symbolic structures; neither one is a disruptive, semiotic language.

Virginia Woolf in *Three Guineas* describes the technology of a new self also, a female subjectivity as outsider who will seek the same goals (substance) as do the male selves of her culture: "freedom, equality, peace"; but the Outsiders' Society wants to achieve these things "by the *means* that a different sex, a different tradition, a different education, and the different values which result from those differences have placed within our reach" (my emphasis). The new means will create interesting experiments, Woolf declares, and she uses the word *experiment* several times as she describes, in effect, the distinctive modifications, the dialogical angle that women will bring to old discourses. She approves, for instance, of the "extraordinarily interesting experiment" of women athletes playing a game for enjoyment rather than for its expensive cups and awards.[26]

Such an interplay of established discourses and muted ones could be expected in periods of major change in a society. Sometimes the linguistic play will be conflictual and contradictory. Indeed, Marianne DeKoven discusses modernist texts (constituted as "self-contradictory") as vitally dualistic, the oppositions always in deconstructive tension and never being resolved.[27] Yet the tension is sometimes that of hybrid complexity and unexpected transformation rather than a deadlocked, deconstructive opposition. Teresa DeLauretis suggests in her *Technologies of Gender* that ideologies may evolve, new discourses emerging and becoming sources of power; she notes that women have historically adopted various discourses and lifestyles, and Marianne Hirsch advises that as differing cultural groups gain "access to the symbolic" we will "need to develop a more complicated model of identity and self-consciousness."[28]

In my examination of the fiction of Woolf, Pym, and Brooke-Rose, I explore such a model, a more flexible one that can respond to the intrasymbolic play of discourses (as well as play between symbolic and semiotic) in twentieth-century texts. Any given ideology in our time has difficulty maintaining an uncorrupted script. In complex societies, it is hard for the institutions and the Laws of the Fathers to keep tight inventory on the languages selected for men and those "wild" ones (like gossip and affectionate language), among which women have sometimes been allowed to glean and scavenge. Many discourses, many ideological choices now impinge on people in ways that would have been impossible in preindustrialized societies.

As William Goode emphasizes in *World Revolution and Family Patterns*, people now often face new obligations in society and in the family. Thus, people must develop their own "system of role relationships," and these may be challenging, "simply because there has been little prior socialization and experience" to prepare them for the new roles.[29] Because of the changing patterns of socialization and the multiplicity of available paradigms, it is more difficult for society, subcultures, or parents to shape a self in the modern world. Jeremy Hawthorn finds the source of this difficulty in "the contradictory values which the individual in our society is supposed coherently to internalize to construct a self."[30] When there is little standardized socialization for new roles, there is the considerable opportunity for dialogic experimentation among the contradictory values.

This may be especially true for women, if, as Homans argues, women are not so exclusively committed to just one model of discourse. As Sondra Farganis argues in *The Social Reconstruction of the Feminine Character*, "sexual identity is more deconstruction and reconstruction than were the sexual ideas and ideals of earlier, more traditional societies."[31] There is no one pattern for young women in their twenties, for instance, as Grace Baruch notes in *Lifeprints*, nor for single women; the widow's role is undefined, or as Starr Hilz says, it is "a roleless role."[32] There is no longer just one pattern or "technology," as Foucault might say, for constructing the subjectivities of women. The girls of the "Brodie set" in Muriel Spark's novel made the thrilling discovery that "it was possible for people glued together in grown-up authority to differ."[33] In modern societies, the glue of the symbolic is cracking, and there is now a diversity even of institutionalized, official ideologies.

There may be a further reason for the development of an experimental subjectivity in women and for the emergence of appositional discourses and selves in the fictional characters and voices among women writers. Showalter, as I noted earlier, and others have argued that women speak in and for two languages and cultures; they have a "double voice." Within the subjectivity of one person, this relationship of the muted language to the dominant one may be a very creative form of *unsuccessful* socialization. In their classic study, *The Social Construction of Reality*, Peter Berger and Thomas Luckmann describe the phenomenon of an inadequate inoculation, as it were, with the culture's ideology. As they explain, the "possibility of 'individualism' (that is, of individual choice between discrepant realities and identities) is directly linked to the possibility of unsuccessful socialization." The unsuccessfully socialized person "has at least the potential to migrate between a number of available worlds"; such a person has "deliberately and awarely constructed a self out of the 'material' provided by a number of available identities."[34] Modern structuralists would be cautious about the notion of people deliberately constructing identities for themselves. Modifying and updating the rhetoric of Berger and Luckmann slightly, we might say that the unsuccessfully socialized subject is aware of being inscribed by more than one discourse and is therefore less likely to capitalize one of them as "The Discourse," or the Law of the Father. Such an experimental self or subject would be more open to possibilities, more likely to appreciate and use the heteroglossia of available discourses.

The concept of unsuccessful socialization epitomizes the relationship of women to their society. In this relationship, women have a kind of built-in disloyalty or mistrust, which several feminists have noted.[35] Only if women perceive themselves as peripheral to a society are they accepted as part of it. They are invited in only if they accept their uninvited status. Presuffrage cultures offer an obvious example; women (and other groups) were members of the society but not members of its political center; they could not vote. They were *inside* only by virtue of being defined as *outside*. They belonged on condition that they not really belong.

Christine Boheemen illustrates this disloyalty-within-loyalty when she writes that a "typical precondition for woman's assumption of a place in society is the rejection or denial of her autonomy whether with regard to sexual reproduction or to her use of language."[36] In Western societies that advocated and supported autonomy (and one could add freedom and equality), women were often asked not to practice these values. They may still learn not to fit in—as a very condition of fitting in.

That is, if women are *successfully* socialized, they will as a result of that success be *unsuccessfully* socialized. Women have a built-in dialogism, since, in terms of political and economic power, they are in effect legal aliens within most societies still. Women virtually have to be translators for the languages within their own subjectivity. As Boheemen implies, a woman's dialogical angle on the discourse of autonomy may be different from a man's; when women play the game, these unsuccessfully socialized selves or subjectivities may engage a distinctive means or rationale, as Woolf indicates in *Three Guineas*.

To appropriate dialogically another's language, then, is not simply to purloin it. The discourse is altered by the infringement and by the purloiner whose ideology may warp or subtly change the appropriated language. When one group decides to infiltrate another group's discourse, or even to live another's ideology, the means of access, or the rationale for living the new life, will probably be quite distinctive and transformative. For instance, when women began to think of themselves as individuals, as selves, as persons of agency who might found a settlement house or agitate for suffrage, their actions (and memoirs) did not constitute a massive adoption or usurpation of some male-defined discourse of individualism. As the detailed studies by Martha Vicinus and Sheila Jeffreys demonstrate, these women were transferring the ideology of a "feminine" compassion to the realm of social and political reform.[37] The technology of this newly constructed female self and discourse was a dialogic and appositional one; an experimental female self emerged as a "hybrid construction," to use Bakhtin's term. This self was constructed of discourses that included the Victorian language of woman as nourisher and helper. Yet these angels no longer used the house as a means of serving humanity; they used the settlements and colleges (where a few of them—very few—also pursued careers).

They adopted and adapted certain discourses from "male" traditions appositionally along with discourses linked to "female" traditions. These women did not suddenly become male egos.

Not all men became male egos either. That is, not all men who have lived in Western societies in the last two hundred years or so have been successfully inscribed or socialized into a discourse of individualism, one that means exploitive capitalism, imperialism, an egotistic self-fulfillment, and the oppression of colonial cultures along with women. A binary model of difference (arrogant men/ relational or semiotic women) is simply not an adequate description. As Ashis Nandy argues, there have always been "other Wests" or an "alternative West." The Western colonizers had to emphasize some of their traditions and ignore others when they sought a rationale for conquest; Nandy observes that it would be hard to find such a rationale in the discourses defined by St. Francis, Johannes Eckhart, John Ruskin, or Leo Tolstoy.[38] The discourses that have become part of the (Western) symbolic do not constitute a monolithic, monologic (or even masculine) ideology. They instead contribute to a complex heteroglossia, some of the discourses being appositional and offering nuanced modifications of each other while some are oppositional, belonging to virtual countercultures.

Recalling what sociologists have said about the multiplicity of roles and life-structuring discourses now offered to modern people in the West, I think we can agree with Jean-François Lyotard that the great totalizing ideologies of the past no longer prevail. A defining characteristic of the "postmodern condition," Lyotard argues, is the demise of the great discourses that have in the recent past structured socialist revolutions, capitalist industry, and intellectual endeavor. In the light of a prevailing "incredulity toward metanarratives," toward great stories or myths that offered "totalization" of meaning, many smaller discourses have emerged and will continue to do so; instead of the grand narratives, there are now many "little narratives," dispersed "language elements" or "language games— a heterogeneity of elements."[39] In this prevailing heteroglossia of discourses, it is very difficult for a single West, a monolythic Western Law of the Father, to claim all the vocal territory and all the ideological space.

Gender narratives, especially if they are metanarratives, grand narratives (or theories), have only limited applicability in the heterogeneous twentieth century. In any case, the totalizing paradigm that reads and writes the feminine as semiotic and dialogic, while the masculine is assigned the monologic and the symbolic is not flexible enough for the experimental subjects/selves in the work of Woolf, Pym, Brooke-Rose, and others.

The Implied Individual(isms)

Appropriation, heterogeneity, and hybridization are everywhere in a complex modern culture where symbolic structures themselves multiply and mingle dialogically. Indeed, some feminist scholars fear that too much mingling will occur. These theorists are concerned that women, women writers, and narrated female selves or characters, are in danger of succumbing to a destructive individualism if they adapt in any way the symbolic structures once dominated almost exclusively by men. Because the several discourses concerning the individual are very much a part of Western ideologies about the self, I will conclude this chapter by loosening the mortar around this symbolic concept, the grand narrative of the individual, a narrative that has perhaps all along consisted of many diverse "little narratives."

In her collection *Sex, Class and Culture*, marxist Lillian Robinson asserts that bourgeois ideals generally exalt the individual struggle and that capitalist, bourgeois art respects only the separate, the unique, the "individual achievement"; we noted earlier Robinson's attack on *A Room of One's Own*. Gayatri Spivak also discerns an ominous trend of female individualism in the character of Jane Eyre, whom she suspects of engaging in the "imperialist project" of feminist self-fulfillment. In her attempt, Jane uses what Spivak calls the "grammar of the creative imagination." This grammar, its roots in Keats's "soul making," is infected with Western "individualism."[40] The soul maker as hero (and thus perhaps individualist), however, probably owes more to Lionel Trilling's reading of Keats's soul-making passage than to Keats himself.[41] In fact, Trilling's reading, as well as Spivak's reading of *Jane Eyre*, are instances of dialogic play between different eras and traditions.

The self as individual, and the related ideology of individualism, have never been pure and monologic, inherited like an unmutated genetic code. Yet Jessica Benjamin asserts that "our culture knows only one form of individuality: the male stance of overdifferentiation."[42] While it is true—according to Chodorow's studies noted earlier in this chapter—that the psychosocial development of some men may lead to a defensive need for establishing difference by means of an emphatic ego, such a process and such a result are apparently not universally the case. There is more than one West, and more than one ideology of individuality, of becoming a distinct identity. Even men (to state the obvious) vary in the degree of separateness (from affectionate relationship on the one hand, to criminal mysogyny on the other) required to maintain their sense of self. To affirm that there is only one egotistic, exploitively self-fulfilled, autonomous, woman-denying, imperialistic mode of individuality is not only to generalize about men. Such an oversimplification also makes the very notion of selfhood a strenuously heroic and oppositional one; it becomes then a moral negative in the symbolic order and something to be eschewed by women.

Notions or discourses of individuality (and individualism) in the West constitute a complex heteroglossia with a long and rich history. Since my concern in this study is modern subjectivity, I will pass over the scholars who have seen glimmerings of the individual and of increasing interiority in Hebrew writing of the Exile period or others who have identified a concept of the distinct person, the individual, as a discovery of the ancient Greeks.[43] I will also reluctantly disregard Linda Georgianna's interesting discussion of the nascent individuality (as personal reflection, self awareness) that emerges in the medieval *Ancrene Wisse*.[44]

Yet the interiorized and religious self is a good place to begin, since an interiorized individuality (and the request for the privacy of a "room of one's own") is often the subject of feminist concern and attack. Staying within the English tradition, since my writers are English, we can recall that the dissenting religious groups of the eighteenth and nineteenth centuries encouraged both self-reflection (personal "conversion") and social action, prison reform and pacifism being part of the ideology of the Quakers, for instance.[45] In this ideology of the individual, the symbolic discourses of privacy and of social responsibility were in dialogic apposition, not opposition. Indeed, as David Martin demonstrates, the rhetoric of the British Labor Party in the twentieth century mingles social issues with the traditional evangelical individualism of Nonconformity.[46]

This evangelical discourse, which integrated the language of individualized self-reflection dialogically with a sociopolitical language, also included originally certain assumptions about property and economics. These assumptions are thoroughly detailed in C. B. MacPherson's study, *The Political Theory of Possessive Individualism*. In a tradition that MacPherson finds adumbrated in British philosophers such as Hobbes and Locke, but also in the dissident Levellers of Cromwell's time, the concept of ownership is a major construct or substance in the technology of the self. The Levellers, who did not own property, claimed to own their labor, their services, and these could be sold for income; in addition, with language familiar to most Western people, this dissident group advocated an "inalienable" civil right, that of owning one's person, one's self. While thus advocating an economic (and psychological) system that allowed capitalism to flourish, the Levellers also encouraged a strong community commitment; they envisioned a spiritual, intellectual, and economically enterprising society.[47]

MacPherson, Martin, and others are not describing a monologic caricature of individualism. They are describing the ideology of a complex self, an ideology constructed of several appositional discourses. Historically, this dialogic subjectivity was an experimental anti-Establishment self. In its capitalist version, it has been largely a self available to males only, as Elizabeth Fox-Genovese emphasizes.[48] Yet even this version was not the sole, pure discourse in the socializing or construction of every Western man.

Some have suggested that a complex "liberal" self needs to be distinguished from the strictly exploitive, "instrumental" self described by Martin Green in his study of imperialism in British fiction. Not all feminist theorists will accept the distinction he makes between "the humanistic belief that individual fulfillment is the ultimate moral criterion" and the instrumentalist exploitation of subordinates by the administrators of Britain's empire. Empire wrote the self as an authority, Martin Green argues, that encouraged an administrative imperialism in church, society, and family (as well as in the colonies).[49] Unlike the instrumentalist discourse, the liberal discourse was a dialogic amalgamation of personal growth, social reform, and economic freedom. Yet when E. M. Forster described his twentieth-century revision of this complex discourse, he argued that economic laissez-faire led to "the capitalist jungle," and he implied that some regulation might be necessary. In effect, he created a dialogic hybrid; he inscribed a self constructed of several Western discourses in creative apposition to each other. He acknowledged that he could accept government regulation in the marketplace but not "in the world of the spirit," since freedom in personal relationships was such a prominent element in his discourse or technology of the self.[50]

Perhaps as Edward Engelbert argues, the modern "elegiac" discourse of despair and alienation emerged from an overly confident liberalism, an idealized belief in human agency and in the capacity for self-fulfillment; similarly, Charles Glicksberg, looking at the work of Strindberg, Huxley, and others, finds images implying that the machine has led to despair, or the collectivized, bureaucratic nature of modern life has done so. Both of these scholars perceive the modern alienated, even nihilistic, self as all-pervasive, as virtually the only extant discourse, the only kind of Western individual. Engelbert writes, "Not only are we unhappy with the world, on which we heap our scorn, but also with ourselves: frustrated, angry, resentful, disappointed, despairing."[51]

We? Our? Ninety-nine percent of the literary works examined by these scholars of the alienated self, the individual-as-bereft, are written by men (Engelbert does look at *Mrs. Dalloway*). One could well ask, Where were women when the lights went out on Western civilization? They were not "in the dark." While some prominent male writers yearned to retreat to the bee-loud glade, and others were elegizing the loss of an idealized individualism, some women were, as we noted earlier, founding and administering settlement houses and colleges. Further, among women writers, a distinctive ideology of the individual was emerging. Nancy Armstrong, in her *Desire and Domestic Fiction*, sees the emergence of a nondominating ideology of the individual in the eighteenth and nineteenth centuries. As a counterpart to Ian Watt's argument that a capitalistic and Nonconformist individualism contributed to the novel's development, Armstrong emphasizes that the novel's primary audience was female; she argues that a distinctive discourse emerged when the novel did, a discourse that both men and women understood as valuing the personal self, pleasure, relationships, the emotions, and the "qualities of the mind." Women presided over this cultivated, relational sphere. Armstrong finds enough evidence, in English fiction, to assert that "the modern individual was first and foremost a woman."[52]

Armstrong's individual is constructed by a discourse that is in apposition (not in polarized opposition) to certain discourses later enunciated by male liberals and humanists of the nineteenth century. Men had also partaken of and contributed to this low-key, nonpossessive discourse of the self. The cultivation of the "qualities of the mind," of pleasure and the affections, are among those activities and values that John Stuart Mill commended as an antidote after his breakdown. He speaks in his *Autobiography* of the need to balance his skills of intellectual analysis by nourishing his emotional responses to people, landscape, poetry, and music; he becomes attentive "to the internal culture of the individual," including himself as an individual.[53] Mill's newly discovered values belong essentially to the discourse of "Hellenism," as Matthew Arnold called it, the encouraging of a "spontaneity of consciousness," a "free play of thought" that allows for culture; these values Arnold opposes to the simplistic insistence on personal liberty, on the making of money and the saving of one's soul.[54] (Content with his own dialogical angle on the humanistic self, Arnold is not sympathetic to the tactics of civil protest being used by the oppressed Chartists who were demanding—according to their discourse of possessive individualism—their "inalienable" rights.) It is interesting that Arnold expressly criticizes individualistic self-assertion and that the focus of Mill's individualism is not an Emersonian self-reliance (or extreme male differentiation, we could say). Instead, Mill's discourse of the individual means the training of the affections and of each person's response to a shared, communal heritage of art and thought.

The discourse that Armstrong describes as arising from a feminine culture is not precisely the same as the official, symbolic discourses by which Mill and Arnold counter yet another symbolic discourse—the ideology of a muscular nineteenth-century materialism. Yet the "feminine" domestic discourse and the highly academic, educationally privileged, "masculine" one of Mill and Arnold do share some common territory. They are appositional to each other rather than opposed in polarized difference. Both of these symbolic discourses (neither one is semiotic) counter greed and a possessive, domineering stance toward one's "self" and toward the selves of others. Both are modifications of a discourse that defined a small subculture within the larger prevailing culture of materialism and imperialism.

This modified, perhaps feminized, liberal discourse plays an important part in the structuring of the experimental selves in the texts of Woolf and Brooke-Rose, both of whom retain a dialogic, ambivalent respect and affection for the male culture that gave them Herodotus, Percival, Shakespeare, humanism, marxism, and even the middle-class individual, including the privacy and solitude that sometimes characterize this mode of the self.

In a domesticated and religious mode, a liberal discourse merges dialogically with the mild, yet witty, discourse of gossip in Pym's novels where women characters once again, in Armstrong's sense, develop into varied and complex versions of the "modern individual." Most of Pym's women characters have appropriated and cultivated the generally humanistic tradition defined by the English poets. The great and the minor poets are often quoted by these women as a kind of apocryphal scripture and used as a sort of proof-text for defining love, making decisions, and indeed, for constructing the self. Yet the individuality that the characters define in relation to that tradition is not one of "possessive individualism"; only a few of Pym's characters "alienate" (i.e., sell) their labor and attempt thus to achieve, to develop a career that would add their stories or books to a (male) tradition of inquiry and creative insight. They live the tradition or discourse daily rather than exploiting it and turning their contribution to it into a marketable product.

And yet, suppose a woman does enter the market and offer her research or writing or typing skills for sale? A few of Pym's characters do so, and Brooke-Rose's contemporary men and women have careers as a matter-of-fact circumstance of their very experimental postmodern lives. Does this mean that the woman's strategy for constructing a self has succumbed to the worst sins of a male-defined discourse of greed, possession, and consumption? As we noted earlier, when a woman enters a profession she may not necessarily adopt the entire cultural package of egotism and ambition that may have belonged to the male professional. Her career discourse (or discourse of "quest") is likely to be in dialogic apposition to the discourses that structure the careers of men.

Certainly, in the imaginative texts under scrutiny in the following chapters, the women characters are constructing "alternative selves"—to use a phrase from Patricia Waugh's book on postmodern fiction by women. In the texts of women writers, Waugh finds a modification rather than a rejection of the "liberal conception of subjectivity." Indeed, women's fiction can "be seen not as an attempt to define an isolated individual ego but to discover a collective concept of subjectivity which foregrounds the construction of identity *in relationships*" (original emphasis).[55] Such a concept of subjectivity involves maintaining a dialogue among several Western discourses of the self as these are creatively appropriated and modified into new, appositional structures.

The textual strategy of the novelists in the current study is a kind of splicing of the available paradigms of the self, a conversational interplay of ideologies, an exercising of the dialogic imagination. The experimental selves and voices in these texts speak many discourses. Most of the major characters or narrators could be described as unsuccessfully socialized, and as a result, they resist society's oppositional gender paradigms. Speaking a variety of hybridized discourses, the voices are ideologically mobile. They create alternative languages and in the process critique and transform the "self" as several traditions have variously constructed the concept.

2 *Virginia Woolf*
Feminizing the Symbolic

In *Three Guineas*, when Virginia Woolf describes the women athletes who play for enjoyment rather than for expensive trophies, she offers the tentative remark that such an "experiment" could perhaps "bring about a psychological change of great value in human nature," a change that might even reduce the likelihood of war (116). In this polemical pacifist text, Woolf adopts the courageous view that human beings are indeed ideologically mobile; they are experimentally open to a variety of discourses. In a letter written in 1940, she again muses on the potential for change, particularly with regard to the attitudes about gender; she asks, "How far is the women's movement a remarkable experiment in that transformation?"[1] Woolf seems to have understood human subjectivity as open to change, the "psychological change" that might result from the presence and practice of a new discourse.

Her own texts inscribe an experimental character or voice by placing in dialogic apposition several discourses, often drawn from traditional symbolic structures, which variously "infect" or transform each other. When Woolf's narrators and characters *relate* the symbolic, they make it more relational as well. In relating the authorized symbolic languages, the narrating voice is often relationalizing them or—we could say—feminizing them.

Woolf is a dialogic gymnast. My argument will emphasize that she does not simply or always deconstruct one version of a symbolic discourse by disrupting it with one version of a "feminine" or semiotic discourse. Instead, Woolf's relational language (we could call it a nondeconstructive version of the dialogic) transforms, hy-

25

bridizes, even revitalizes a number of symbolic discourses. Rather than being bipolar, her language is more like the many-sided flower perceived (and constructed dialogically) by the dinner guests in *The Waves*.

Yet Woolf criticism tends to follow an ideology of polarity or difference—perhaps inevitably, since it is necessary to identify distinctions even if one argues that these result in dialogic appropriation and a multifaceted experimental language of hybrids. Aside from the early studies of difference as androgyny in Woolf's fiction, more linguistically oriented recent studies have, like Joan Lidoff's, identified Woolf's fluid style with a woman's subjectivity, and Patricia Laurence argues that Woolf's texts draw upon a (feminine) "semiotics of silence" (ellipses, unspoken remarks); Makiko Minow-Pinkney's Lacanian argument finds subversion in Woolf's semiotic (pre-oedipal, nonsymbolic) discourse, while Ellen Rosenman perceives a concept of "communal" art emerging from the "invisible" maternal presence in Woolf's life as well as from a woman's literary tradition.[2]

On the other hand, Gillian Beer observes in Woolf's texts the concerns and even the style of prominent male writers such as Ruskin, Darwin, and Tyndall, while Richard Pearce argues that a "male narrative hegemony" prevails (in *The Waves*, for instance,) in spite of Woolf's effort to shape a female authorial voice; similarly, Anne Herrmann's Bakhtinian study finds Woolf successfully deconstructing the (male) subject yet losing her struggle to free (from men's language) the subordinate feminine text, although Keith Booker's study (also Bakhtinian) concludes that Woolf's key dialogic scenes demonstrate the "inability" of patriarchal language to control discourse.[3]

Woolf's prose is rich; her dialogic texts result in dialogic (even polyphonic) criticism as the foregoing two paragraphs testify. My purpose in this study is not so much to examine the conflictual polarities of Woolf's discourse as it is to look at the multiple and experimental transformations that her fiction's characters and voices create, particularly as they dialogically *relate* languages (and themselves) to each other. I am less interested in deciding which language wins (male or female), less interested in oppositions, than in a text's rich appositions, many of which are appropriations and transformations of symbolic structures, that is, of structures usually identified by Woolf's critics (and sometimes by Woolf herself) with the negative, the patriarchal, and the masculine.

Woolf's texts do incorporate some discourses that are inherited from the largely male-designed symbolic order and others that derive from a variety of neglected discourses largely used by women. Among the latter are several that intrigue Woolf as she examines the gossip and daily concerns of female (and male) diarists and letter writers. In such materials, a relational concern is prominent; there is a preoccupation with the familiar and ordinary (though an occasional focus on an eccentric hobby). Generally, the discourse is one of caring and curiosity. Joanne Frye, for instance, asserts that women's writing often privileges "dailiness," and she finds that "relationality" is a prominent aspect of a female, first-person narrator's subjectivity.[4] Yet such relationality can also emerge in third-person narratives (and in texts narrated by male voices); certainly this is the case in Woolf's fiction. There the relating and relational voices draw even the venerable and traditional symbolic structures into dialogue.

Occasionally, the linguistic interplay can appropriately be called oppositional or subversive—a female discourse taking over or deconstructing a male one (or vice versa). Such a linguistic conflict occurs with remarkable impact near the end of *Jacob's Room*, for instance. Yet Woolf juggles an amazing heteroglossia of discourses, and the process of their interaction is most often a transformation or evolution, the distinctive discourses recognizable yet transformed as they accumulate or coalesce in apposition to each other. Woolf was a novelist, essayist, diarist, letter writer, and conversationalist. Doing all these things well, she was certainly acquainted with the linguistic culture of both men and women, and—more importantly—with several discourses within each of these cultures.

The textual and political result is the emergence in Woolf's fiction of many experimental discourses and voices. The language of these experimental subjectivities shows—I will argue—a relationalizing of the symbolic. We can also call this a feminizing of the symbolic. Yet feminizing implies a link between a discourse and gender, and though such a link may prevail in current psychological studies and in some of Woolf's texts, it does not prevail in an absolute way. So, even though I find the word *feminizing* helpful, it should be understood here to indicate a loosening, a relationalizing, of the discourses of symbolic authority embodied, for instance, in Mr. Ramsay or Percival. Employing a dialogic and appositional discourse, certain characters such as Lily and Bernard appropriate, and transform or feminize, the inscriptions of authority and agency.

In Woolf's two most radically experimental novels, *Jacob's Room* and *The Waves*, the feminizing process is a major part of the narrative's structure. The traditional linguistic and narrative authority structure, the bildungsroman, is present in *Jacob's Room*, and the heroic quest (for grail or empire) resides in the figure of Percival of *The Waves*. Yet in both novels these symbolic narrative structures are muted; in these novels, Woolf relegates a famous masculine ideology to a feminine position narratively. Woolf gives narrative prominence instead to the nonfamous, the unimportant, the gossipy and trivial world of ordinary life. In these two novels, which will be the focus of this chapter, the voices of relationality do not usually deconstruct a male discourse. Instead, the relational discourses transform and feminize even as they relate, or comment on, the (narratively) muted structures of the symbolic.

Relating Subjectivity: Woolf

Before turning to *Jacob's Room* and *The Waves* (with some remarks about the other novels), I want to look more closely at Woolf's understanding of discourse, relationality, and the self. As an example of someone whose "life had been an experiment from the start," for instance, Woolf described Mary Wollstonecraft's willingness to abandon some of her revolutionary theories (those against marriage) and marry Godwin ("Four Figures," *CE*, 3:199). Wollstonecraft did not perceive herself as defined by one political discourse. Calling Mary's life with William her "most fruitful experiment," Woolf declares that Mary "is alive and active, she argues and experiments, we hear her voice and trace her influence even now among the living" (*CE*, 3:199). Woolf often describes the self as experimental, or certainly as being constructed of varied theories or values—what we can now call "discourses." In 1924, during the writing of *Mrs. Dalloway*, she speaks of herself as inconsistent and paraphrases as precedent Montaigne's view that "one is various."[5] In her essay on Montaigne, she describes his approach to self-understanding or, indeed, self-construction. "By means of perpetual experiment and observation of the subtlest he achieved at last a miraculous adjustment of all these wayward parts that constitute the human soul" (*CE*, 3:26). Virginia Woolf's concept of human nature as experiment, then, seems to suggest a capacity to change, to appropriate, and to dialogically combine various discourses that construct human consciousness.

Writing about George Crabbe, for instance, she described this clergyman and poet as well-educated, urbane, and witty; yet he often sought out his rural roots in a sea village where he went to look for fossils and shells. As Woolf says, "Crabbe's nature, indeed, included more than one full-grown human being" (*CE*, 4:19). So did Montaigne's nature or subjectivity, and so did Mary Wollstonecraft's. As Bernard puts it in *The Waves*, everything "is experiment and adventure. We are forever mixing ourselves with unknown quantities" (118). Usually, people share dialogically several discourses that are available to them in the social and political environment; one's language is "half someone else's," as Bakhtin observed. For Woolf, subjectivity is "various"; it is "experimental" and dialogic, as several languages mingle in apposition.

Although Woolf shared with her era an artistic preoccupation with consciousness, especially with the flexible, various, or even illusory self, she was not philosophically a thoroughgoing skeptic. When she uses the word *soul*, she consistently implies a center or essence, as Mark Hussey has argued, and possibly a "transcendence," as compared to the more variable characteristics of a person.[6] On the other hand, Woolf speaks of her soul as being repressed and "diminished" during a long social evening as she listens to uninteresting people (*D*, 2:235). So the discourse of others can be mixed uncomfortably, even with one's own most intimately self-constituting discourse.

Woolf seems to have adhered pragmatically to some concept of agency, a central soul, yet she clearly did not think there was a "master narrative" (to use again Lyotard's phrase) that could define the ideology of one's life or of an entire culture. In contrast, Beatrice Webb believed herself to have been "secreted by the Time Spirit," as Woolf phrases it, after reading Webb's autobiography in 1929 (*D*, 3:74). Woolf also observes that "there were causes in [Webb's] life: prayer, principle. None in mine" (*D*, 3:62). There was no master narrative or "mistress narrative," no single discourse in either the masculine symbolic order or among the several feminine discourses that was for Woolf all-encompassing—a linguistic force capable of the foolproof socializing or inscribing of a modern person.

Though she maintained an empiricism that acknowledged a nonhuman world, an "it" (*D*, 3:62), Woolf saw discourse as experimentally and variously constructing the consciousness of Wollstonecraft or Crabbe. She says also of Joseph Conrad that he, too, "is not one and simple; no, he is many and complex"; in his mature novels, he brings "these selves" into relation with each other ("Mr. Conrad: A Conversation," *CE*, 1:310). Although Woolf resisted the idea that she was influenced by a "Time Spirit," her concept of several selves as theories or ideologies within one person is close to a prevailing epistemology of "perspectivism," which Avrom Fleishman claims for Woolf, and it may bear a resemblance to T. S. Eliot's elaborate theory of "points of view," many such viewpoints being necessary if the world is to become real for the self.[7]

Yet for Woolf the notion of several viewpoints or discourses entering into the construction of one subjectivity is also distinctly Bakhtinian. Such modes of discourse have traditionally been linked to the feminine (though not of course limited to female persons, as Woolf's discussion of Conrad and Crabbe demonstrates). Discussing her ongoing research into the structuring of the subjectivity of women, Carol Gilligan observes that the girls in a recent study tend to assume that listening to others and depending on their concern in return is "part of the human condition." For the girls, "the central metaphor for identity formation becomes *dialogue* rather than mirroring; the self is defined by *gaining perspective* and known by experiencing *engagement with others*" (my emphasis).[8]

Woolf's remarks about the "social side" of her personality, a characteristic she says she inherited from her mother (*D*, 2:250) indicate engagement, something closer to participation than mere curiosity. In September 1930 (during the period in which she was writing *The Waves*), she describes her response to her friends: "I use my friends rather as giglamps: There's another field I see: by your light. Over there's a hill. I widen my landscape" (*D*, 3:316). Her language here hints of manipulation ("use"), but her statements about the benefits of relationship seldom do this, and David Cecil perceived her social side as unselfishly attentive. He describes her as "an extraordinarily unegotistic talker. She seemed much more interested in what other people said than in what she said herself."[9]

For those who wanted to write, Woolf is emphatic about the necessity of acquiring more than one discourse and thinking of oneself as more than "one single person." As she says in "A Letter to a Young Poet," a dedicated writer is a "continuous character" made up of all the poets of the past; one needs then to grow "by imagining that one is not oneself but somebody different. How can you learn to write if you write only about one single person?" (*CE*, 2:184, 193). Like Conrad or Wollstonecraft, a writer needs a relational and ideological flexibility unavailable to an individualistic identity.

Woolf does not suggest that aspiring poets broaden their reading and their experience in order to fulfill themselves. The "technology of the self" that Woolf recommends to the young poet does not include as rationale the humanistic goal of self-realization or self-development. Instead, the writer's "self" needs to be intimately acquainted with many discourses in order to be creatively responsible. Woolf occasionally speaks of finding her own voice or style, as Bette London argues.[10] Yet Woolf is not preoccupied with this concern, and her own novels are quite varied. Like most complex writers (Joyce, for instance), she never lapses into a repetition of former achievements. What some have seen as a prevailing Western indulgence in individualistic self-fulfillment is not Woolf's strategy for art or for living. The "young poet" instead needs a generous responsiveness, a relational openness, and a dialogic variety of discourses and of selves.

When she emphasizes the poet's openness to many discourses,

Woolf may have been thinking of her relational, feminine inheritance (where identity is linked to dialogue, as Gilligan suggests); her advice parallels to an extent T. S. Eliot's urging that writers know the "tradition"; she may also have derived her negative view of the sufficiency of "one single person" from G. E. Moore. Moore insisted that good cannot be defined and that mercy, justice, and freedom are simply means to an end; he also denied any ultimate metaphysical reality to the self. It too is a means. Many times in his *Principia Ethica*, he returns to his antihumanist argument that the realization of one's "true self" cannot be a goal or an ultimate good.

Self-realization is an inadequate concept, Moore argues, because the notion implies an eternally existing self out there that one must then "realize."[11] In the paragraph immediately following one of these denunciations of self-realization, the *Principia*'s most frequently quoted passage occurs, the passage in which Moore declares that the most "valuable things" in life are "states of consciousness," especially those states ("good in themselves") constituted by "personal affection and the appreciation of what is beautiful in art or Nature."[12] Moore's influence on the Bloomsbury group was complex, and some of them may have understood him in a neo-Platonic (and essentialist) way. Yet Virginia Woolf's understanding of the dubious value of self-realization parallels that of Moore.[13]

In 1908, after reading the *Principia*, Woolf writes to Vanessa Bell and pronounces the philosopher "humane in spite of his desire to know the truth" (*Letters*, 1:364). The desire to know the (one) truth or to know just one self narrows a person's humanity, Woolf implies, and narrows a writer's creative responses. She attributes the lack of complexity in F. L. Lucas's "uninteresting mind," for instance, to the predictable and simple trajectory of his early adulthood: "He deliberately vowed to be pagan, *to be individual*, to enjoy life, *to explore his own sensations* when there wasn't much matter to go on. Hence the repetition, *the egotism*, the absence of depth or character" (*D*, 3:257; my emphasis). Woolf here censures the (symbolic) discourse of individualistic rebellion and self-realization as rigid and limiting. Contrary to such individualism is Woolf's more flexible concept. She speaks of the individual as one discourse among several that may mingle in the constructing of human consciousness; in "Evening Over Sussex," she playfully identifies several interior selves, the third (among six) speaking of the "disappearance and death of the individual" (*CE*, 2:290–92).

Although several of her most famous characters—such as Mrs. Dalloway and Mrs. Ramsay—seek time alone as a means of understanding themselves and others, they always return to their friends, their responsibilities, or even the socially crowded party. Even the disastrously withdrawn Rhoda in *The Waves*, who is scornful of the "antics of the individual," still acknowledges that a self or individuality of some kind is important as an aid to *relationship* and to the enjoyment of beauty. During the second dinner party, her reasons for entering into the conversation and the world of her lifelong friends are significant:

> But since these rolls of bread and wine bottles are needed by me, and your faces with their hollows and prominences are beautiful, and the table-cloth and its yellow stains, far from being allowed to spread in wider and wider circles of understanding that may at last . . . embrace the entire world, I must go through the antics of the individual. (223–24)

In addition to the necessity of nourishment, the beautiful faces of her friends draw Rhoda in, as does the perhaps impossible hope (to her) of fuller understanding, communication, embracing. These values are reminiscent of Moore (beauty, personal affection), but they also belong to discourses with a long history among women (the social gathering that affirms relationships and encourages conversation, communication, or even gossip). The self and self-fulfillment are not the values or goals here. The self is a discourse, an ideology (for Rhoda, it is a mere experimental antic), in fact a means that facilitates the celebration of friendship and shared lives.

Because the modern world has lost the security of belief and conviction that Woolf saw prevailing in the nineteenth century, she notes in "How It Strikes a Contemporary" that modern novelists can offer in their work a characterization or fictional self of greater depth and complexity (*CE*, 2:158–59). Yet this lack of a dominant ideology or master narrative may also lead to a kind of egotism, to the possibility of a writer who "will only tell us what it is that happens to himself" (*CE*, 2:159). Listening to the young Robert Graves talkatively and defensively expand on his lifestyle, Woolf suggests that it is "our age" that puts "this burden of proof" on people (*D*, 3:13–14). That is, she acknowledges that egotism, a narrow clinging to "one single" self, and a defensive self-indulgent individualism might be a hazard of modern life.

At the same time, her own enthusiasm for the more complex self, the experimental self of dialogic and multiple discourses, prevails in her fiction and nonfiction as well. Woolf obviously did not believe that subjectivity and discourse had been confined to a rigidly exclusive male territory. That is, she did not perceive the "subject" as being irretrievably taken over by patriarchal authority. Her view was not as absolute as Luce Irigaray's, who asserts that "any theory of the subject has always been appropriated by the 'masculine.' "[14] While Woolf acknowledged in *Three Guineas* that science "is a man" (139) and society is or recently was "a father" (135), she would not have agreed with the European feminists, briefly discussed in my first chapter, who argue that for a woman the "subject" position is virtually lost; women must find instead a rhythmic language of semiotic images and phrases or a radically experimental *écriture féminine*.

Contrary to this view, the narrator of *Orlando* asserts that women, when deprived of men's company and conversation, do not just "scratch,"[15] bereft of linguistic subjecthood. There are languages, ideologies, that men have more or less ignored, and these languages not only inscribe the self in Woolf's texts but enter into dialogue with patriarchal, symbolic ideologies, modifying, reappropriating, and feminizing them. Among these relational languages is the gossip that Orlando, Nell, and the other women of problematic reputation engage in when they are alone together, free of male company. The women's discourse here is close to being what Spacks calls "serious gossip," a conversation that defines a subcultural community as well as the identity of each person in the group, as interpretations, judgments, and understanding are clarified.[16] Having invited Orlando to join their society, Nell and the others share their life stories along with "fine tales" and "amusing observations" (*Orlando*, 219).

Are the life stories reflective, and are the "amusing observations" interpretive? Do they evaluate and clarify identity and community? The narrator only sketches these conversational gatherings, and perhaps they do not rise to community-forming "serious gossip." Yet serious gossip, or what I would rather call "cooperative discourse," is the prevailing discourse during the latter half of the two dinners in *The Waves*. Here both sexes share their life stories, interpret (and accept, reject, or modify interpretations given by the others), and confirm their continuing identity as a small community of close friends. As they do so, they dialogically take up and develop each other's phrases and images. They cooperate in creating a text that the entire small community has produced; each contributing, they "write" the kind of shared understanding or text that Jennifer Coates has described as typical of a small group of women engaged in gossip.[17]

A cooperative text is also produced in *Mrs. Dalloway* at Lady Bruton's luncheon, a subtly amusing occasion of serious gossip. Lady Bruton, descended from a military family and concerned in past and present with political causes, is herself a dialogic mix of discourses. For instance, when she asks Richard about Clarissa, this relational inquiry (not entirely perfunctory) is lightly mocked by the narrator; Lady Bruton's question "signified recognition of some *feminine comradeship* which went beneath *masculine lunch parties*" (my emphasis).[18] We expect *feminine* lunch parties and *masculine* comradeship, but the narrator offers instead some dialogic juxtapositions and in effect gives us a linguistic sketch of Lady Bruton (Lady Brute) as manly "fem-speak."

The dialogically humorous mix of gender ideologies here ("feminine comradeship," "masculine lunch parties") presages the feminizing of the entire occasion. Although Richard and Hugh help Lady Bruton with her letter to the *Times* about immigration, the focus of the lunch is their gossip about Peter Walsh's failure at love and life. His return to England is "vaguely flattering to them all" (*Mrs. Dalloway*, 162), as they each interpret Peter's character, his moral outsiderhood, while at the same time confirming their self-satisfied communal identity, their own (mocked, comic) companionable rectitude. No single consciousness or speaker supplies the discourse for this event, but all present contribute to the constructing of the cooperative, gossipy, identity-confirming and group-confirming text. The relational language of such episodes is not a semiotic or pre-oedipal lyricism; yet it does not speak the Law of the Father either. The symbolic order is for the occasion dialogically and comically misappropriated by the voice that relates and relationalizes it.

In addition to the cooperatively produced text, there is in Woolf's fiction the relational or feminine discourse described by Carol Gilligan—a language of sympathy and relationship where identity formation and the resolution of moral issues depend especially on engagement with another person's feelings and point of view. When employing this discourse, which usually evolves only two voices, the speaker considers the effect on the other person or the way in which the listener may respond. Woolf in effect describes this kind of responsiveness in her observations on letters and memoirs (of male as well as female writers). In "Lives of the Obscure," she speaks of minor women novelists and obscure writers of letters and memoirs as sharing with more significant authors (such as Jane Austen and Madame de Sévigné) a female tradition of writing to "give pleasure" and "to entertain" (*CE*, 4:129).

Such letter writers are responsive to the person who will eventually read the letter or novel. As Woolf says of the correspondence between Horace Walpole and William Cole, "good letter-writers feel the drag of the face on the other side of the page and obey it," a responsiveness that results in a "mingling of voices" ("The Humane Art," *CE*, 1:102). She also speaks of the letters between these two "antiquaries" as being full of gossip, the daily details of life (102–3). In "Two Antiquaries: Walpole and Cole," Woolf examines the antiquarian gossip as the shared avocation of friends (*CE*, 3:113). If they are good letter writers, Woolf implies, both men and women adopt a relational, dialogic discourse that responds to the interests, preferences, and indeed the subjectivity of the other person. Patricia Spacks also suggests that letters, memoirs, and even some fiction belong to a kind of gossip.[19]

Again, I would emphasize that the dialogic style of the letters and memoirs that Woolf is describing is not a radical *écriture féminine*. It is not a violent subversion of the symbolic; nor is it lyrical, nonsensical, or semiotic. As Woolf describes them, the letters of Madame de Sévigné show her responding to "the wit of La Rochefoucauld," while Josephus, Pascal, and romances are "embedded in her mind. Their verses, their stories rise to her lips along with her own thoughts" ("Madame de Sévigné," *CE*, 3:66–67). The subjectivity of Mme de Sévigné is ideologically complex. Her discourse is dialogic, incorporating appositionally into a feminine concern for her daughter even the symbolic discourses of privilege and authority, yet appropriating these, feminizing them, for her own relational purposes. The "humane art" of letter writing has a civilizing effect, Woolf implies. The dialogic discourse of a Sévigné can transform or feminize even the symbolic discourses that once belonged only to the urbane tyranny of the prerevolutionary French court, the philosophers, or the professionals.

The discourses, then, by which Woolf constructs texts and subjectivities (in her imaginative reviews as well as in her novels), are varied and subtle. One cannot fit them easily into a scheme of binary difference. Unlike many discourses that have been called "feminine" (and that are so different from the dominant symbolic), the relational discourses used by Woolf tend dialogically to infiltrate and modify the "masculine" ideologies that inhabit the same text. It is, after all, a characteristic of relational discourse, as in personal letters, to respond to the other speaker (and the other's language). Relational language (unlike the semiotic or the *écriture féminine*) does not declare open opposition and revolution. It does not inevitably deconstruct; instead, relational language, as a mode of the dialogic, retextualizes all other language. The young women in Gilligan's study, *A Different Voice*, often retold in relational terms the ethical dilemma that was described to them.[20] That is, they retextualized (dialogically misappropriated) the story in a way that privileged relationships rather than laws and rules.

Although Woolf said that women writers need to think back through their mothers, she also affirmed that the mind of the mature writer "can think back through its fathers or through its mothers" (*Room*, 101), and she evidently in her own work thought back through many writers, men and women, and many kinds of discourses. Woolf was intimately and appreciatively acquainted with writers who used the dominant, and often dominating, male discourses of the symbolic order. Just as Stephen Dedalus was, according to his friend Cranly, "supersaturated with the religion" against which he was rebelling,[21] so Woolf was supersaturated with a male literary and cultural tradition against which she was, in many ways, rebelling. She was also supersaturated with the writings of women, and she was imbued with many different kinds of discourses used by women (novels, diaries, poetry, memoirs, letters). Being a relational, dialogic subjectivity herself, she could speak not only the language of men and the language of women but many of the various dialects and idioms of each tradition.

Feminizing the Narrator: *Jacob's Room*

Like Virginia Woolf, the female narrator of *Jacob's Room* is also well acquainted with symbolic discourses and with discourses more usually designated "feminine." In Woolf's first experimental novel, the central narrative ideology (the male bildungsroman) is so completely understated that it is virtually mute. Into this blank, this lack, this wild area, pour a variety of relational idioms, discourses derived from women's traditions; these discourses feminize the male text that they are relating. The female narrator (who often draws upon the observations of subnarrators, mostly women) appropriates the position of subject in the text. As Patricia Waugh summarizes traditional narrative, the inscription of subjectivity, "historically constructed and expressed through the phenomenological equation self/other, necessarily rests masculine 'selfhood' upon feminine 'otherness'."[22] In Woolf's novel, however, Jacob becomes, in a reversal of the Lacanian description of discourse, the other, the blank, the lack, the absence against which the narrator's subjectivity develops and grows.

Jacob's Room could well be called "Mrs. Woolf and Mr. Flanders." Just as Woolf in "Mr. Bennett and Mrs. Brown" asks all the male realists to consider with more subtlety the complex and mysterious "Mrs. Brown" (*CE*, 1:324–37), so the narrator in *Jacob's Room* resolves to understand and portray this strange, unknown person, this young English male. It is as though Woolf counters Freud's famous question, but the gossiping, analyzing narrator of *Jacob's Room* asks, "What do *men* want?" And the construction of the novel itself (female narrator as strong subject, character Jacob as mystery) pushes the implications of that question into further questions: do they want Shakespeare? a tour of Greece? love? war? That is, the usual concommitants of the symbolic order (of most masculine discourses and life myths) are cast by the questioning narrator into the realm of strangeness, peculiarity, otherness. One way in which the narrator feminizes the entire novel is in retextualizing the ordinary symbolic structures as strange; reading these structures from her more relational culture and point of view, she sees them as *not* natural or customary but as odd, rigid, oppressive, sinister. Indeed, these structures destroy Jacob.

The contrast of the masculine structures and the more relational ones is acknowledged by the narrator herself. She notes the difference in age and sex; she is ten years older than Jacob, and a woman.[23] Yet she is well acquainted with the masculine and symbolic discourses that are shaping the young man's life, or at least she seems to know many of its texts: Shakespeare, Shelley, Virgil, Plato, and others. Like Jacob, she also has made the tour of Greece and Italy. Although they share a discourse to some extent, her dialogical angle is different. While Jacob is often bored and disappointed with his tour (and numbly distressed once he falls in love with the married Sandra Williams), the narrator offers brief lyrical meditations on the Mediterranean landscape—on the Acropolis, for instance (*Jacob's Room*, 160–61). She interjects, fondly recalling the "lonely hilltop" in Italy "seen by me." Meanwhile, Jacob has just been considering "doing Greece," and then he might "knock off Rome"; possibly then he could write up his thoughts on civilization, "something in the style of Gibbon" (136). Jacob's casual colloquialisms here suggest that for him the privileged symbolic discourse of education and travel is routine; something that he perceives as an expected pattern, easily understood and summed up.

And yet Jacob resists, though somewhat casually, being summed up. Unlike his teacher, the priestlike Sopwith who is adept at "summing things up" (41), Jacob tries to ignore being categorized by his education and the socialization process generally. He resists his "interpellation" (to use Louis Althusser's word), that is, his subjection to the social apparatus that is "hailing" him,[24] pulling him in, calling him to his vocation of male subjecthood in a war-making state. The narrator's understanding of discourse, however, is the very opposite of the perspective of Jacob's tutors and his patriarchal society. She insists often that one cannot "sum people up" (31, 154); one cannot know Jacob, though all his acquaintances offer opinions (70–73).

As an explanation for her more open view of human beings, the narrator offers a very Bakhtinian description of discourse. After tentatively portraying some of Jacob's words, gestures, and thoughts, the narrator says that the representation is still incomplete:

Moreover, *part of this is not Jacob but Richard Bonamy*—the room; the market carts; the hour; *the very moment of history. Then consider the effect of sex*—how between man and woman it hangs wavy, tremulous, so that here's a valley, there's a peak, when in truth, perhaps, all's as flat as my hand. *Even the exact words get the wrong accent on them.* (73; my emphasis)

Jacob's language (in fact, his "self") is in part someone else's, to paraphrase Bakhtin; Jacob's language is partly that of his friend Bonamy, of the institutions of his time, and of the genderized perspective of male subjectivity. Although the conscientious narrator claims to draw upon many sources, even if she quotes (the exact words), the accent will be wrong. When she tries to read this muted other, the dialogical angle of her discourse may skew the result.

As a text, *Jacob's Room* is massively invaded, appropriated, by feminine voices. Jacob's narrative room is full of women. Indeed, William Handley argues that Woolf's pacifism (and her modernist aesthetic) is embodied in the tension between the female narrator's very personal discourse and the militaristic, dehumanizing culture that objectifies and kills Jacob; but as Jane Archer notes, "We never escape the perspective of the woman and writing" in this novel. And Virginia Blain emphasizes that the many feminine voices in effect develop a "female perspective as the norm"; as Rachel Bowlby suggests, the narrator is like Mrs. Norman, the woman who observes

Jacob on the train and who concocts outrageous stories about him.[25] The text is a gloss of gossiping feminine commentary. Although one narrator gives us the overall text, she constructs it as though it were a group-derived text like those described by Coates in her studies of discourse among women.

The text about Jacob begins with the "voice" of Betty Flanders, the words of her letter, as she refers to her husband's death. Her first spoken words are, "Well, if Jacob doesn't want to play" (7), words spoken to her son Archer whom she sends to find Jacob on the beach. And Jacob doesn't want to play: he never seems to play the patriarchal game seriously. He is, in a sense, orphaned by the symbolic order. The "law" of his personal biological father is absent, so Jacob, as a result, is perhaps more relational, more vulnerable to feminine discourses, and more problematic as a man of England. Yet his brother calls him on the beach, hails him, and it is the masculine discourse that finally incorporates Jacob into his country's military discourse and kills him. Although the narrator, and so many feminine voices, try to "write" Jacob or re-vision him, in the end he becomes the male-as-absence, a dead soldier, a mysterious other to the observing and speaking feminine subject, the narrator.

Jacob's voice, or his male subjectivity, begins only four of the fourteen chapters in the novel: chapters 5, 8, 12, and 13. The reader is continually asked to look elsewhere and to listen to women's voices especially. The first chapter that begins with Jacob's thoughts or words is chapter 5, in which he is in his London rooms and trying to identify a quotation. Immediately, however, the narrator begins several pages of description and reflection about London, before telling us that Bonamy visits Jacob that evening and they decide the quotation is from Lucretius, not Virgil (69). Chapter 8 begins with a brief, almost parodic sketch of Jacob's day at the office before the narrator develops her reflections on letters, especially those from Mrs. Flanders. Chapter 12 is almost Jacob's chapter, as he travels in Italy and Greece; there is occasionally some nearly conventional rendition here of his subjectivity through free, indirect discourse. Although most of chapter 13 concerns other people's comments about Jacob, it does begin with a short conversation between Jacob and Bonamy when Jacob returns to London. Thus, in a novel supposedly about Jacob, much of the text asks us to look away from Jacob and instead to consider the miscellaneous concerns of minor characters and of the narrator.

The turning points of the novel (the beginnings of chapters) do not usually ask the reader to turn toward Jacob. Most chapters begin with the voices or thoughts of women. The first two chapters are dominated by Mrs. Flanders, though the second chapter also begins in Scarborough's gossiping female voices with their opinions about the interesting widow. Jacob is at college in chapter 3, but the chapter begins with Mrs. Norman's misreading of Jacob in the railway carriage; chapter 4 begins with the narrator's response to paper editions of Shakespeare along with her observations on how handsome Timmy Durrant is (47), as he and Jacob sail near the Scilly Isles. After chapter 5, which actually quotes Jacob in its first sentence, chapter 6 begins with a description of the Guy Fawkes bonfire, then Florinda's face and her words as she declares to Jacob how unhappy she is (74). The enthusiastic narrator describes the woman's world of paper flowers and calling cards at the beginning of chapter 7. After the token description of Jacob's day at the beginning of chapter 8, the next three chapters begin in the consciousness of women—the countess who has Jacob to lunch (100), Fanny Elmer who falls in love with Jacob (114), and then Mrs. Flanders at her letter writing (125). At these conventional transition points in the novel, we hear the relational language of women as they talk about Jacob; most of them like him, wonder what sort of person he is, and offer fragmentary interpretations of him as he walks past their lives.

Just as the novelist will note the character of Mrs. Brown "imposing itself" ("Mr. Bennett and Mrs. Brown," *CE*, 1:324), so these women sense Jacob briefly imposing himself on their very feminine world and discourse. Yet their discourse virtually defines subjectivity in this novel. Woolf thus turns the tables on narrative practice. In order to find words, and to declare its subjectivity, the "male" sentence in this novel must first acquire a feminine "infection," a female voice willing to draw Jacob into the conventions of signification, conventions controlled for the most part in this text by the language of women: relational concern, gossip, dailiness, and the communal construction of a story.

Part of the wonderful humor in this novel, an element that I have discussed elsewhere as a bildungsroman parody, derives in addition from a strategy very close to narrative transgression.[26] There is a highly self-reflective play between the narrator and Jacob. It is almost as though they overhear each other. In this self-conscious narrative, the masculine Jacob has no choice but to succumb dialogically to the feminine narrator's interpretation. (What else can he do!) The narrator, for instance, is well acquainted with the feminine domestic tutoring that started "the Greek myth," the discourse that makes every young man think he must tour and idolize Greece. The "governesses" start it, and "we have been brought up in an illusion," explains the narrator to the reader (138). Confidently, she affirms that the bored Jacob probably agrees, and sure enough, we then hear him say: "But it's the way we're brought up" (138). Jacob is not allowed to attach his boredom to a more masculine discourse of world-weariness, the language, say, of modernist alienation. Instead, the source of his boredom is feminized; we are invited to believe that his loss of faith in the discourse of governesses is the root of his *accidie*.

The voices of the governess, of the mother and the motherly, of the curious or romantic female, control most of Jacob's text. Yet much of the poignancy of this very subtle novel results from the fact that the apparently peripheral masculine voices (those "prophesying war") do eventually invade the text, but this happens like a slow shock. We learn, even through the female narrator, that Jacob is educated among men who control and categorize—men who sum up. When we (as readers) seem to get Jacob to ourselves, so to speak, during the conventionally narrated beginning of chapter 12, there is a rich amalgam of discourses. At the start of Jacob's tour of Italy, the female narrator maintains the nearly conventional neutrality of indirect discourse. We hear Jacob noticing a "motor car full of Italian officers" (135). Jacob has always been conscious of himself as the "inheritor" (45) of Western, masculine culture, and threads of literary discourse emerge as he notes the "trees laced together with vines—as Virgil said" (135). After thus footnoting his observations, he passes a train station where there is "a tremendous leave-taking going on" in preparation for war, though Jacob offers no footnote commentary to this effect. He is still musing on Virgil, and he thinks, "It was the custom of the ancients to train vines between elms." The bland reverence of symbolic authority here (custom, ancients) could be a quoted note from a Latin reader. Then Jacob irritably responds to the discomfort of the journey, the Italian trains being "damnably hot with the afternoon sun on them" (135).

In a few minutes, a few sentences, Jacob moves through at least two discourses that have a masculine accent—his pedantic yet poetic recollection of pastoral Virgil and his youthful, nonchalantly violent "damnably hot." Is the "full" car of officers merely an objective observation of Jacob? (But why "full"? Why not just a "car of Italian officers"?) Do the "full" car and the "tremendous" farewell suggest that these observed scenes are making a greater, more alarming, impression on Jacob then he is willing to acknowledge? He can deliberately link his subjectivity to literature, to Virgil, to an Italian landscape; however, he does not yet see that he, as inheritor of Italy and the West, is also hailed, called, or subjected to the responsibilities of symbolic discourse and to the heroics of war.

Yet a feminine voice also follows Jacob, even in these initial paragraphs of chapter 12 where the narrator is less intrusive than usual. In the midst of his irritation about the heat (and perhaps his suppressed alarm about war preparations), a distinctly maternal voice suddenly describes the laboring train: "Up, up, up it goes, like a train on a scenic railway" (135). This is a motherly voice reading a story to a child: up, up, up. These first three paragraphs of the chapter, from which I have been quoting, are intricately dialogic. Several voices contend, as it were, for Jacob's soul. Surrounded textually by the subjectivity of women, Jacob often draws an interpretation from the domestic and relational tradition, even while a patriarchal discourse prepares the text and Jacob for war.

Near the end of the novel, the narrator's persistently relational concerns and her feminine discourse accumulate some very sinister language and imagery. If the character overhears the narrator, the narrator also overhears the character. In the last two pages of chapter 12, the narrator is describing her own mental passage from the Mediterranean back to England, to London churches, streets, and banks. It is as though the narrator, having given Jacob his necessary tour of the origins of Western civilization, has collected from patriarchal discourses a militaristic souvenir or two as she went along. Although she has infected the male traditions of discourse, these have also begun to infect her language. In the final paragraph of chapter 12, she says that sunlight "strikes" the "shaving-glasses," and she goes on to describe the summer sunshine:

> The bright, inquisitive, *armoured*, resplendent, summer's day, which has long since *vanquished* chaos; which has dried the melancholy medieval mists; drained the swamp and stood glass and stone upon it; and equipped our brains and bodies with such an *armoury of weapons* that merely to see the *flash* and *thrust* of limbs engaged in the conduct of *daily life* is better than the old pageant of *armies* drawn out in *battle array* upon the plain. (163; my emphasis)

The pacifist voice of the narrator profoundly deconstructs itself here. At this point in the text, the narrator's feminizing vision becomes conflicted. The deliberately posed *oppositions* (war and daily life) both speak in military images and so undercut the contrast.

The narrator cannot prevent the discourse of armor and conquest from infecting her lyric praise of daily life (the "armoured ... summer's day" that "vanquished chaos" and the mental "armoury of weapons" against primitive conditions). The narrator's praise of the civilizing effects of enlightened pragmatism and control dips into images of weaponry and conquest. Perhaps this dialogic tension indicates the inability of Western civilization to limit its control to the conquest of swamps and mists: it must conquer everything else as well. Although the phrases try to make a contrast, the contrast becomes problematic as armor and thrusts and conquest infiltrate the entire passage.

Yet more than a contrast is asserted. The narrator also makes a value judgment: ordinary life is better than war. Does the deconstructive activity in the passage suggest that the narrator does not quite believe that daily concerns are really better, more valuable, than heroic conquest? Are the daily concerns of shaving, watching the sunlight, and the "flash and thrust of limbs" (with perhaps a hint of lovemaking) not as valuable as the great public, historic, symbolic discourses of heroism, politics, and military logistics?

Earlier in the novel, the narrator herself asks a question similar to mine. Although the narrator affirms the value of letters for easing loneliness, for communication, she questions their typical, ordinary subject matter: dinner, tea, news, social life. The narrator muses, "And yet, and yet . . . when we go to dinner, when pressing fingertips we hope to meet somewhere soon, a doubt insinuates itself; is this the way to spend our days?" (93). Although "the notes accumulate," the narrator briefly questions whether their daily, social concerns are a valuable discourse. By 1929, Woolf herself suggests in "Women and Fiction" that women novelists may want "to alter the established values—to make serious what appears insignificant to a man and trivial what is to him important" (*CE*, 2:146). The women writers will feminize, even trivialize, the (masculine) "serious," and they will see as valuable what his discourse has inscribed as merely female and trivial. The narrator of *Jacob's Room*, however, seems unable to share this confidence in the value of the ordinary and the feminine.

Nevertheless, the narrator is an experimental subjectivity, acquainted with both the trivial and the serious, the (feminine) discourses of social dailiness and the (masculine) discourses of public history, Western literary culture, and war. The narrator assumes subject status for herself, and by placing Jacob in the subordinate narrative position of other, she necessarily feminizes his story, his career, his muted subjectivity. Although this narrator apparently doubts whether her feminizing and relational discourses are "better" than the renowned ideology of empire, which eventually inscribes Jacob, yet her narration still critiques that symbolic ideology by dialogically teasing it and rendering it almost mute.

The narrator's complex relational discourse, drawing upon the gossip of others, crowds the discursive "room" with her language and effectively evicts Jacob from his own story. By the time the narrator describes Mrs. Flanders asking Bonamy what to do with Jacob's shoes, the dead Jacob has been reduced to an absence, an empty narrative space, a man whose feet do not need the vacant shoes (176). He is defeated by his manly subjection to the symbolic discourse of war (the political value of which disturbs the narrator's language). Yet Jacob is throughout the text distanced from any narrative affirmation of that discourse of empire, because he is paradoxically inscribed as uninscribable. That is, Jacob is given the narrative position usually reserved for the female character; he is muted and other, a shadowy subjectivity in a male subculture, while a woman's voice, from the *narratively* dominant feminine culture, dialogically tells his story with a relational curiosity and concern.

Feminizing the Symbolic: *The Waves*

Woolf's first experimental novel virtually turns narrative practice upside down, as the dominant female narrator transforms the male symbolic of quest, empire, and war into a muted, strange, unspeakable otherness. In the next two novels, the major female characters also borrow and transform symbolic structures, but their dialogic hybridizing of these structures is less drastic than the operations of the narrator of *Jacob's Room*. Like this narrator, however (and like the voices in *The Waves*), Clarissa Dalloway, Mrs. Ramsay, and Lily Briscoe primarily seek to appropriate and transform the symbolic, rather than explosively shattering it with semiotic oppositions or deconstructions. For this reason, a brief look at the experimental discourse and subjectivity of these women will be a helpful preparation for my discussion of *The Waves*, which also is a feminizing of several symbolic life structures.

Again here, and throughout this chapter, my concern is not so much with the radical, polar oppositions of discourse in Woolf's texts (though such discourse is there and has received well-deserved critical attention). Instead, my focus is the subtle hybridizing and retextualizing of the symbolic structures, the (often male-derived) discourses that Woolf was—like Stephen Dedalus—supersaturated with, even though she subjects them to her critique and to her transformative, dialogic prose.

Although the distraught veteran Septimus has been described, by Minow-Pinkney, as breaking into a liberating discourse of semiotic rhythms and images,[27] his narrative counterpart, Clarissa Dalloway, begins to speak a more subtle, and less oppositional, experimental language. I am not convinced that the visions of Septimus free him into a pre-oedipal and liberated subjectivity; indeed, he is floundering in the still very manly, but garbled, symbolic order. His persistent subjection to this order where Dr. Bradshaw and the empire define manhood becomes very clear when Septimus realizes that he, "the lord of men," is "called forth" to be sacrificed, "given whole"; when he asks, "To whom?," the voices answer, "To the Prime Minister" (*Mrs. Dalloway*, 101–2). The state is still God for Septimus. He does not have a religious, prophetic vision but a parody of one; his madness is a distorted affirmation of the war ideology that has destroyed him.

To some extent, Clarissa shares his desire for cultural affirmation and discursive legitimacy. Both wish to be heroes, though gender writes Clarissa as the heroic social impresario, the "perfect hostess." As a young woman, Clarissa felt the derogatory scorn when Peter called her the "perfect hostess" (93). She is a good example of the unsuccessfully socialized woman that I described in the first chapter. She has been successfully socialized, successfully incorporated into her society on condition that she not really be incorporated into it (into its centers of power). Her gender places her in the contradictory subjectivity of hostess, a feminine self that will be taken seriously only on condition that such a self not be taken seriously.

Within this problematic, contradictory subjectivity, Clarissa understandably experiments with discourses that might explain her to herself and others, that might defend her ideological legitimacy. She tries out some official, "masculine" words; she appropriates and feminizes language drawn from the symbolic as a way of demonstrating to herself that she and her parties are important or valuable. The closest she comes to a symbolic rationale for her parties is that they are an "offering" (184–85); yet this word could drag in all the manly baggage of religion, conversion, and God—the components of an oppressive discourse that Clarissa rejects (191). Unlike Septimus, she does not sacrifice her sanity and life as an offering to the prime minister, though the potential parallel is part of her admitted "corruption" (280–81). Instead, Clarissa dialogically hybridizes the word *offering*. She warps it into relational and egalitarian discourse. Her party is "an offering; to combine, to create; but to whom?" In Clarissa's nonreligious discourse, there is no "to whom," no hierarchy, no god. "An offering for the sake of offering, perhaps. Anyhow, it was her gift" (185).

The symbolic word *offering* is already mutating when it enters the phrase "offering for the sake of offering," because the word's ritualistic (symbolic) tradition implies petition, propitiation, exchange, and request. Within symbolic discourse, an offering requires a "to whom," and the "whom" is an authority, the Law of the Father, God, or the prime minister. From Clarissa's feminizing of symbolic discourse here, a dialogic hybrid results, an objectless offering, in fact a gift—as Clarissa declares, appositionally amending her experimental discourse.

Unlike the narrator of *Jacob's Room*, Clarissa evidently assures herself of the value of a feminine or relational discourse (and life). She adapts and warps symbolic discourse to her own needs. Unlike Miss Kilman and Dr. Bradshaw, Clarissa does not seek to convert anyone—not even herself—to the political and linguistic order that yet enables her to be the hostess. At the end of the book, as I noted earlier, she returns to her guests; for her, any dialogic explanations, any self-understanding or self-fulfillment, become chiefly a means of living a relational discourse.

In *To the Lighthouse*, also, there are several experimental subjectivities, ideologically flexible characters. Some of the women in this novel, even though they are adept at discourse traditions deriving from female culture, do experiment with symbolic discourse as well. Elizabeth Abel has described Cam's encounter with her father's language and her eventual retreat from this language that excludes her and her mother.[28] Although not allowed to speak this language, Mrs. Ramsay knows its idiom, and her subjectivity incorporates a manly tough-minded ideology of empiricism. Her "inner speech," as the Bakhtinian school would call it, is much wider than the gracious discourse by which she encourages community among her guests. It is wider than the motherly folklore, which haunts her about the effect on James of the cancelled trip to the lighthouse. "Children never forget," she thinks, as she collects some of the pictures he has been cutting out.[29] As she reflects, sinking into herself and losing "personality" (*Lighthouse*, 96), her inner speech includes, to her annoyance, some remnants of her culture's religious discourse: "We are in the hands of the Lord" (97). In an inner dialogue, she answers this with the ideology of modernist, atheistic disillusionment. No "Lord" could have created such a disordered world, she thinks, in which there is no justice or lasting happiness (98).

Although this pessimistic discourse is a central construct in Mrs. Ramsay's subjectivity (that is, she believes it), she does not speak it aloud. Her experimental consciousness is various (like Montaigne's, like Virginia Woolf's), a mingling of conflicting discourses in dialogic play. Yet her symbolic discourse here, an Arnoldian discourse of nostalgic atheism, is muted in Mrs. Ramsay. It is not supposed to structure the feminine self. So she drops her sad look (and sad discourse), puts on her shawl, and joins Mr. Ramsay for a walk in the yard.

When he inquires about her sadness, she refuses to speak the discourse that it signified; she realizes that "they could not share that; they could not say that" (104). Often in Woolf's female characters what is really muted is not the *woman's* language and culture, but the *woman's acquaintance with the discourses of male privilege* within the symbolic order. Since the dominant society does not perceive a woman as rational (or as an alienated modern), Mrs. Ramsay keeps her inner speech to herself. She keeps in the closet her (illegal) appropriation of these symbolic discourses.

Lily also is an experimental self constructed of more than one discourse. She can engage in dinner-party trivia, though she dislikes succumbing to it and being "nice" (139). She also dislikes the philosophical technicalities of Mr. Ramsay's "work," at least when Andrew describes the focus of his father's book: "Subject and object and the nature of reality" (38). Earlier critics who identified Lily as androgynous in effect acknowledged her subjectivity as inscribed by both masculine and feminine discourses; structuralist readers are more likely to describe the pre-oedipal sources of her subjectivity as Rachel DuPlessis does, or on the contrary to find Lily's art, as Homans claims, modeled on the son's discourse, since a woman's absence (Mrs. Ramsay's death) is required for representation, for art.[30]

Indeed, as Lily begins to identify herself as an artist, she does appropriate a discourse of work or vocation from the symbolic order, but she transforms it and feminizes it. Lily is another one of those failed or mediocre artists that have puzzled readers of Woolf's fiction. Woolf, however, does not argue in *A Room of One's Own* that women's fiction should start providing images of successful women in the professions or the arts; she does not urge positive role models. What Woolf requests of future women writers is that they refuse to limit a female character's subjectivity to one (feminine) discourse only. As she puts it, the representation of women has been "much too simple and much too monotonous. Suppose, for instance, that men were only represented in literature as the lovers of women, and were never the friends of men, soldiers, thinkers, dreamers." (*Room*, 87). Among Shakespeare's characters, Woolf continues, only something of Othello and Antony might be left, and there would be no Brutus, Hamlet, Lear, or Jacques. Yet in literature about women, "love was the only possible interpreter" (87). For Lily, love is not the only possible interpreter (discourse, ideology, narrative). Lily is acquainted with more than one discourse. Her "vision," especially its process, is the important thing, as recent critics like Pamela Caughie have emphasized, rather than the value of the painting itself.[31] Lily is the major dreamer and thinker in *To the Lighthouse*.

Lily's vision does not come easily. Along with her meditative assessment of her relationship to the archetypal gender signifiers, Mr. Ramsay and Mrs. Ramsay, Lily gradually frees herself and her language from Charles Tansley's exclusionary discourse about women painters. While she paints on the Ramsay's terrace before the war, she imagines that her painting will "never be seen; never be hung even, and there was Mr. Tansley whispering in her ear, 'Women can't paint, women can't write' " (75). Although Tansley's words haunt Lily's consciousness dialogically for years, she almost from the first understands that he doesn't believe them. At dinner, she speculates that the negative statements are "for some reason helpful to him" (130). They probably are helpful to the defensive scholar Tansley, who must write his dissertation in an era in which women were threatening the *sermo patrius* and feminizing literature and art.

Also during Mrs. Ramsay's dinner, Lily dialogically appropriates the discourse of work, of *his work*, a gendered phrase that she had previously used only for a man's career or interest. Regarding Mr. Ramsay's dubious success as a philosopher, Lily had always been ready to "think of his work" (38). As the dinner proceeds, we can see Lily appropriating this phrase but adapting it as she does so. When it first occurs to her at dinner, she conventionally applies it to men; she decides that Mr. Bankes "is not in the least pitiable. He has his work." Then she "remembered all of a sudden as if she had found a treasure, that she had her work" (128).

At this moment, in which she feminizes the (symbolic) discourse of vocation and claims it as her language, she decides to change her painting—to move the tree more toward the middle. The imagery of *treasure* is probably important here, as Lily discovers her language and subjectivity, since *treasure* often signifies integrity in Woolf's fiction; Clarissa, knowing that Dr. Bradshaw can force a person's soul, wonders if Septimus died "holding his treasure" (*Mrs. Dalloway*, 281). In appropriating while transforming the symbolic discourse of work, Lily preserves her own treasure; that is, she evidently does not become appropriated by, or infected with, the muscular idiom of work as self-aggrandizement or fame. Although she wishes she were a better artist, there is no indication that she perceives her work as a matter of official documents (like Tansley's dissertation) or an alphabetical ladder of rigorous success. Her subjectivity is not structured on a desperate ambition to move from A to B.

That is, Lily's experimental self is dialogic and appositional. While she adapts from the (male) symbolic a discourse of work or vocation, she also develops a discourse of the woman-as-artist. Like Bernard in *The Waves*, Lily has a vision of a woman writing. After the death of Mrs. Ramsay, as Lily continues to work on the painting, she recalls how she and Tansley once skipped rocks while Mrs. Ramsay sat nearby writing letters. Remembering this scene, Lily recalls that she had become less and less angry at Tansley while Mrs. Ramsay "sitting there writing under the rock resolved everything into simplicity" (*Lighthouse*, 239). Resolving and relating are major activities or structures of Mrs. Ramsay's subjectivity, just as they are also Clarissa's gift. Yet Lily's memory here includes not only such preeminently feminine discourses, for Lily recalls that Mrs. Ramsay is writing letters.

It is significant that Mrs. Ramsay is *not* knitting a stocking in this recollection or presiding at a dinner; here she does not image the semiotic or pre-oedipal, but the adult and post-oedipal, the literate use of the symbolic system. Remembering Mrs. Ramsay and her complex discourses, along with Tansley's discourse of work, Lily reaffirms her own appositional discourse. She invokes the symbolic discourse of quest or work, but she does so experimentally, rejecting the exclusionary rigidity of Tansley's discourse; she thus hybridizes and feminizes the discourse of the artist's calling. In the remembered presence of the woman writing, Lily becomes someone who paints (one of the dreamers and thinkers). Her vision (310) when she completes the painting is as much her re-vision of herself, her dialogic freeing and fashioning of her experimental subjectivity, as it is the finishing stroke that she makes on the canvas.

Lily finds or declares her work, appositionally improvising a discourse of vocation that is not as individualistic as Tansley's yet not as conventional and passive as Mrs. Ramsay's solicitous caring. In *Orlando* and *The Waves*, however, there is less sense that one can define a work or an identity. Lily found a phrase, or several, for her experimental self, but *Orlando* discards almost as many self-defining phrases or discourses as she finds, calling them "illusions" (*Orlando*, 174). In the course of centuries, she changes ideologies, including several masculine and several feminine ideologies, as she appropriates, interrogates, and abandons a subjectivity that continually is being constructed. There is in *The Waves* a similarly experimental discourse of the self. Although Bernard's friend Neville says, "I am a story. Louis is a story" (*Waves*, 37), and apparently agrees that each person is inscribed like a discourse, yet none of these characters or voices sees just *one* story (or one work in life) as being the only (authoritative) symbolic.

These voices seem to inscribe, as most readers have observed, rather archetypal or stereotypical lives. The six friends are written by clichés of the symbolic order: the family man and amateur writer (Bernard), the earth mother (Susan), the madwoman (Rhoda), the homosexual scholar (Neville), the bourgeois capitalist (Louis), the pleasure seeker (Jinny). Each voice or character is indeed almost a *caricature*, the word Virginia Woolf uses as she describes her plans for the book (*D*, 3:300). Yet Woolf's narrative (or antinarrative) style interrogates these basically symbolic life ideologies, and critics have variously examined the decentered subjectivities that result. Several readers have recently suggested that the voices hover (or are constructed) between polarities of some kind. Bernard moves between a masculine symbolic and a feminine semiotic, Minow-Pinkney argues, and Gabriele Schwab finds all six characters caught between society's codes and an "imaginary unboundedness," while Patrick McGee suggests that the Brechtian displacements emphasize history as a process that shapes "the subject as an intersubject, as a composite or hybrid in the symbolic order of everyday life"; more elaborately, Miriam Wallace and Tony Jackson each offer differing and quite subtle interpretations of the polarities of stylistic metonymy and metaphor in the representation of these voices, Wallace emphasizing that subjectivity in *The Waves* is an "inherently relational" oscillation between individuality and the desire to merge.[32]

Since my focus is Woolf's discursive transformation of symbolic structures, I will be calling attention to this creative, relational sharing (among the six friends) of phrases and narratives that are often quite conventional symbolic structures. There is little that is disruptive or semiotic about these six subjectivities (except possibly Rhoda's distress and suicide). Yet the symbolic is transformed—almost transfigured, one might say—by Woolf's narrative and stylistic decisions.

The formal decisions in effect feminize the symbolic material in three ways. In the first place, the style and form (the chantlike statements, the rejection of literary realism, the somewhat dehumanized landscapes of the interludes) narratively displace all symbolic structures. In such a defamiliarized narrative milieu, these six rather conventional (symbolic) lives become other. Somewhat analogous to the feminized textual placement of the bildungsroman in *Jacob's Room*, the six lives in *The Waves* are not given a position of narrative authority and legitimacy; instead, they are alienated from such authority. They are feminized, located as other. They lose narrative legitimation. They glow with artifice and are just "stories."

Secondly, the only element of the usual socialization process that is retained and represented in the novel is that of the lifelong friendship: the "peer group." This text refuses to build up realism's expected context of early parent-child interaction, of detailed scenes and dialogue, of cause-and-effect development of character; instead, we have only the friendship and thus an enormous enhancement of subjectivity as relational, ever changing, creative, dialogic (feminine). The importance of any single story, or of any given symbolic structure, that may contribute to a sense of self, for the six friends, is distantly peripheral to their (unconscious and conscious) sharing. They talk, therefore they are. Finally (and linked to the narrative enhancement of the peer group), the transgressive implications of Bernard's vision of the woman writing, and his own anxiety about writing, suggest that he is a "woman writing," a gossip, a relational friend.

Woolf's care to avoid the conventions of realism still provokes some negative criticism of the novel, Eric Warner insisting that the lack of verisimilitude limits the reader's imagination; with a more political emphasis, Eileen Sypher argues that the absence of social, developmental detail implies that the sex differences (the women are passive, the men assertive) are natural, biological.[33] On the contrary, as I have suggested, the very lack of the conventions of realism prevents anything from becoming essentialist or natural in this novel. Precisely because the sustained, lyric style is never naturalized into ordinary dialogue and idiom, the lives of the characters are never naturalized either. The style dispossesses them of narrative legitimation, thus alienating them from their own (usually symbolic) phrases and stories. The six lives are textually positioned (like Jacob) in otherness, difference, and so in a kind of narrative femininity.

The otherness of the characters or voices is enhanced by the contrasting style of the italicized interludes. The physical world of the interludes is more real (more realistically rendered) than the six voices are. The landscape in these passages acquires a kind of *textual* substance by being described in the ordinary past tense, the tense that is conventionally used in narratives, as Roland Barthes observes, to imply that a story has been told and that something has happened.[34] In contrast, the chapters themselves are narrated in the present tense, except for Bernard's final soliloquy, which is in the past tense and presumably is an attempt to say what has happened. The "pure present" of the chapters contributes to a feeling of timelessness and suspension, as J. W. Graham argues.[35] The use of the present tense also underlines the absence of legitimizing affirmation that would give these more-or-less symbolic stories and lives their traditional place, that is, in the textual center of their own narrative.

The six friends are also experimental selves and feminized subjectivities in that they are vehemently relational. Their whole story *is* their relationship. Further, they seem to be empathic or relational in some unconscious or intuitive way. All of them, including the aloof Rhoda, dip into each other's discourses and images in a manner that suggests Woolf may have been "thinking back" through certain modernist male writers, including Yeats. On a more deliberate level also, these voices are relational, continually inscribing each other into their sustained friendship. In Bernard especially, the language becomes relational, a feminization that he feared as a child; in maturity, he accepts this, as he speaks discourses that Woolf elsewhere employs in her own feminization and evaluation of Joseph Conrad.

In continual relationship with each other, the characters speak as if they agreed with Bakhtin—that everyone's language is partly someone else's. They live and move and have their being in appositional, discursive relationship. They borrow ideology and images but never accent or inflection. Within the nonidiomatic, honed lyricism of the novel, however, the characters do borrow each other's discourse. It is Bernard, for instance, who tells Susan (when they are watching the woman writing) that if discovered they will "be nailed like stoats to the stable door" (*Waves*, 17). Yet Louis, who did not share this childhood adventure of Bernard and Susan, picks up the phrase during Percival's farewell dinner; to be loved by Susan, thinks Louis, would mean being "impaled by a bird's sharp beak" and "nailed to a barnyard door" (120). There is a kind of unconscious dialogic sharing here, since Louis could not have known Bernard's earlier remark to Susan. Yet both men use the same images to acknowledge an ideology of possession. Does Bernard, as a child who will become a writer, recognize that making "phrases" (as the woman is) can be a means of possessing, "nailing" it down? Louis's own control (of his commercial interests and his life) perhaps gives a readiness to his remarks about Susan's possessiveness as wife and mother. Yet it was Jinny's (not Susan's) unexpected kiss that the child Louis experienced as a kind of rape or attack: "I am struck on the nape of the neck. She has kissed me. All is shattered" (13).

Another unexpected sharing, or appropriation, occurs between Jinny and Bernard. Again, the borrowing is not idiomatic, so in this sense it differs from most of the illustrations used by Bakhtin; yet the borrowing is dialogic in that two characters borrow or transform each other's discourses. Jinny first enunciates (as a small child) the imagery of bubbles rising; they "form on the floor of the saucepan" and "rise, quicker and quicker in a silver chain to the top" (11). This early metaphor of Jinny's ardor, her passion and energy, seems to be a meditative, unspoken observation. Yet Bernard over and over as an adult uses variations of this image as a trope for the energy, abundance, and spontaneity of his phrases. His phrases and images rise "like the silver bubbles from the floor of a saucepan" (49); they "begin to bubble up, and I wish to free these bubbles from the trapdoor in my head" (188); "the phrases bubbled up from my lips under the elm trees in the playing-fields" (217). Thus, perhaps Bernard's phrases and stories are an appositional hybrid of conclusiveness (nailing it down) and imaginative disruption, a continual breaking open of possibilities again; his phrases are promiscuous and bubbling, like Jinny's sex life, never committed but always aiming, as Bernard says, to "explore" (16, 240).

Woolf's strategy for representing human consciousness as something shared (either by means of speech or by some kind of unconscious, intuitive perception) may be partly her response to Dostoevsky, as almost all scholars have observed. Indeed in her reading of Doestoevsky and other Russian writers, she finds some of the things that Bakhtin also enunciates. In "Phases of Fiction," she says that too much soul, too much Russian delving into murky philosophical and psychological matters, impoverishes fiction (*CE*, 2:87). Yet Woolf appreciates, as she notes in "The Russian Point of View," the complex mixture of good and evil in the same character where the "old divisions melt into each other" (*CE*, 1:243). In "Modern Fiction," she also contemplates, though with some irritation, the "inconclusiveness of the Russian mind" (*CE*, 2:109). Bakhtin, with enthusiasm rather than irritation, often praises in *Problems of Dostoevsky's Poetics* the "unfinalizability" of the author's heroes.[36] Both the Russian critic and the English one are fascinated by the multiple discourses that melt and mingle in characterization.

Sometimes, the melting and merging occur through conversation, although this novel gives only the soliloquies, which then refer to the ongoing conversations. Still, the friends interact. They talk to each other and in fact gossip a lot, especially about the fascinating Percival. The "communal mode of consciousness," which Malamud observes in *The Waves*, and the search for a "relational conception of self," which Waugh identifies mostly with Bernard,[37] result in part from the continuing engagement of the characters with each other. Although a character is occasionally alone and musing in a genuine soliloquy (especially after the death of Percival), more often two or three are together, and the one who is thinking also refers to, and paraphrases, the concurrent conversation. That is, we are asked to understand that though the style could be called introversive, these six characters are talking to each other much of the time. Their mode of discourse is distinctly relational in that each person depends on the presence of special, lifelong friends for a sustaining sense of identity and community.

In addition, however, some of the dialogic merging of consciousness cannot be explained in any realistic way; it is not the result of conversation but of an unconscious or intuitive understanding. As Maria DiBattista has suggested, Woolf's notion of a shared, "anonymous" level of consciousness may parallel Forster's concept of a realm of general, common experience deeper than personality.[38] Woolf might also have been thinking of Yeats, especially his theory of a "Great Memory," a somewhat Jungian reservoir of cultural images that are the common property of nature itself and of visionary people. Woolf refers to Yeats many times in reviews and essays, quoting "The Lake Isle of Innesfree" in an early *TLS* essay ("Among the Poets") of 1916; she includes several quotations in her reviews of *The Tower* (1928), reviews she wrote during the year of its publication.[39] This is also the year in which she completed *Orlando*, the book that in its conception was linked to *The Waves*. As early as November 1926, Woolf considers plans for a "semi mystic very profound life of a woman" (*D*, 3:118), and she sketches a minimalist plan for the present-tense style of the book in February 1927: "She writes./ They say: She says:/ Night speaks" (*D*, 3:128).

Also late in 1926, Woolf says she is reading sections of Yeats's *Autobiography* (*D*, 3:118–19). The early portions of the *Autobiography* (including the occult, mystical speculations of "The Trembling of the Veil") were published in 1926; this book was part of the library of Leonard and Virginia Woolf, as was *The Tower* and a very early text of psychological and paranormal speculation, Yeats's *Ideas of Good and Evil* (1904).[40] While Woolf was in the midst of writing and revising *The Waves*, she had a long discussion with Yeats and others (in November 1930) about the poet's theories on the "unconscious soul" (as she phrases it in a letter to Vanessa) and his "complete system of philosophy and psychology." Woolf says she agrees "with many of his views" (*Letters*, 4:250).

In *The Waves*, Woolf seems especially to have been interested in Yeats's concept of an *anima mundi*, a world soul, where images are stored and tapped occasionally by those sensitive to them; in "The Tower," the persona tells of seeing dead warriors whose "images" are "in the Great Memory stored."[41] There may be a "nation-wide multiform reverie," Yeats suggests in the *Autobiography*; in *Ideas of Good and Evil*, he had proposed that these often represent a family, or the "genius of the tribe," even "the genius of the world."[42] Percival, who embodies one of the master narratives and symbolic structures of the West, is a kind of "genius" of turn-of-the-century British colonialism as well as the more archetypal seeker of the Grail.

In *The Waves*, this genius of the tribe dies. Woolf may be suggesting that other images will replace the "nation-wide" reverie or dream represented by Percival. Is the woman writing in the garden (an image that haunts Susan and especially Bernard) constructing a relational text that will replace the *sermo patrius*, the varied cultural myth of Parsifal's privileged vision and the mundane but adored administrator of imperial Britain, Woolf's Percival? The woman writing may herself be a new text, a new and feminized discourse; she is a new image of the tribe and one that Bernard finds as he dips his own phrases into the "Great Memory."

Yeats describes also the relationship of the individual and the world's soul in his *Autobiography*, where he asserts that "revelation is from the self, but from that age-long memoried self, that shapes the elaborate shell of the mollusc and the child in the womb, that teaches the birds to make their nest."[43] The prefatorial interludes to each chapter of *The Waves* suggest a kind of nonpersonal or unconscious world, and the fact that Woolf's characters somehow dip into the images and phrases of those interludes implies a Yeatsian unconscious realm that is accessible through an "age-long memoried self." Perhaps the repeated images of shells and birds in those interludes is also a parallel to the imagery used by Yeats, particularly the connection of self and shell. In the fourth interlude, birds pierce the shells of snails (109), and Bernard at the first dinner describes his friends as birds singing their own songs and tapping "with the remorseless and savage egotism of the young our own snail-shell till it cracked" (123). Later, Susan is singing like "an old shell murmuring on the beach" (171), and Jinny speaks of lives or "faces" as "abraded and battered shells cast on the shore" (175). In his summing up, Bernard notes that as one matures a "shell forms upon the soft soul" (255). Living in relationship, the six friends converse dialogically as they consciously or unconsciously repeat and hybridize these shared phrases.

The friends are not individual seers only, drawing up an image from a subconscious level, but they construct communal images or epiphanies among them. Although Bernard begins the story of Elvedon, Susan contributes a phrase to this vision; watching the lady writing, Susan says, "If we died here, nobody would bury us" (17). Several times, Yeats affirms his belief that two or three people can dream portions of one large dream and then construct it by discussing each person's contribution.[44] Woolf is referring to this notion—though not very seriously in a letter to Ethel Smyth—when she describes Yeats and Walter de la Mare in conversation tossing "between them higher and higher a dream of Napoleon with ruby eyes. And over my head it went" (*Letters*, 4:253). This is the same meeting, however, that Woolf describes to Vanessa, affirming agreement with many of Yeats's ideas. The communal, or relational, epiphanies of *The Waves*, unlike the single-observer epiphanies characteristic of Joyce, seem to be constructed along the lines of Yeats's shared dreams.

One of these communal epiphanies is a response to Percival, a kind of Yeatsian genius of the tribe. He is a trope for the symbolic order itself. As Keith Booker emphasizes, Percival's mastery on the playing field in cricket encodes him as a master of empire as well, since he is perceived as nearly a deity, like Conrad's Kurtz; indeed, Jane Marcus and Kathy Phillips see in Percival (and the novel itself) Woolf's radical critique of imperialism.[45] This critique is most particularly imaged in Percival, because he is narratively inscribed as strictly a myth. Percival is not even a voice; he is a sort of (impossible) metasubjectivity.

Percival offers no spoken discourse about his culture's assumptions; instead, he *is* the discourse, the mute embodiment of those assumptions. Yet we have a fragment of written discourse from Percival, a revealed text, as it were, a Dead Sea scroll. So it is not quite true that he is the still center of a turning and speaking world. He is not entirely silent, because this god of the tribe does send a letter to Neville. The novel's own text "purloins" Percival's words so that we almost miss them. They come through Neville's subjectivity as he looks at the letter after Percival's death: "I am about to play quoits with a colonel, so no more" (*Waves*, 152). Does this mean that there is a narrative transgression and that Percival speaks, and thus is not really a symbol, a shared dream and mythic sign of cultural discourse? No, because his only words declare his silence ("so no more"), and the reason for his silence is that he goes to play a game.

Percival is the game. He is the game plan of the symbolic order as imaged in a masculine British ideal of his time; Percival is the colonial servant and the empire is the moral quest. His six friends at the dinner acknowledge that he is a shared, unifying symbol. Bernard reflects, during the first dinner, on the single flower, "seven-sided," to which "every eye brings its own contribution" (127); then the friends construct an epiphanic "moment" out of this "one man" (145). Each contributes several phrases as they build up their vision of Percival. Louis affirms, "Something is made" (145) as they discuss Percival; Jinny speaks of "this globe whose walls are made of Percival," and the "moment" made of him; Rhoda sees forests and the landscapes of "far countries" in this communally constructed vision; Neville contributes images of ordinary happiness in a room that has a "table, a chair, a book"; Susan offers the rural landscape that is part of the vision (145–46). And Bernard identifies them all as creators of this moment; it is "created by us from Percival" (146).

Percival is here the center of a relational or communal epiphany. The narrative representation of the event recalls a Yeatsian shared dream in which parts of the total vision are contributed by several people. Percival is the cultural genius of his era, a master narrative. Appropriately, when this friend and hero dies, Neville's language dialogically stylizes the cadences of the Apostle's Creed ("Was crucified, dead, and buried"), since Neville summarizes: "Percival fell; was killed; is buried" (152).

When this icon of the tribe is killed, when this central text of the symbolic order is erased, the remaining six friends must reconstruct their discourse of community and identity. They must again make phrases, experiment, build up a collective discourse. At the second dinner, they do so in a way that again could be called Yeatsian, or we could describe the process as the relational discourse that women engage in as they build up a communal text. The six friends develop or inscribe their vision dialogically, repeating and altering each other's phrases; their chorus of reflection is appositional, not conflictual and disruptive.

After Rhoda identifies the "still mood, the disembodied mood" that they share (228), Bernard gives it an image—the "six-sided flower; made of six lives" (229). Louis adds to the collective text by saying that the flower (or the communal vision itself) is a "mysterious illumination" seen against "yew trees," and Jinny adds, "Built up with much pain, many strokes." Then Bernard adds his perceptions about family, friends, travel, death, as he looks at the vision "we have made"; dialogically confirming the pluralistic quality of their shared text, Bernard reiterates Louis's notion that it is a light blazing against yew trees (229).

The subjectivity being represented in this episode, and frequently throughout *The Waves*, is collectively structured. Whether we describe this structuring as a feminine or relational text shaped by a community, or see it as dialogic, or perhaps as a Yeatsian communal dream, the characters here merge and mingle, experimentally building both identity and community. Although each of the selves or characters has chosen (or is inscribed by) a conventional life pattern, a symbolic structure that seems not to challenge prevailing gender myths, yet the style and form of this novel imply a large reservoir of "inner speech," to use Bakhtin's term. The unconscious speech, and in fact the consciousness, of the characters provide for each of them a broad and varied resource.

Their relation to the symbolic order, to their defining tradition and culture, is very different from Charles Tansley's relation to it, or William Bradshaw's. Neither of these men experimented with discourse. They already knew what "human nature" was; they knew who should fight, who could paint, who could not, and who must write a dissertation. The characters or voices in *The Waves*, by contrast, seem to know that the patriarchal sentence is not the only one. The symbolic order, historically defined and inscribed by men, is itself only a discourse; it is as fragile as any of Bernard's phrases, as fragile as any text. It can die, and its death is represented by Percival's death.

Yet his death is only the largest, most upsetting loss of meaning, that is, of discourse, experienced by the six friends. They have to rewrite their lives, restabilize them, after the loss of that central text, but they respond to various, less drastic losses along the way as well. On these occasions, too, they subtly revise the texts they are living by. Susan, for instance, whom Bernard (and almost every reader of *The Waves*) identifies as "wholly woman, purely feminine" (248), is not "purely" and rigidly caught up in her simple, rural life of sensuous maternity. During the first dinner, she very carefully hedges her life discourse; she says, "I shall never have anything but natural happiness. It will almost content me. I shall go to bed tired" (131). The "almost" anticipates her dialogical revision of her own life, for she eventually admits that she is "glutted with natural happiness" (173).

All are glutted or dissatisfied, however; Bernard is dissatisfied in the end because he has "no more appetites to glut" (285). Either one has too much, or one is disillusioned because one no longer even wants to have too much! Either way, the life story requires revision, and all the characters do revise, if not their lives, their perceptions of their lives; that is, they experimentally adjust and evaluate the discourses that shape subjectivity.

None of them believes that his or her version of human nature is the only one, and perhaps this insight arises from their continuing fellowship with each other. Together they construct images, and they dialogically share, repeat, or reshape each other's phrases, as they build the text of their lifelong friendship. Although the past-tense narrative of Bernard's final soliloquy may give special emphasis to his disillusionment with phrases and to his request for a simpler "language," he is not the first to discover such a language. He wants the "little language" of lovers and the "one syllable" words used by children (238, 287, 293, 295); even "a howl, a cry" would be better than "false phrases" (295), he says. But it is Louis at the first dinner who tells Rhoda that the others were talking "a little language such as lovers use" (143).

Perhaps, Bernard as an elderly man wishing for a cry is recalling the elemental quality of Susan's childhood passion. At that earlier time, he had said, "I heard you cry, 'I am unhappy' " (15). Though he observed that she did not cry or cry out, he perceived the wordless, phraseless mode of her expression (14). Jealous about Jinny's kissing Louis, Susan as a child identified "love" and "hate" (15) in the "single words," which she prefers to Bernard's phrases (16, 18). She has known this language all along, and the limitations as well as the satisfactions of a simple, nearly nonverbal life are eventually acknowledged by Susan.

This novel is not condemning all rational syntax (all "big language" or symbolic structures) as masculine, rigid, and negative, while approving semiotic cries as feminine and good. Instead of falling into the error of presuming any single worldview to be the only one, the six friends meet often and share discourses. Throughout life they hear each other. The most defensive and self-enclosed (Louis? Rhoda?) continue to be relational within the group and to join the others in constructing revisionary texts of both identity and community.

Even Rhoda defines herself in relation to the group. She has an affair with Louis, and she is in love with Percival. She and Bernard dialogically share the imagery of flinging words or seeds: Rhoda sees birds rising "like a fling of seed" (10–11), and Bernard compares his mind or "identity" to a "fling" of seed (217, 262). Rhoda's phrases, however, are unwritten and usually unspoken; they are dreams: "I flung words in fans like those the sower throws over the ploughed fields when the earth is bare," because, she says, she wants to fill the night with "dreams" (205). Yet her dreams often begin in a communal context—while she is with her friends. At the first dinner, after a vision of a shape, a white arm, a column, she says, "But these pilgrimages, these moments of departure, start always in your presence, from this table, these lights, from Percival and Susan, here and now" (139). As I noted earlier, she is willing to accept the "antics of the individual" in order to join her friends—though not always and not finally; she kills herself because she can find no ultimate dream, no absolute text or symbol.

Having difficulty learning mathematics, Rhoda feels "outside the loop of time" (21–22), but she is not really outside language, not outside symbolic structures absolutely. It is evidently numbers for which she has "no answer," and she cannot write the answers when the others do (21). Rhoda certainly does learn to read, and in fact seems fascinated with certain master narratives of the symbolic order. As a small child (in her first long soliloquy), she sees herself as an explorer, a searcher; she rocks petals in a basin of water and imagines the other ships sinking in high waves while her own explores exotic islands (19). (She could be Orlando imagining Shelmerdine surviving the high seas as he rounds the Horn.) Later, as a schoolgirl, she abandons her daydream of being a fearless, conquering empress and instead reads a book: "I will go now into the library and take out some book, and read and look; and read again and look. Here is a poem about a hedge" (56). Rhoda then develops a fantasy of moonlit landscapes, flowers, and a garland she wants to give to someone; she asks three times: "Oh! to whom?" (56–57) Since this happens before she meets Percival, it is not only the death of Percival that makes Rhoda realize there is no absolute text.

Rhoda's relation to the symbolic order is ambivalent. On the one hand, she fails or refuses to accept the (necessary) limitations of a life as phrase, as language, as a written subjectivity. On the other hand, she does try to appropriate symbolic structures, in fact to appropriate one of the most famous master narratives—the Shelleyan quest for an eternal ideal of beauty or truth. Beverly Schlack's identification of the repeated Shelleyan texts in Rhoda's soliloquies[46] is important for an understanding of Rhoda's "self" or lack of it. Rhoda especially is looking for a final, secure truth, the ultimate genius or soul of the world.

Her discourse, like that of Septimus, seeks completion, a "whom," an object in a text that the others come to recognize as forever unfinished. While Lily has appropriated the text of vocation ("my work") from the symbolic order, Rhoda demands The Work, the security of a totalizing, all-encompassing quest, one that she hopes to find evidently in the texts of poetry she reads. Beside her great hope and quest, the mere gestures of identity—doing arithmetic, aligning herself with the socially constructed (feminine) behavior of dressing and dancing—all seem either threatening or foolish.

She admits as a young woman, "Identity failed me" (64), and much later she says, "I have no face" (223); she despises "the antics of the individual" (224). But so did Shelley, as Virginia Woolf noted. In a review written in 1927, Woolf describes Shelley as pursuing an endless quest for something eternal, an ideal that he thought he found temporarily in several women. She sees in this quest "something inhuman about Shelley"; she also quotes William Godwin on the generalized nature of Shelley's poetry, a feature that made Shelley—in Godwin's words—"not an individual character" to his father-in-law (" 'Not One of Us,' "*CE*, 4:23). Woolf in her review cites with evident agreement Godwin's interesting diagnosis of Shelley as being deficient in individuality, and she implies a link between this restricted subjectivity and Shelley's obsession with the large quest for ideal beauty.

Like Shelley (or Woolf's view of him), Rhoda is an absolutist of the imagination. She has this in common with some mystics and some poets. To an extent, Bernard also is a visionary. Although he recalls occasionally his general and archetypal visions of the woman writing and of the empty world during the eclipse, the world "without a self" (*Waves*, 287), yet he returns also to particular phrases and to the task of building up a daily subjectivity in relationship with his friends. After Percival's death, Bernard in his grief felt "outside the sequence," outside the customary perceptions and habits (the "myths," Barthes might say) that made life seem natural. Like Rhoda, outside the "loop of time," Bernard also temporarily is "outside the machine" (158) of everyday meanings, but unlike Rhoda, he wants to return in spite of his grief. He says, "But now I want life round me" after the "exhaustion" of this "revelation" (158).

Rhoda, in contrast, wants revelation, "a world immune from change" (107), an ultimate text that does not die. Although in Draft I of the holograph, Rhoda feels a brief "identification" when she sees the statue of Artemis one evening,[47] in the published novel, her fragmentary visions (white shapes, a "white arm" resting on a knee, a column) are not named (139). In the published novel, there is little to suggest that a more feminine world, culture, or language would have satisfied Rhoda's quest. She is not an alienated woman defeated by the (male) symbolic order. The mysterious statue, "column," or figure "makes no sign, it does not beckon, it does not see us" (139). Rhoda has a vision of a cosmos that simply is not interested in human beings. Unlike Septimus, she finds no prime minister as the goal of her "to whom," and unlike the comfortably agnostic Clarissa, Rhoda cannot make an offering for the sake of the offering.

Rhoda is one of those dreamers and thinkers whom Woolf recommended, in *A Room of One's Own*, that women novelists portray. An experimental subjectivity, Rhoda has appropriated a traditionally masculine (Shelleyan, symbolic) quest for the absolute. She is, of course, a poor role model, but then so was Shelley. Neither one, in Woolf's view, ever achieved a responsible individuality. Yet Rhoda's subjectivity is creative and lyric; as a text, she is a radical and experimental voice.

Bernard's vision of the "fin" far out in a "waste of waters" suggests that he also looks impossibly for some final truth. As he jots the fin into his phrase book, he hopes to formulate eventually "some final statement" (*Waves*, 189). Although Bernard never finds this totalizing phrase, he does not despair. Like Virginia Woolf, he can enjoy reentering the particularized, social world of phrases, of constructed illusions. Returning home in June 1929 after visiting Vanessa in Spain, Woolf describes a "sense of nothingness" resulting from the travel and her "not going round in the mill yet" (*D*, 3:233). Then she takes up the responsibility of constructing her world and herself:

I must somehow brew another decoction of illusion. . . . I must make human illusion—ask someone in tomorrow after dinner; and begin that astonishing adventure with the souls of others again—about which I know so little. Is it affection which prompts? (*D*, 3:234)

Yes, it probably is affection, and a generally relational subjectivity, that prompts Woolf to "make human illusion." The same thing also prompts Bernard as well as the other characters in *The Waves* to construct and reconstruct illusion, phrases, their lives. All of them are experimental in that they are so affectionately and dialogically conscious of each other's perspective. A soliloquy by one of the voices almost always mentions, and sometimes quotes, one or two of the others. The friends dialogically feminize the very process of achieving subjectivity, because (in the experimental psychology and sociology of this novel) they arrive at themselves primarily through their constant relational discourse with each other.

Bernard's first major soliloquy, for instance, uses the "different voice" that Gilligan describes, that is, a feminine or relational discourse. In contrast, Louis, the outsider, the Australian (who is given the first long soliloquy in the book), emphasizes his difference and solitude. His first observation is: "Now they have all gone . . . , I am alone" (*Waves*, 11). Bernard, however, is moved to "speak" (to think, to make extensive use of language) in response to Susan's furious, grieving jealousy over the kiss Jinny gives Louis. In his initial long soliloquy, Bernard's first words are about someone else, not himself: "Susan has passed us.... She has passed the toolhouse door with her handkerchief screwed into a ball. She was not crying, but her eyes, which are so beautiful, were narrow as cats' eyes before they spring. I shall follow her, Neville" (14). Only at the fourth sentence does Bernard say "I." He explains that he follows her partly out of "curiosity" and also "to comfort" her (14). His motive is the writer's (or the gossip's?), since he is curious, and his ethic at this early stage in life is relational and feminine; he wants to comfort Susan.

Bernard has uttered brief, evocative (semiotic?) sentences earlier, as have the other children. Yet his growth into articulate symbolic consciousness occurs in sympathetic response to another person's unhappiness. His subjectivity and his motivation are usually relational. The exceptions occur when Bernard is in love and when all are asserting their egos during the early part of each dinner. Bernard admits that he once threw a "tremendous battery of phrases" at the woman, he says, "who made me Byron" (249–50), and the newly engaged Bernard dialogically mangles the peaceful imagery of Wordsworth's "Composed upon Westminster Bridge." As Bernard's train approaches the "sleeping," feminine city's domes and cathedrals, images repeatedly suggest a military/sexual invasion; the "missile" of the train will "explode in the flanks of the city like a shell in the side of some ponderous, maternal, majestic animal" (111).[48] Perhaps the discourse here indicates Bernard's anxious response to modern machinery as much as his "reading" of his own sexual vigor, but this exception complements the fundamentally relational quality of his discourse. He acknowledges that he as a young man saw himself as "the inheritor" of Western civilization but especially of its literary heros; his "self" was built temporarily on Hamlet, Shelley, a hero of Dostoevsky, Napoleon, and Byron. Yet as Bernard says, "I changed and changed" (249), becoming "I, I, I," Bernard, rather than these models (253–54).

He "changed and changed" mostly in response to his friends,

not to his books. On page after page, in every soliloquy, we see him thinking about Neville, Percival, Jinny, Susan, and the others. Books (and the symbolic inheritance of Western civilization) may almost be enough for the scholarly Neville, but not for Bernard. He tries to gain inspiration from a page of Byron but realizes that "the stimulus of other people" is necessary (79–80); he says, "I need an audience" (115). Out of "curiosity" and "greed," he says, "I think of people to whom I could say things; Louis, Neville; Susan; Jinny and Rhoda. With them I am many-sided" (116). His remarks about the dialogic effect of other people on his character and his discourse resemble those of Woolf herself, noted earlier, when she said that the perspectives of others provided for her a fresh light on the "landscape" (*D*, 3:316). Bernard says his "character is in part made of the stimulus which other people provide" (133). Although all his friends also respond to each other, Bernard over and over identifies this relational characteristic as central to his own subjectivity.

It is appropriate, then, that Bernard sees, or describes the fantasy of, the lady writing. His discourse with Susan and about her was relational or feminine, and then—in Susan's company—he saw an image of his own discourse: the woman writing. In some respects, his verbal gesture of describing Elvedon is maternal, for he does what Mrs. Ramsay does when she reassures Cam with a story of mountains and valleys and birds and antelopes (*Lighthouse*, 172). Bernard's story, however, is not reassuring; this vision that he and Susan share is frightening to both. It may be, as Gilbert and Gubar suggest in *No Man's Land*, that the "vocabulary of anxiety" here reflects Bernard's ambivalence about women becoming writers.[49] His anxiety may also be the result of his having described *himself* (in describing the woman writing), because his use of language is quite relational, quite "feminine"; Bernard wants to help, to comfort, to explore out of curiosity.

Bernard is himself a woman writing. Both children feel frightened at what could happen if the male gardeners see them, but it is Bernard who feels that he has indeed been observed: "Run! The gardener with the black beard has seen us! We shall be shot!" (*Waves*, 17) Does Bernard sense that making phrases in order to "melt" into the other person, to comfort, or to "explore" with curiosity (16) is not a sufficiently important or manly use of language? Perhaps a real "inheritor," a male, should not entertain others with fantastic stories. It is as though Bernard perceives even as a child that "real men" don't write like ladies in gardens.

And yet they do. Woolf appreciated the dialogic, responsive style of both Walpole and Mme de Sévigné, as I mentioned earlier. She also affirms the importance of the relational and loquacious Marlow who was part of Conrad's "double life" as an author. In the essay, "Joseph Conrad," which she wrote just after Conrad's death in 1923, Woolf describes Marlow as the one who analyzes and reflects, "sending after his smoke beautiful rings of words" (*CE*, 1:304–5). The "sea captain," however, Conrad's other voice (*CE*, 1:304), is more severe and judgmental. Woolf especially contrasts the two voices in another essay of 1923, "Mr. Conrad: A Conversation." One of the characters in this "conversation," Penelope, describes Conrad as "not one and simple" but "many and complex" (*CE*, 1:310). She contrasts the sea captain in Conrad, the narrator who is "simple, faithful, obscure," with the other voice or narrator, Marlow:

Then again, Marlow is a man of words; they are all dear to him, appealing, seductive. But the sea captain cuts him short. "The gift of words," he says, "is no great matter." And it is the sea captain who triumphs. In Conrad's novels personal relations are never final. Men are tested by their attitudes to august abstractions. ("Mr. Conrad: A Conversation," *CE*, 1:311)

Marlow is "subtle, psychological, loquacious" (*CE*, 1:311). His is the voice of "personal relations," Woolf suggests, or what Gilligan might identify as the "feminine" ethic, and the sea captain is the voice of judgment and principle, which are the typically masculine criteria of value (in Gilligan's studies).

Like Conrad's narrators, Bernard is a dialogic blend of many voices; these include Marlow and, less frequently, the sea captain. Indeed, Bernard and Marlow sometimes intertextually make the same phrases. Bernard asks for an audience, as Marlow does, and the discourse of both is relational or feminine, even gossipy. (As I noted in the first chapter, Spacks argues that Conrad's Marlow is basically a gossip.) Bernard wants a companion to hear his subtle, psychological, loquacious effort to "sum up," and he thinks he has met this person once "on board a ship going to Africa" (*Waves*, 238). (Maybe Bernard's dinner companion *is* Marlow?) The relational Bernard does not like solitude and silence.

Much earlier, in the company of others on a train, Bernard notes that "words at once make smoke rings—see how phrases at once begin to wreathe off my lips" (67). When a man on the train speaks, a "smoke ring issues from [Bernard's] lips" and the two travelers are in "contact" as a result (68). Later, Bernard reflects: "When I cannot see words curling like rings of smoke round me I am in darkness—I am nothing" (132). Other people allow him to see "how lovely the smoke of my phrase is, rising and falling" (133). And as we saw just above, Woolf described Marlow as "sending after his smoke beautiful rings of words." Marlow might suddenly perceive an object, Woolf also writes, "and then complete in its burning *ring of light* that thing flashed bright upon the mysterious background" (*CE*, 1:305; my emphasis). Bernard's first perception (the words that begin the book) is of "a ring . . . a loop of light" (9).[50]

Yet Bernard also echoes a phrase that Woolf uses to describe the more stern voice of Conrad. She suggests, in "Joseph Conrad," that many readers will prefer the Marlovian emphasis on the "heart" and on human beings in their "relationships" rather than Conrad's stern vision of "the waste of waters." (*CE*, 1:306). Bernard also has a vision of the "fin" that turns "in a waste of waters" (*Waves*, 189) as he glimpses a reality distinct from human relationships. Perhaps this vision is "mystical," as Woolf called it, when she described in 1926 her early inspiration for *The Waves* as a haunting perception of "a fin passing far out" (*D*, 3:113).

Bernard, the inheritor of his author's thorough acquaintance with male traditions of literature and with the discourses of women as well, is usually a relational Marlovian in discourse. Perhaps, however, as he faces death he regresses to a stern, manly subjectivity of "difference," a reprehensible ideology of oppression and conquest? With his (phallic) spear "couched," he gallops, his hair flying "like

Percival's," the administrative imperialist in India: "Against you I will fling myself, unvanquished and unyielding, O Death!" (*Waves*, 297). Even though he has just abandoned his phrase book, it is significant that Bernard does not fling a spear at death but flings a story instead. Keith Booker observes that "Bernard narrates himself into a typical scene of knightly heroism," but Judith Lee emphasizes that Bernard is only using metaphor here, and the battle imagery implies a transformed self that resists death (not a military enemy).[51] There is a joyful irony in the fact that Bernard is still making phrases (presumably, close to the moment of death). He says, "I will fling myself"; he is the phrase he flings. He has often thought of himself as a "fling" of seed (217, 262), and he has constructed himself and the identities of his friends my means of phrases.

Bernard turns even this final event into a phrase and into a (fantasy of) relationship. He does not go to his death in manly silence as does Conrad's arrogant "Lord" Jim. Although Bernard knows there are no stories (187), no totalizing truths, he makes one more story as he draws upon traditional symbolic structures of Western myth. Yet his appropriation of these structures is dialogic; Bernard's fight with the ultimate enemy, and his "like Percival's," bring to mind a polyphony of intertextual discourse: friendship (and Bernard's grief at his friend's death), British colonialism, the Grail quest, religious quest, allegorical psychomachia, and knightly ordeal. Even more important than the dialogically mingled yarn of Bernard's final story is the fact that he told it. In the end, he does for himself what he did for the distressed Susan at the beginning of his articulate subjectivity: he tells a story.

Bernard's discourse remains basically relational, feminine, and dialogic throughout his life. Although his ambition had been to find "the one story to which all [his phrases] refer" (187), when he abandons his book of phrases, he is acknowledging finally what he has suspected earlier—that the world or life has no "self," no reliable identity-defining discourse. As Sandra Kemp and Patrick McGee have argued (both using varieties of Lacanian discourse), *The Waves* presents, impossibly, what is not representable or interpretable.[52] Like the world during the eclipse, human life offers no all-explanatory, sufficient discourse that supplies identity or subjectivity once and always. Not only is there no master narrative (with Percival dead) in Bernard's "old civilization" (184), but the minor phrases as well are similarly fragile and temporary. Bernard realizes that his book has "recorded merely changes" and "shadows"; even "those fabulous presences, men with brooms, women writing" are made of "dust that changed" (285).

Bernard, in some ways the sequel character to Orlando, makes an observation similar to Orlando's. Bernard asks, "How can I proceed . . . without a self, weightless and visionless, through a world weightless, without illusion?" (285). Orlando had answered this question by realizing that she loses some illusions only to acquire others. One does not proceed at all without discourse of some kind, whether it is a "little language," a semiotic and subversive playfulness, a discourse of career, heroic quest, family, pleasure, writing, or a dialogic and even communal construction of a cooperative text or epiphany. Although the voices in *The Waves* draw largely upon symbolic ideologies as they develop and share the discourses of their lives, these symbolic structures are displaced into narrative otherness by such formal devices as the chantlike, present-tense utterances and thus lose the narrative authority we would expect of such conventional, symbolic life structures.

In Woolf's dialogic narrative contexts, where there are many stories, Jacob's (symbolic, heroic) story is obscured, feminized by the many women's voices that gossip about, and inscribe, this male-as-other, even though their relational discourse cannot free him from the symbolic discourses that kill him. While Clarissa, Mrs. Ramsay, and Lily experiment with the symbolic, appositionally appropriating it for a woman's use, the friends in *The Waves* relate, relationalize, and feminize everything. The formal and ideological modus of this experimental novel is the device of the six voices, talking and developing in relation to each other. It is as though the friends belong to a sort of primal alumni group, the six graduating into discourse at about the same age and then continuing their relational phrases and friendship for the rest of their shared and dialogic lives. All of the symbolic structures that the six voices engage (or abandon) are drawn into relationality, becoming feminized by a community that authorizes—finally—no single (dominant, masculine) phrase but instead writes and rewrites itself experimentally. Even Bernard's summing up is a many-sided flower of discourse, dialogic with his friends, with Percival, and with the woman writing.

3 *Barbara Pym*
Textualizing the Trivial

If there is a meaning to the ordinary and the trivial, it is that the trivial has no meaning, or very little. A discourse of the trivial attempts *not* to be a discourse. We may acknowledge with Jacques Derrida that there is "nothing outside the text."[1] That is, there is no discourse outside discourse. Yet the trivial, by definition, attempts to signify something that is insignificant. To the extent that a discourse of the trivial approaches this pure and rudimentary status (and of course it cannot completely shed all signification), it is quite elusive; it evades the ideology of textual value itself. The ideology of the trivial is that it has no significant ideology, belongs to no master narrative, no great codes of quest or romance, and no *sermo patrius*.

As spoken discourse, trivia is throwaway conversation, the casual remarks people might make while eating or waiting for a bus. Etymologically, trivia is the discourse of two travelers while passing each other at a crossroads (*trivia*). Although Oedipus killed his father at a crossroads, most crossroad encounters are not of mythic or archetypical significance. Indeed, in the novels of Barbara Pym, the discourse of the trivial persistently aligns itself with the ordinary and the everyday. Sometimes her fiction aligns the trivial with the "feminine," but this is not always the case.

Again, in this chapter, as in my discussion of Woolf, I am less interested in making binary distinctions between a feminine and a masculine language. My argument continues to be that a multiplex of appositional discourses shapes the language and the experimental selves (the novel's characters or voices) in my three writers. In Pym's generally realistic narrative style, the language spoken by most of her women characters is almost never anything that fits the category of the semiotic. Instead, the concerns of domestic life are typically spliced into discourses drawn from the symbolic, but these symbolic discourses are ones that are peripheral to the modern West. No longer heavy with the economic and political authority of, for instance, competition, self-fulfillment, or marriage, the symbolic discourses that enter the hybrid language of Pym's characters tend to be somewhat marginal, not highly valued (perhaps outdated); they are codes and life structures that belong to an "alternative" West—to use again Ashis Nandy's concept.

The most prominent of the discourses that, along with domestic language, characterize the trivial or the ordinary in Pym's work are varieties of Christian discourse and the character's reading and misreading of English literature. As preparation for looking at these (trivial) discourses in Pym's novels (especially *Less Than Angels* and *Quartet in Autumn*), I want to emphasize and clarify Pym's radical undertaking and experiment—to give a text to the ordinary, to give a text to the (by definition) text-less life and self.

Textualizing a Non-Text

By its own inscription, the trivial resists inscription. The in-significant by definition lacks significance, lacks the signifying capacity. In Pym's writing, the trivial emerges as a dialogic complex of discourses. Having no value, no noticeability as a text, the in-significant must—if it is to speak at all—appropriate a discourse of some "significance," though this may be a discourse that survives only on the margins of contemporary culture and society.

Thus, when the characters in Pym's novels respond to the richness of ordinary life, they often engage in a hybrid, experimental discourse. Sometimes this discourse is oppositional. A character may offer a "multi-voiced" resistance to intrusive forces, as Barbara Griffin suggests; Pym's single women in particular, according to Laura Doan, emerge through a "dual-voiced" narrative that allows a critique of social structures. Orphia Jane Allen also observes that the "polyphonic narrative style" of Pym's work is a result of the tension between the individual's plans and social expectation.[2]

In addition to these oppositional strategies are the dialogic reflections and remarks that mesh the trivial (and occasionally feminine) with the official or significant. Such linguistic appositions are my main concern here; they allow the in-significant to piggyback into significance, into reality, so to speak (indeed, in order to speak). But the hitchhiking trivia subtly alters the direction of the (serious, important) symbolic, sometimes deconstructing it, more often transforming and realigning its implications. Pym's most vital characters are highly aware of language; they experimentally appropriate and transform a variety of discourses as they enunciate and affirm the rich subtleties of the ordinary.

One facet of the ordinary has been given a historical definition in British fiction (and in critical studies of it). By looking at the everyday lives of mid-twentieth-century people, Barbara Pym identifies herself as belonging to the postwar generation. Although there is an occasional Samuel Golding or Muriel Spark, British novelists of the fifties and sixties, unlike the great modernists, generally wrote a more conventional, realistic prose, probed ordinary middle-class or working-class experience, and eschewed the lyric, epiphanic visions that illuminate the pages of Woolf and Joyce.[3] Pym's characters also belong to an era of reduced expectations. In her novels, the men and some of the women must earn a living in dim offices or libraries; they buy groceries, flowers, and plan meals; the women do the washing up. Pym's characters are generally conscious of a postwar "diminishment" in their lives, as Robert Long observes, and Michael Cotsell declares that the "minor events in minor lives" of Pym's fiction belong to the postwar context in which "something major—Britain—became minor."[4]

Yet the experience of the "minor" life, or the element of ordinariness, in Pym's work is featured as such. Jane Cleveland, the pastor's wife in *Jane and Prudence*, hears "with delight" the gossip about the personalities and tensions in the new parish; she is fascinated by such "richness." Later, her unmarried friend Prudence eagerly anticipates "the experience of being in love with such an ordinary young man as Geoffrey Manifold."[5] Other characters perceive a value in what they describe as the ordinary or trivial, and Pym's readers have variously tried to clarify or define the everyday world (the discourse) of her novels. Edith Larson draws attention to the ordinary comforts and "security" of family life, while William Greenway notes the often unsatisfying routines of both home and work; Robert Graham argues that Pym's narrative accumulation of small joys and sorrows shapes an overall theme of deprivation and loss, but Allen sugests that Pym's irony and wit infuse the ordinary with energy, "thus validating the trivia of women's lives."[6]

By speaking of validation, Allen pinpoints the most radical and powerful element of Barbara Pym's work. Pym validates the ordinary, makes it recognizeable as it virtually writes or constructs the self. Pym's characters emerge from a dialogic textualization of matters presumably so unimportant that they have nearly evaded sign and text. The subjectivity inscribed by a discourse of the trivial is an experimental one, as the in-significant tries out a variety of significations in the process of entering discourse.

Yet Pym's characters would not refer to themselves as "experimental." Dierdre Swan, a student of anthropology in *Less Than Angels*, is uncomfortable when she hears about the "light-hearted experimenting," as she puts it, of a visiting French anthropologist who attends a different English church each Sunday.[7] Scientific metaphors or discourse (such as experimenting or anthropological study) are often negative in Pym's fiction. Instead, her dialogically active characters bring the trivial into enunciation by linking it to discourses that are not (at present, anyway) central to Western culture.

As Pym begins to enunciate the discourse and value of the ordinary, she is attentive to the language of other writers who have also worked with this elusive concept. Among these are Denton Welch, perhaps Virginia Woolf, certainly Logan Pearsall Smith, Charlotte Yonge, and John Keble. These writers constitute an extremely mixed bag, and a brief look at Pym's responses to their discourse of the ordinary will indicate the complexity, subtlety, and experimental flexibility of her own discourse of the ordinary.

Several times in her journals and letters, Pym records her fascination with the trivial, with the details of everyday, noncrisis activities. Referring to novelist Denton Welch's request for more details (about food, homes) from writers, Pym suggests that a reader is most interested in these things not because they supply sociological information but "because they are pleasing in themselves."[8] The everyday experience is not only interesting but valuable. Her romance writer, Catherine Oliphant, says as much in *Less Than Angels*: "The small things of life were often so much bigger than the great things, she decided, wondering how many writers and philosophers had said this before her, the trivial pleasures like cooking, one's home, little poems especially sad ones, solitary walks, funny things seen and overheard" (104). As she suspects, other writers have indeed affirmed her pleasure in the small or trivial; it may be that Catherine is recalling Virginia Woolf. In the novels and journals, Pym several times quotes or responds to Woolf who advised in "Modern Fiction": "Let us not take it for granted that life exists more fully in what is commonly thought big than in what is commonly thought small" (*CE*, 2:107).[9] In *A Room of One's Own*, which Pym quotes in her journal, Woolf gives a gendered discourse to the big and the small; Woolf points out that men's activities are generally considered "important" while those of women are perceived as "trivial" (*Room*, 76–77).[10] Both writers affirmed the value of the small, even the trivial, although the narrator of *Jacob's Room*, as I suggested, may be questioning or doubting the importance of everyday social activity such as eating and letter writing.

Barbara Pym does not doubt the value of the trivial, and she seems especially concerned to define this discourse in a heterogeneous, maybe contradictory, way. She refers often to Logan Pearsall Smith's *Trivia*, and her own discourse of the ordinary shares some features with his. On the other hand, his brief prose poems are quite different from her own perspective on the ordinary. Pearsall Smith's concentrated little paragraphs almost always have a sudden turn in the meaning and they conclude with a distinct insight, an epiphany of discovery or a challenge to the reader. A diary entry in 1943 shows that Pym's interest in the trivial is very different from his. Hers is more miscellaneous, less focused. Pym has been describing her pleasure at finding some pre-Raphaelite tombs:

You (reader) may say, Why do you make such a thing of it all? To which I will snap (like Trivia) Well, what about your own life? Is it so full of large, big wonderful things that you don't need tombs and daffodils and your own special intolerable bird, with an old armchair or two and occasional readings from Matthew Arnold and Coventry Patmore? (*VPE*, 118)

The "intolerable bird" is very close to the unusual epithets of *Trivia*, and the challenging attack on the reader's supposed opinions also echoes Pearsall Smith.

Yet Pearsall Smith's paragraphs hone the reader's attention to the specific insight, the discovery that the author has made in something trivial. Pym's concern is, we can say, with the discourse of the ordinary itself. Pym contrasts the discourse of the ordinary with those "large, big wonderful things," and thus identifies trivia as precisely not any of those things. Her interest is with the minor and the nonwonderful, with just those things that have escaped being defined as important (or escaped being defined at all?). The voice in the diary passage implies that her critic (the reader) adheres to an ideology of a life that is "full"; it is even fulfilled, supposedly, with culturally defined wonderful plans, goals, or loves. The speaker instead advocates a grab bag of little things; even those things that might be considered solemn and wonderful (perhaps Matthew Arnold and the tombs?) are trivialized by being thrown together with birds and Coventry Patmore. In her most radical use, the ordinary is noteworthy *because* it is ordinary and because it remains ordinary; it does not burst into epiphanic luminosity and signification.

For Pym's fictional characters as well, the ordinary is special in itself. I have already noted the fascination, for Prudence, of the very ordinary Geoffrey. Mildred Lathbury, by the end of *Excellent Women*, has dialogically redefined one of the "big" texts of the West: self-fulfillment or the "full life." For Mildred, the phrase implies a flexible, open-ended discourse that is linked, in part, to domestic trivia. She re-visions the concept of a full life as she reflects on the likelihood of becoming the wife of Everard Bone. After dinner at his house, when he asks her to consider doing a little proofreading and indexing for him, Mildred asks herself whether any man is "worth this burden," and she feels "despair" at the unfamiliar proof sheets.[11] And yet, Bone's reserved, severe appearance had attracted her from the beginning; he is not "romantic" but "perhaps just a little splendid?" (*EW*, 64–65) Mildred also is quite interested in Bone's eccentric mother and her odd pronouncements about apologies, "worms, birds and Jesuits" (255). Like Pym's list of daffodils, furniture, poetry, and other items necessary to an involved subjectivity of the ordinary, Mildred's interests here tend to evade categories, especially any "big" and "wonderful" structures of quest or love.

With her nontotalizing openness to experience, her decision to marry the "splendid" Bone probably does not mean a narrow, oppressive life for her. She speculates that with her church work, proofing, and the interesting mother-in-law, she may have "what Helena called 'a full life' after all" (256). Yet the anthropologist Helena Napier meant "full life" in the "accepted sense"—as she phrased it earlier (238). She means a full life in the traditional, liberal, and rationalist sense. Helena is a scientist, a woman with a career, a husband, and an affair with Bone. Even her husband, however, had dialogically nudged the phrase "full life" more toward the domestic and the ordinary. Earlier, he had argued that Mildred's life of service and church work was a "*full* life" in itself (238). With his remarks, the phrase "full life" has lost its monologic signification; it is now "two languages, two belief systems"—as Mikhail Bakhtin describes a "hybrid construction" (*DI*, 304–5).

When Mildred uses the phrase in the last sentence of the novel, "full life" is a complex appositional construction. It is ironic, but the irony goes both ways. That is, it is ironic that Mildred's full life is not one—in the "accepted sense"; yet it is also ironic that Helena's traditional understanding of the phrase is so limited. The notion of a full life has been dialogically revised, re-textualized in terms of the richness of the everyday world of domesticity, inept clergy, church sales, eccentric personalities, and Mildred's probable marriage to Everard. Mildred's life will be full, but full according to a very heterogeneous discourse of trivia.

Nevertheless, some of Pym's characters do perceive the ordinary as nonfulfilling, as distinctly a lack. Yet, as the elderly Letty Crowe notes in *Quartet in Autumn*, a life of "not having" might be a positive feature. Close to retirement and reflecting on her life, Letty wonders: "Might not the experience of 'not having' be regarded as something with its own validity?"[12] In terms of narrative development, *Quartet in Autumn*, as I will argue, emphasizes and in fact proves Letty's point. The text enacts Letty's observation, for she, with her sense of "not having," is more open to change than are her office colleagues; lacking a large and noble meaning in her life, she more readily experiments with new discourses and a new life. This very lack of a clear (symbolic) myth of meaning or fulfillment engages Letty and Pym's other responsive characters in a continuing dialogic openness.

The validity structurally and textually in not having (not having a significant discourse) lies in the openness, looseness of structure, and the possibility of several alternatives. This is a spartan or ascetic narrative ideology, and it evades the totalizing conventions of a "wonderful" great code or a quest for truth, fulfillment, and love. Unlike Pearsall Smith's discourse of the trivial, for Pym the trivial and the ordinary have validity because they remain ordinary. When Catherine Oliphant in *Less Than Angels* offers her opinion that life (and evidently her own stories) are often indefinite, she compares the ordinary with the traditional and definite structures of most texts. Life, Catherine indicates, in qualified agreement with her hostess Mabel Swan, is not always unpleasant: "It's comic and sad and indefinite—dull sometimes, but seldom really tragic or deliriously happy, except when one's very young" (89). For Catherine, the great tragic readings of life do not correspond to her experience of work, housekeeping, and intermittent romance. Her indefinite life, in its miscellany and lack of definition, falls outside what Lyotard (as we saw in the first chapter of this study) describes as a "grand narrative."

Instead of such a totalizing ideology, Pym and her most alert characters turn to the indefinite and intriguing mix of daffodils, tombs, chairs, Jesuits, poetry, and other trivia; in this narrative site, any sort of structuring of ordinary life is more challenging and more open, more peripheral to the great ideologies that generally govern (and by implication limit) social and personal life. Unlike the great texts whose "accepted sense" constructs most lives and selves, the trivial teases the imagination and draws the person into exploring a new subjectivity.

Pym's discourse of the trivial can be located in the wild area, which is on the fringes of a society's governing, and generally male-designed, codes. The link between the feminine and the muted, identified by Ardener and Showalter, obtains also in Pym's texts; that is, the trivial is sometimes, though not always, associated with a female subculture. In *No Fond Return of Love*, for instance, Dulcie is about to give room and board to her niece. Dulcie reassures herself that she and her niece will have something in common. Since both do routine editing and proofing, "their work and the domestic trivia that bound all women" will at least provide conversation.[13] Unlike this muted (and by definition unimportant) discourse, the discourse of men usually verbalizes the big, wonderful issues, those designated as noble and worthwhile. Catherine, for instance, describes the letters of her former lover Tom Mallow as she and his more recent girlfriend Dierdre exchange news of him. His letters are "terrifyingly occupied with such momentous things," as Catherine says, adding that she and Dierdre wouldn't want him to be any different (*LTA*, 231). Catherine herself, as we saw earlier, prefers the "trivial pleasures like cooking, one's home, little poems especially sad ones, solitary walks, funny things seen and overheard" (104). Catherine's list, like Pym's in her Pearsall Smith imitation, is a wide-ranging mix, an indefinite collection. Although the trivia that interests Catherine includes Dulcie's "domestic trivia," Catherine's discourse extends beyond this. In Pym's novels, the discourse of the ordinary is not limited to domesticity but draws a lot of other things into a sometimes indefinite heterogeneous hodgepodge.

From this very indefiniteness, most of the serious negative criticism of Pym's work has emerged. Although she provides a lot of detail, her apparent realism seems incomplete to Penelope Lively and Robert Liddell, since the descriptions are usually spare except for food and interiors.[14] Even those who appreciate Pym's focus on the minutiae of everyday life have observed a very understated structuring of descriptive details—if indeed there is any pattern at all. In these "almost plotless novels," as Jane Nardin says, the descriptions and images do not always coalesce into a consistent pattern; commenting on Letty Crowe ("black") and Marcia Snow (also "Snowey," her cat), Nardin concludes that the details of darkness and light cannot be integrated into a clear pattern of moral implications.[15] The most severe appraisal of Pym's reluctance to restrict or clarify her discourse of the trivial comes from Robert Long. He can isolate an occasional moral insight in the novels, but he sees the middle-aged Bede sisters as repressed, existing only in a "domestic half-life" in Pym's first published novel, *Some Tame Gazelle*. He asserts that there is no "significant moral action" in that novel; indeed, "moral awareness is not at the center of [Pym's] novels as it is in Austen's."[16]

Yet there is significant moral awareness and action in Pym's work. Such awareness is even at the center, but readers do not habitually link moral considerations to a discourse of domestic or eccentric (perhaps *decentered*) trivia. The obscurity or indefiniteness that flourishes in the rich trivia of Pym's work results in part from her dedication to writing the ordinary as ordinary. Unlike Sandy Stranger in *The Prime of Miss Jean Brodie* who titled her moral treatise "The Transfiguration of the Commonplace,"[17] Pym almost always refuses to transform the commonplace into the epiphanic. The trivial does not glow, even though it may delight and comfort, and the structuring of decision and action remains extremely subtle. Major crises or life decisions typically occur at the periphery of the narrative. A novel ends just when a couple's relationship may be developing, as in the case of Mildred Lathbury and Everard Bone. In later novels, we hear about this married couple only in truly crossroads conversation—the trivial exchanges over coffee, during parties, or while sorting items for a jumble sale.

Even within a novel, a crisis is often given parenthetically only. For instance, in a manner very reminiscent of Woolf's bracketed relating of the deaths of Mrs. Ramsay, Prue, and Andrew in *To the Lighthouse*, Pym describes the death of anthropologist Tom Mallow during his second visit to Africa. Almost as an afterthought to Catherine's discussion with Dierdre about Tom's "momentous" letters, the narrator observes in a poised yet conversational idiom: "Catherine did not know, indeed how could she, that before Tom could post his Christmas cards, he would be lying dead, accidentally shot in a political riot, in which he had become involved more out of curiosity than passionate conviction" (*LTA*, 231). Just as Woolf's narrator relates conversationally, regarding Prue's death, that "people" had said "everything . . . had promised so well" (*Lighthouse*, 199), Pym's narrator also glances at the listener for an aside, "indeed how could she," how could Catherine have known? The large event or the narrative material (deaths, marriages) that could provide a novel with a more conventional structure, a big, mythic discourse, and perhaps a more recognizable moral significance, are sidestepped.

In a sense, Pym's novels can be described as a "writing beyond the ending"—to use the title of Rachel Blau DuPlessis's study of the closure conflicts in women's narratives; indeed, Jean Kennard, citing DuPlessis, suggests that Pym's texts write beyond a romantic ending by offering an "ideal of community" instead.[18] Yet the strategy of Pym on textual closure is more likely to be an *ending before the writing*. That is, she stops her novels before the writing (the signification) takes over, before the literary and cultural scripts of marriage, quest (or a "full life" in the "accepted sense") can impose their structures on her characters. Unlike Woolf's Bernard, who for most of his life wanted to find a phrase and make a story that would explain things, Pym's narrators and her most vital characters want to *avoid* a phrase. They evade a story, evade a "momentous" or "wonderful" symbolic script.

Perhaps Jane Cleveland, the pastor's wife in *Jane and Prudence*, is the most active in this regard. Jane Bold Cleveland's maiden name aptly describes her keen sense of linguistic adventure and experimentation. Her observations usually jostle open the traditional expectations of others. Being new to a parish, she says, is like entering a theater while the film is in progress; you get only a whispered "garbled synopsis" (*JP*, 19). Jane herself enjoys garbling meanings. When a visitor collecting old clothes for a sale remarks (with Jane's dress in mind) that "ladies like to keep old things to wear in the mornings," Jane further disconcerts him by saying that she will wear her present dress all day; she explains, "My days don't really have mornings as such, not in that way, I mean" (144–45). Here she tries to soften the statement by drawing it back ("that way") to suitable dress for a suitable hour. Yet her assertion about not having "mornings as such" implies a cosmic deconstruction, as though the earth's rotation, and thus mornings, could be merely a matter of verbal and social taste; Jane declines mornings. She evades not only dress codes (and codes about morning activities suitable for British clergy wives), but she also appears to eschew basic symbolic structures as old as day and night; she will not be written into them.

Although Jane's capacity to dislodge meanings is extreme, it is only an exaggeration of Pym's subtle strategy, a strategy that evades (or ends before) the expected phrase or structure. This narrative tactic will of course obscure, or certainly complicate, the moral closure, the conclusions and implications of her fiction. The expected textual structuring has been evaded. With Jane's remarks, the ordinary (the non-text of Jane's anomalous decisions about dress) wobbles into an eccentric and astonishing textuality.

Domesticating Western Culture

The subtlety of Pym's novels results not only from their understated structure and their rich dialogic conceptualizations of trivia but from the peripheral nature of the discourses that are employed to define or characterize the trivial. For this, Pym relies on discourses that are not at the center of Western tradition. We are not used to responding to these discourses; we are not even used to perceiving them or their implicit structure. These discourses, although part of the Western symbolic, are among the alternative traditions, linguistic and conceptual formulations that are no longer fashionable.

After looking at Pym's language of the domestic and mundane, I will consider more fully the discourse of contemplative dailiness that Pym found in Anglo-Catholic hymns and in Charlotte Yonge's fiction. Then I will briefly consider Pym's response to English literature, especially the links between this everyday humanism and John Keble's advocacy of English literature as an aid to Christian faith and life. Although my discussion of these discourses includes an ongoing discussion of Pym's novels, I will examine in detail only *Less Than Angels* and *Quartet in Autumn*. In the former, the writer-character Catherine so well embodies or "inscribes" the creative and experimental qualities of a subjectivity that derives from the subversively unimportant; Letty, of *Quartet in Autumn*, shows the resilience of the trivial as discourse, even in a modern world of fossilized or retired discourses.

In Pym's novels, the discourse of domestic trivia is almost always positive—caring, relational, and steadying; it sometimes inspires creative work. As we noted earlier, Dulcie saw trivial conversation to be a solidifying, communal link for women. Like gossip (and domestic trivia can become gossip), the language about home life, meals, and gardens (one's own or the neighbor's seen through a window) in Pym's fiction often draws people together, as Patricia Spacks claims for gossip. Domestic trivia, then, constructs a communal subjectivity, a self that finds its identity in shared everyday activities or observations. Indeed, Catherine acknowledges after Tom moves out that a "gossipy tea" with a woman would be "comforting" (*LTA*, 154). Differing from Pym's other female characters, Catherine is a commercially successful writer of romantic fiction; she finds in housework an inspiration for her stories (28), even though "everyday life" is "tough meat" and must undergo "mincing" before she gives it to her readers (7).

Catherine resembles Barbara Pym who, as she herself and most readers have observed, detailed in her fiction the daily trivia rather than the big wonderful things. As Pym remarks in an interview, inspiration comes from the everyday world of home or work: "All these things like journalism, politics, and the rest, the blue bugloss, thistles, and poppies—a lot of these are what a novelist's material comes from I should have thought. The daydreams and the sex. . . ."[19] Pym's interview statements about the writer's materials do expand trivia beyond the domestic sphere and perhaps beyond the strictly trivial; politics is certainly public, and political discourse is assumed to be important—if not quite big and wonderful.

Yet in the interview, Pym continually takes pains to downplay the importance of even the important. The tensions in the interview are instructive. The interviewer, Iain Finlayson, has an "agenda"; he keeps returning to Cyril Connolly's book *Enemies of Promise*, where Connolly argues that certain "enemies" (such as a novelist's doing journalism) interfere with the writer's creative gift and promise. Barbara Pym, however, persistently evades the notion of a great artist's being deterred from producing a masterpiece simply because of salaried work or other pragmatic obligations. She does not see herself, or novelists generally, in terms of the discourse of heroic masterpiece-producers. She says of herself, "I'm not a professional writer—I never have been, really. I've always had to earn my living in some other way" ("Interview," 3,5).

Pym in effect domesticates and even trivializes, in the best possible sense, the Western notion of the artist as hero. Arguing that the only real hazard for a writer is "success," she points out that during the war Connolly's journalism, his editorship of *Horizon*, "was a great service to people," even if he never produced a masterpiece of fiction ("Interview," 3,5).[20] Pym's implied values here are usually read as domestic and feminine values—flowers, daydreams, service; yet she appositionally includes politics as an implicit element (discourse) of art. She indicates no soul-destroying conflict between domesticity and being an artist. Similarly, in the experimental subjectivities of her fictional characters, *culture* becomes a household word.

On the other hand, both Pym and her characters venture negative appraisals of domesticity and everyday experience. Most ordinary activities seem "useless," Belinda Bede remarks in *Some Tame Gazelle*; Caroline Grimstone, heroine of the sketchy, imperfect novel, *An Academic Question*, is the only character in Pym's fiction to express frequently her dislike of the trivial, though her friends do have such interests and she acknowledges that the trivial matters of food and contraception availability cause riots among students.[21] Although Pym herself found a positive delight in everyday concerns, she admits in April 1940 that domestic activity with "a little time for reading" still "isn't *really* enough"; she needs to be writing fiction (*VPE*, 103). For Pym, for Catherine, and for certain peripheral women characters (for instance, the scholar Beatrix Howick in *A Few Green Leaves*), the satisfactions of ordinary private life inspire public and even published expression. Pym's remarks about masterpieces and service, however, indicate that for herself and most of her female characters, the construction of the self is not intimately linked to public recognition or to the writer-as-hero myth. Daily trivia suffices to comfort, to unite friends, and even to inspire creative expression.

For most of the women characters, the discourse of trivia is enhanced by, and dialogically combined with, the meditative dailiness of a distinctly Christian discourse, and with a feminized humanism or literary discourse. The meditative or Christian dailiness is a distinctive version of the ordinary, as Pym's language indicates when she introduces, in her diary, the passage from *Trivia* (a passage often quoted by critics). In 1943, trying to recover from her affair with Gordon Glover, Pym comments on having managed a "detachment" from her "pain." Then she writes, "It is a *wicked* thing to want time to pass and not to try *to enjoy one's days*. Now I try *to make things to look forward to*, however small" (*VPE*, 114; my emphasis). Pym condemns a nonresponsive, dulled consciousness, and she places a moral value on assertively fashioning "things to look forward to," even small, trivial things. She then quotes from *Trivia* the second and final paragraph of a brief insight, which Pearsall Smith entitles "The Coming of Fate":

So I never lose a sense of the whimsical and perilous charm of daily life, with its meetings and words and accidents. Why, today, perhaps, or next week, I may hear a voice and, packing up my Gladstone bag, follow it to the ends of the world. (qtd. in *VPE*, 114)

Pearsall Smith is here emphasizing his discovery that one must be alert to destiny; otherwise, one may miss it. The "so" states the result of the insight developed in his first paragraph. In that paragraph, he describes his minimal response to life's possibilities. "Slight the impulse that made me take this turning at the crossroads, trivial and fortuitous the meeting" with a friend.[22] He points to the element of chance and mystery in such crossroads or trivial encounters.

In contrast to Pearsall Smith's discourse of the trivial, on this occasion Pym develops a distinctly religious language. She precedes her quotation of *Trivia* with a moralistic discourse, denouncing the reprehensible attitude of dull-heartedness, and she emphasizes responsibility for the anticipation of a continuing openness in daily life. One looks for the whimsical and perilous charm, but one also tries to construct things "to look forward to." Her language carries an edge of duty and agency that is lacking in the *Trivia* passage (and lacking in Pym's imitation/parody of *Trivia* quoted earlier). There is a moral obligation, Pym says, to enjoy life and to fashion an attitude that allows one to respond to the uncertain charm of daily experience.

Pym's more ethically strenuous discourse of the trivial is usually a dialogic hybrid of domesticity and a pervasive religious discourse. Church services, parish jumble sales, and even prayers are ordinary activities for most of Pym's characters. Clerics are major and minor characters in her fiction. Several scholars have commented on Pym's own absorbing interest in the high-church liturgies of Anglo-Catholic tradition, an interest that pervades the novels, or certainly the earlier ones. Yet Pym's texts are never structured by conversion, spiritual quest, or vision. Though a "Christian writer," she never offers an "ultimate answer," Jane Nardin observes, and Janice Rossen emphasizes the significance for Pym's characters of the ritual and antiquarian aspects of their Anglo-Catholic tradition.[23] Certainly on a first reading, Christianity seems to be largely a part of the furniture in these novels, a background or setting, rather than a major factor in the structuring of subjectivity.

Yet Christianity, especially Anglo-Catholicism, is one of the most important discourses in Pym's work. It often merges into, and characterizes, her discourse of the trivial; indeed, Anglo-Catholic spirituality insists on a link between the ordinary and the holy. Anglo-Catholicism is best known for its incorporation of Catholic liturgies, but it also promoted a very Catholic (even Roman) doctrinal focus. The Anglo-Catholic doctrinal discourse, originating in the Oxford Movement, is not at all vague, and in Pym's novels it subtly changes the discourse of domestic trivia into one of Christian meditation and relationality. The trivial becomes an understated sacramentalism that acknowledges a blessing in the physical and the ordinary.

There is no great vision expected in the everyday experience—just a divine blessing or presence that is implied in the doctrine of the Incarnation. In his detailed history of Anglo-Catholicism, W. S. F. Pickering acknowledges the increasing emphasis on ceremony, celibacy of the clergy, and the prevalence of a distinctive vocabulary among high-church members. Equally important is the more traditional doctrine. Pickering traces the prominence given by Anglo-Catholicism to the dignity and goodness of human beings (instead of their "depravity"—a Calvinistic or more Protestant concept); the sanctified Christian community, being an "extension of the Incarnation," practiced its faith with the celebration of all seven traditional sacraments, including confession.[24]

The great hymn-writer of the Oxford Movement, John Keble (often quoted in Pym's novels) especially tried to promote greater participation in the sacraments, as W. J. A. M. Beek emphasizes in his study of Keble's contribution to theology and literature. Keble's sacramental theology interpreted the Mass as a "sacrifice"; Christians were united to Christ's sacrifice by celebrating the liturgy and by accepting sacrifice—submitting to God's will—in everyday life.[25] Anglo-Catholic doctrine thus offered Pym a discourse that made the trivial something more than a grab bag of minor, secular curiosities and domestic activities. The trivial, the physical, the everyday experience, and crossroads conversation (rather than the great love or quest) become the site of moral growth and of the constructing of caring, community-oriented selves.

In some respects, Pym was not a thoroughgoing Anglo-Catholic. The Anglo-Catholic movement, with its Marian hymns and encouragement of a celibate clergy, was a somewhat subversive subculture. Most Anglo-Catholics regarded the mainstream parishes of the Church of England as too conventional, comfortable, and above all too much identified with an "English way of life."[26] Yet Barbara Pym enjoyed the Englishness of church life. She portrays married clergy and vicarage life with as much detail and care as she does the celibates of the "clergy house," for instance, in *A Glass of Blessing*. Jane Cleveland, the pastor's wife in *Jane and Prudence*, pauses when she sees four women gathering in the church to decorate it for a harvest celebration; it is an "English scene," she reflects, "and a precious thing" (26).

On the other hand, Pym, like so many of her fictional characters, read the *Church Times*, which generally supported the Anglo-Catholic movement.[27] Further, Pym was well acquainted with Keble's hymns, and these reiterate the sacramental discourse of Anglo-Catholicism. In one of her mock-Stevie-Smith letters, Pym (as this "queer old horse, this old brown spinster") refers very lightly to *The Christian Year* (*VPE* 69), one of Keble's most popular books of liturgical poetry. During a discussion of Anglo-Catholic hymns in *An Unsuitable Attachment*, Rupert Stonebird criticizes Keble as a hymn writer and cites two lines from one of the Marian hymns in *The Christian Year*.[28] Edwin also refers to "one of Keble's less felicitous hymns" in *Quartet in Autumn* (73). Apparently, neither Pym nor her fictional judges think Keble was much of a poet, yet her discourse of the ordinary or the trivial incorporates Keble's sacramentalism.

Pym also found the same spirituality (that is, the same Anglo-Catholic and sacramental discourse) saturating the novels of Charlotte M. Yonge, who was a great admirer and promoter of Keble's hymn-poems. Yonge wrote a series of reflections on *The Christian Year* and on *Lyra Innocentium* (the latter being Keble's doctrinal poems about childhood), and she often draws her chapter mottoes in *The Daisy Chain* from Keble's Christian poetry. Pym was very keen on the fiction of Yonge and in 1943 called *The Daisy Chain* "so well written" (*VPE*, 116–17), even though Yonge herself expressed doubts on this point, apologizing in her preface for the length of the novel and its plethora of characters.[29] Pym refers to other fiction of Yonge as well, but *The Daisy Chain* attracted her both early and late in her career; she still finds it "very readable" in 1971 (*VPE*, 260). Her qualified acknowledgement of Keble and her enthusiasm for Yonge gave her a double dose of Christianity as a domesticated discourse of sacramental attentiveness to the trivial.

This discourse is the subtle agent of moral perception for many of her characters, including Jessie Morrow, Dulcie Mainwaring, and the very ironic Belinda Bede. In *Crampton Hodnet*, Jessie Morrow finds Keble's phrases in her thoughts as she prepares to help clean up the room recently vacated by Mr. Latimer, a curate whose cold, pragmatic proposal she had rejected. Readers naturally see in the words *trivial* and *common task* a keynote of Pym's discourse of the ordinary. Keble's phrase, from the hymn "Morning," points to a special kind of ordinariness, however. The entire stanza reads:

> The trivial round, the common task,
> Would furnish all we ought to ask;
> Room to deny ourselves; a road
> To bring us, daily, nearer God. (93–96)

Jessie reflects her way through this stanza, perhaps reluctantly and ironically at first, as she admits having "no right" to ask for anything since she is Miss Doggett's "companion"; she is "lucky to be able to occupy herself with those things that would furnish her with all she needed to ask."[30]

Jessie's words here misappropriate and hybridize the symbolic morality (and theology) of the hymn stanza. Her rereading (all she "needed") of Keble's morally stringent "ought" suggests that she does indeed find her circumstances sufficient and not oppressive. She goes on to quote to herself the last two lines of the stanza, lines that speak of life providing "room to deny ourselves"; Jessie feels "no sentimentality" for the rejected Latimer, and concludes that she "was really a very lucky woman. It might well have been otherwise" (*CH*, 157).

Her present restrictions (being a single "companion") still offer her a lot of positive "room" and space for decision; by denying herself marriage, she has also freed herself *from* Mr. Latimer. Having "room to deny" oneself is patently a little different from having "a room of one's own," but the metaphor of space is present in both discourses. Woolf's metaphor privileges a notion of creative space, the economic and psychological space a writer needs. Jessie's use of Keble's tricky phrase (and here for once he is almost a poet) deconstructs the notion of room altogether. Self-denial implies *no room* rather than any kind of space and room; the text of subjectivity here seems to be a non-text.

Yet Keble's contradictory room (that opens into a road in the next phrase) exactly characterizes the trivial of Jessie's life and of Pym's novels about the ordinary. Just when there is no room, there is really the greatest room. When one denies oneself some great text of one's culture (some symbolic structure such as marriage, profession, producing a masterpiece), then there is freedom to perceive other things. The apparently unexpansive dailiness of most lives is precisely the only room that matters in the discourse of faith. It is the room of the minor but practical insights that renew the self; these opportunities for growth, opportunities that evade the imprisoning grand narratives, construct a maturing subjectivity.

Such everyday opportunities for renewal (even if they are not always responded to) are central to the discourse of Christian dailiness for Keble, Yonge, and Pym. The word *new* is repeated six times in the central portion of the hymn (lines 21–28), and in a line not usually included in hymnals, though it belongs to the original poem, Keble refers to the apocalyptic Christ of Revelation who "makes all things new" (20; Rev. 21:5). Keble's straightforward, doctrinal poem is quite clear about the link between Christ's sacrifice and the "new" in everyday life. As Keble admonishes, "If in our daily course our mind / Be set to hallow all we find," then God will provide valuable "treasures" for "sacrifice" (29–32). The human mind, human subjectivity, united in faith with Christ's sacrifice, will "hallow" or make holy all it sees. Everything becomes blessed and is given, offered, sacrificed daily. It is made "new every morning."

In this Anglo-Catholic (and Roman Catholic) sacramental discourse of "Morning," one perceives God in everything; "in all t'espy / Their God" (43–44), says Keble. So the "trivial round" becomes the focus of moral growth. One does not need to pursue a great love or a great quest (or a career as an anthropologist in Africa). For Keble, one need not reject "neighbor" and "work" or enter the "cloister'd cell" (49–50); this would be "to wind ourselves too high" (51). Neither the heroic quest is expected nor the great visionary call or sudden conversion. As Pickering emphasizes, Anglo-Catholic spirituality encouraged a gradual conversion or change in character; it did not expect a "sudden, emotional spiritual change."[31]

Following in this tradition and this discourse, Pym's characters almost never have epiphanic renewals or conversions. There are some mild exceptions such as Wilmet's sense of "hope" and "new" life in response to the light and fire of the Holy Saturday liturgy, and her increasing openness to people not of her class or interests, especially during her visit to a retreat house where, in a fertile "pagan" part of its garden, the birds seem larger and the bees unexpectedly swarm.[32] On the other hand, we hear nothing further in *An Unsuitable Attachment* about "the uncomfortable and disturbing sensation" that accompanied Rupert Stonebird's regaining of his faith (35). We don't learn much about these episodes, and Pym herself said that she had never had a "rich spiritual experience" (*VPE*, 100). Such an experience would not have been part of her Anglo-Catholic tradition or discourse. In contrast to the modernist fiction of Woolf, whose texts offer sustained visionary reflection, subjectivity in Pym's texts is constructed from precisely the nonvisionary yet "hallowed" trivia of everyday life.

The discourse of a hallowed dailiness prevails also in Charlotte Yonge's fiction. John Keble was the vicar of Yonge's church, and her novels link the Oxford Movement to the popular style of "domestic realism," which emphasized the character-building moral struggles of everyday life.[33] In Yonge's *The Daisy Chain*, when the teenaged Ethel May begins to teach school, a visitor to her family comments on what he sees as an improvement in her impetuous character: Ethel's school teaching, being "good homely work," has made her more attentive, he says, to "home duties." In response, Ethel's sister Margaret (invalid and family adviser) sketches her perspective on the construction of the self. She notes that the "many little details" of daily experience "form the character more than the great events" (135–36). The plot rather self-consciously illustrates this notion, and after four hundred more pages of "many little details," one is not surprised to read that another visitor to this very religious family is impressed with Ethel's attentiveness to everyday concerns. There "is *so much soul* in the *least thing* she does, as if she could *not be indifferent* for a moment" (560; my emphasis).

For Ethel, theology has become a household discourse, a domestication of her culture. She has learned "to hallow all" she finds (as Keble advises), even the least things, the trivial. Her siblings have learned to do the same, along the way overcoming any temptation to fame and wealth; instead, the men (and especially the women) learn the value of being "useful" and of sacrificing one's own pleasure or will (62–64, 405). In the end, the unmarried Ethel (an excellent woman—she has built a church!) knows that she can never expect "to be first with any" (593). Her thought is echoed by Pym's Mildred Lathbury who acknowledges, "I was not really first in anybody's life" (*EW*, 39).

In this Christian discourse of sacrifice (a traditional, symbolic discourse, though hardly mainstream in modern times), the trivia of ordinary events and activities resonate with value; they are hallowed. While Anne Wyatt-Brown sees Pym as paying a high price for her "obsession" with Yonge's fiction, this psychoanalytic biographer may be misreading the Christian discourse that was so important to Pym. Wyatt-Brown argues that Pym's passive heroines and her "eccentric perspective" on social life are a result of the novelist's unresolved depression and repressed emotions; clinging to "the rituals of daily life" limited the perspective of Yonge and of Pym.[34] This is probably true, in its way. Psychoanalytic discourse is certainly one of the grand narratives of our time; that is, it seems "true" to us, or "natural," as Roland Barthes might say. Yet it is not the only "technology of the self" in the West, and it may not "read" Barbara Pym very well. Foucault argues in *The History of Sexuality* that there have been other discourses that structured the self or identity.[35] Among these alternative discourses is the Christian sacramentality that in Pym's novels often gives a text, gives a voice, to the ordinary.

On the other hand, Pym certainly recognized that the discourse of psychoanalysis was part of modern culture. Yet she grew up in an era dominated by a quite conservative psychoanalytic discourse, one that urged marriage and motherhood for women rather than a career, as Sheila Jeffreys has documented.[36] Although Pym knew the discourse of psychoanalysis, it was not her mode of self-fashioning, and she treats this discourse with some irony (as she also treats Christian discourse).

In *Less Than Angels*, for instance, the narrator offers an amusing sketch of a room full of young anthropologists who have not yet written up their field notes. They are indulging in psychoanalysis as the discourse of the victim-hero. They feel hampered by economic, family, and psychological difficulties (they are encountering "enemies of promise," Connolly might say). These highly theoretical apprentice-scientists are ready with the best modern discourse by way of giving an account of their problems, for "they were by no means inarticulate themselves, often gathering in this room or in a nearby pub to talk of their neuroses and psychological difficulties which prevented them from writing up their material" (49).

The narrator goes on to mock also—and hinting of religious discourse now—the passive role of the women "devoted" to these men; the women have learned "to bear love's burdens, listening patiently to their men's troubles and ever ready at their typewriters, should a manuscript or even a short article get to the stage of being written down" (*LTA*, 49). With an evenhanded, light touch, the narrator apportions the serious grand narrative, the modern discourse of psychoanalysis, to the men and gives the muted Christian, burden-bearing ideology to the women, her irony mocking both discourses (as well as the briefly sketched characters).

Although Pym echoes Yonge and Keble often, she does so with an irony not present in Yonge's novels or in Keble's poetry. In *No Fond Return of Love*, Dulcie, at the conference for indexers and editors, hears a lay reader suggest that everything "can be done to the Glory of God," even making indexes and bibliographies. "His small congregation heard him say, almost with disappointment, that those who do such work have perhaps less opportunity of actually doing evil than those who write novels and plays or work for films or television" (30). Even dull professional tasks can be hallowed and offered to God, but the speaker (or the congregation) seems disappointed with this ethic's narrow range of opportunity for good or ill.

In response, Dulcie finds it easier to hallow domestic trivia rather than professional tasks. "But there is more satisfaction in scrubbing a floor or digging a garden, Dulcie thought. One seems nearer to the heart of things doing menial tasks than in making the most perfect index" (*NFR*, 30). Perhaps her affirmation of domestic concerns here carries with it a hint of something besides a sacramental femininity. Even by herself as she gardens or scrubs floors, the nonreligious Dulcie senses a special quality in these activities, so close to "the heart of things"; the near-Wordsworthian phrase is her substitute for the "Glory of God" one is supposed to manage by writing a good index.

The more intellectual (and theologically sophisticated) Belinda Bede of *Some Tame Gazelle* is more imaginative in her dialogic rereading of a woman's domestic responsibilities and of Christian self-denial. Laboriously kneading ravioli dough, she doubts if "Keble *really* understood" a woman's domestic tasks when he affirmed the sufficiency of such trivia; "did it furnish *quite* all we needed to ask?" (227). On the other hand, Belinda accepts blame readily, sacrificing her own opinion. Yet she does this very much for her own reasons. Early in a dinner party, she takes the blame for failing in two womanly responsibilities: congenial conversation and offering the sherry in a timely fashion. Her manners were lacking, she tells her guests "quite sincerely, thus taking upon herself the blame for all the little frictions of the evening. But it was so obvious that women should take the blame, it was both the better and the easier part" (119).

Sacrificing her sense of justice here (a guest's late arrival has been partly responsible for the tension), Belinda modifies this action of a humble hostess by dialogically rewriting and carnivalizing a gospel text. In Luke's story, Jesus says Mary (unlike her busy sister Martha who is preparing the meal) has "chosen that good part," that is, of listening to Jesus (Lk. 10:42). Belinda dialogically echoes this story but overturns its moral content. For Belinda, the better part is also the *easier* one. By implication, she reinscribes Mary's decision as being the lazy option (which *was* Martha's accusation in the first place).[37] Like Jane Cleveland, Belinda likes to dephrase a phrase. She also undercuts any ethic of gracious "feminine" or Christian self-denial when she accepts blame.

Belinda accepts blame simply because it is the easiest social gesture. She is avoiding hassle, and her dialogic garble of scripture renders her ethic practical, not deeply accepting or self-denying. Thus Belinda, Dulcie, and many of Pym's other women maintain an appositional colloquy with the symbolic discourses available to them in their culture. Their reflections are sometimes an ironic dialogue with certain muted and alternative discourses, discourses that they on the whole accept and live.

In addition to the discourses of domestic trivia and of sacramental dailiness, the self-fashioning of Pym's characters usually includes a feminized or domesticated humanism. All readers have observed how constantly Pym's men and women draw courage, comfort, or just an apt phrase, from English literature. Indeed, as I indicated in the first chapter, Pym's women characters are twentieth-century descendants of the "modern individual," the cultivated eighteenth-century woman of playful intellect who exercises mind and heart largely in the domestic sphere of relationships.[38] In addition, Jane, Catherine, and others have that "spontaneity of consciousness" that Matthew Arnold advocates in the structuring of the humanistic ("Hellenistic") self, a self free of materialism and economic competitiveness. In Pym's fiction, poetry is comfort and insight, not a career. Her humanistic discourse belongs partly to the tradition enunciated by Arnold when he argued that poetry may someday perform the functions of religion.[39] Indeed, Catherine Oliphant seems to be living this concept when she quotes Arnold's "Dover Beach" as a consolation to Tom on his loss of "faith in anthropology" (*LTA*, 105).

Frequently, Pym's response to literature also reflects that of Keble. For Keble, the English poets, especially Wordsworth, supplied a crucial element in the technology of the self, that is, in the construction of the Christian self. Keble's own poetry is fuzzily Wordsworthian, often affirming the contentment to be derived from flowers and trees and usually discerning in nature the mark of something divine. For Keble, who lectured and wrote on Wordsworth, poetry as well as nature had a healing effect; as Beek suggests, "poetry was for Keble something akin to religion, a *kind* of sacrament."[40] The person who reads and quotes poetry is employing a discourse that, according to Keble, leads to a gradual healing, or even to a slow and sure spiritual maturing.

Barbara Pym and her characters often speak of literature's healing effect, though they also lightly mock this idea. Herself a romantic college student, Barbara Pym broods about Henry Harvey's inattentiveness, and she says it's a sign of the seriousness of her state when she gets "the Oxford Book of Victorian Verse out of the library" (*VPE*, 29); similarly, Belinda (the "Barbara" representative in *Some*

Tame Gazelle) sees this book as a literary aspirin when she must stay in bed with a cold (185). Pym is evidently quite serious, however, when she asserts that she usually finds *Marius the Epicurean* very "soothing" (*VPE*, 157), and she offers a virtual ideology of reading (and writing) when she describes her interest in Ivy Compton-Burnett's fiction. In a letter written in 1940, Pym says that even such a powerful influence "passes (like so much in this life) and I have now got back to my own way such as it is. But purified and strengthened, as after a rich spiritual experience, or a shattering love affair" (*VPE*, 100). While she goes on to doubt whether she has ever had a great spiritual experience, her rhetoric affirms (using religious discourse) literature's self-fashioning effect. Her "own way," of writing herself and her fiction, has undergone a significant spiritual change.

Her new subjectivity as a writer, Pym notes parenthetically, resulted from an influence that "passes (like so much in this life)." She and her fictional characters often make remarks of this kind, reiterating a doctrinal truism of their faith. The effect of such an attitude on Pym's discourse *about discourse*, in her Compton-Burnett appraisal, is subtly to subvert the importance of any single discourse or any given writer's influence. Compton-Burnett's prose may have had a major impact on Pym's writing (like a spiritual experience), but even so important an influence is only a step or stage in an author's continuing expectation of development.

Pym's fictional characters share this openness to discourse. Although they find comfort, especially in a crisis of love, from a favorite passage of literature, they turn to it as they might turn to a cup of tea. They do not see English literature as some kind of scripture (nor do they see scripture as "scripture"). Again, Jane Cleveland's appropriation of the Bible and of literature is representative as well as distinctive. She doesn't just appropriate; she kidnaps her quotations or objects of parody. She is not an inheritor but a purloiner of texts. She develops her most amusing and extended dialogic borrowing when the member of parliament Edward Lyall tells her that he occasionally travels to London by train instead of a car. Jane begins a parody of T. S. Eliot's "Journey of the Magi":

"You mean you want to know what your constituents have to endure? The tea too weak or too strong, the stale sandwich, the grimy upholstery, the window that won't open, the waiting on the draughty platform . . ." Jane could have gone on indefinitely, feeling like one of our great modern poets, had not Edward interrupted her with an embarrassed laugh. (*JP*, 219; original ellipsis)

Jane's language not only teases Edward Lyall, but it dialogically mocks Eliot's cadences as well along with the narrative of the great quest. (And the detail of trivial inconvenience in Eliot's own poem already undercuts the notion of a great quest by great heroes.) Jane's re-visioning of Eliot's poem carnivalizes even the trivial—even the everyday nuisance of the "wisemen's" travel.

Jane's reminiscences of scripture show a similar irreverence. She echoes the words of Jesus ("For ye have the poor always with you," Mt. 26:11) when she notes the clergyman's expectation that women will reliably supply food. "And the clergy are always with us where meals are concerned," Jane comments (*JP*, 30). By using the rhetoric of the famous statement, Jane completely reverses the position of the privileged male clergy. They become instead "the poor," the neglected outsiders who constitute a dependable social problem, a reliable nuisance that deserves compassion but not moralistic obsession.

Jane's brief scenarios and dialogic phrases consistently carnivalize the big or wonderful structures of meaning. And yet if Jane is so unconventional and creative, why hasn't she published more than one book, the collection of essays on seventeenth-century poets? She herself feels that her marriage ended her career (11), and her young friend Prudence thinks Jane's life of parish work is "wasted" when she has "great gifts" and "could have written books" (102).

In one of those rare self-reflexive (almost postmodernist) scenes in Pym's fiction, we come close to the answer to this question, or to its lack of an answer. On the strength of her single publication fifteen years earlier, Jane still attends the meetings of a literary society. At the literary meeting in *Jane and Prudence*, we have in a nearly surreal scene the representatives of two other versions of Jane herself; or rather, we have *three* versions of the "implied" narrator/author all talking with each other about being writers.

Jane's "old college friend," Barbara Bird, is finishing her seventeenth novel; in quoting her reviewer, she uses a phrase from a review of one of Pym's novels (117).[41] An unnamed young author is sketched in with hints of Barbara Pym's physical appearance: "a tall, youngish woman with large eyes and prominent teeth" (118). She is not well known yet and has published just two novels (as Pym had—before *Jane and Prudence* became the third). This deferential young author at first mistakes Jane Cleveland for the famous Barbara Bird, and then the three of them discuss writing, publishing, critics.

These experimental subjectivities, these fragments of authorship and authority, have stepped aside from the novel's action briefly in order to offer comment—like a chorus—about women writers. These three reflect each other. When the young novelist decides to "plunge boldly" (119) to speak with a poet (featured on the program), she enacts adverbially Jane's own maiden name; Jane herself had "boldly" opened the vestry door when she tried unsuccessfully to settle a quarrel among members of the Parochial Council (114). None of the three women is censorious or envious; none implies that the others have lost their integrity because of writing more or less than someone else. And most importantly, the implied author behind the implied author (Pym herself) obviously decided to feature, in *Jane and Prudence*, the puzzling and puzzled Jane, the verbally eccentric one-time scholar now married, instead of featuring the new "youngish" writer or the very successful Barbara who quotes the review of Pym's novel. These "major" characters, that is, successful writers, have only cameo entrances; although their lives might be expected to inscribe a symbolic pattern of significant quest, they are relegated to minor status in this narrative.

In her narrative preference, Pym is like her character Jane Bold Cleveland who prefers not to join the author-admiring, author-centered groups at these meetings; instead, she likes "to wander freely and observe others with what she hoped was detachment" (117). The narrative on the periphery of the big (author-centered, hero-centered) event is free from the restrictions of a closed plot, a quest or romance.

One could almost say that the implied ethic of the three discourses (the three trivia-hybrids) that Pym features is this freedom, this flexible openness to change. The languages of domesticity, faith, and literature intermingle, become new, and change in a world where all texts are mortal and merely experimental. All texts construct the self anew, but temporarily only, since human subjectivity (according to Keble's rhetoric) continues to find the trivial round, the crossroads experience of self-sacrifice and growth, "new every morning."

When human subjectivity resists renewal, or the consciousness-constructing texts are closed or fossilized, Pym's narratives imply moral danger. The most extreme instance of the noncaring (and nonexperimental, nonopen) discourse is Leonora Eyre's rigid self-fashioning. In *The Sweet Dove Died*, Leonora attempts to protect her late middle age, to "arrange" it like furniture or her collection of Victoriana. She even tries to arrange the life of the bisexual James into an exclusive passionless companionship for herself.

James's uncle, Humphrey Boyce, who is more than platonically interested in her, accurately observes that she has "this romantic view of the past—and of the present."[42] She does; her social conversation is a "tedious" recounting of what she sees as "romantic episodes" from her past (*Dove*, 17). Her trivia is not the throwaway remark about the everyday and the eccentric; her conversation instead describes what she sees as a big and wonderful text. As she explains to Humphrey: "One feels life is only tolerable if one takes a romantic view of it," including a romanticized, idealized view of Victoriana (91). Leonora's solace is the opposite of Dulcie's in *No Fond Return of Love*; Dulcie recommended turning to "trivial things" as a comfort after "one great sorrow or one great love" (167). But Leonora, who is atypical among Pym's heroines, is stuck in her own version of a great text of romantic, attractive feminine elegance. When her friend Meg calls her "gracious and elegant," Leonora says, "You make me sound hardly human, like a kind of fossil" (56). Indeed, Leonora tries to fossilize herself.

Leonora tries to fashion herself as a beautifully frozen discourse; she *wants* the text of her life to be monologic. She tries to cage herself just as she hopes to keep James in the barred room (and former nursery) in her house. Even her language nearly entraps him. He is vulnerable and caring, open to the "infection" of her sentence. He hears her say, "One does try to arrange one's days so that one visits as many agreeable places as possible" (9), and later he deliberately uses the word *agreeable*, knowing she likes it (47). Still later, he is evidently using the word as though it were his own when he decides not to stay the night with Phoebe. Waking up in her dirty and cluttered cottage "would certainly not be agreeable, he decided" (64). Leonora attempts to write his subjectivity, indeed, to subject it to her own.

None of the three discourses that are usually most active in Pym's novels is active in Leonora's subjectivity; she is distinctly not an experimental self. She dislikes the "cosiness" of female acquaintances like Meg; she has no meditative and renewing faith-discourse and no active relationship with English literature. Unlike Pym's characters who enjoy domesticating and hybridizing the symbolic texts of religion and literature, Leonora does not want to render these texts "new every morning." Her moral failure is linked to the fact that she understands these symbolic discourses only in their most rigid, fossilized form.

Less as More: *Less Than Angels*

In contrast, Catherine Oliphant of *Less Than Angels* is dialogically engaged with language as she fashions both her own stories and her experimental self. Her stories have a loose, minimal structure. Like Barbara Pym's fiction, Catherine's stories seem to end before the writing, that is, before an implied marriage or other obvious plot-culminator. Catherine finds in domestic trivia and other muted discourses a creative language that keeps her free of rigid symbolic structures and, in addition, a language that allows her to challenge and free others.

Although she had "imagined that her husband would be a strong character who would rule her life" (*LTA*, 27), at age thirty-one she hasn't found that person yet and clearly does not feel bound to this great text of feminine passivity. When her lover Tom Mallow leaves her for the young student Dierdre, and especially after his death in Africa, Catherine is distressed. Yet after spending a couple of weeks with Dierdre's family, she longs "for her flat and her typewriter and her odd solitary life"; she is full of ideas for stories and wants to return to her work (248). Her aloneness is never the loneliness of pathos or emptiness. That is not how she "reads" her "odd solitary life," although Tom (and some critics) do read Catherine's life as one of sad, solitary deprivation.[43] Catherine is commenting on the "loneliness of men" when Tom argues that more women than men are lonely; yet Catherine says, "Loneliness can often be a kind of strength in women, possibly in men too, of course, but it doesn't seem to show itself so much" (90–91). Catherine is not a sociologist or anthropologist citing data here, but her discourse of loneliness is interesting because of what it says about her. As she later reassures the concerned Dierdre: "I never mind being alone" (255). She reads aloneness in women, and presumably in herself, as a discourse of strength, not of passive forsakenness that needs a classic male rescue.

In fact, she requires a certain amount of psychological aloneness or privacy in order to write. Early in his acquaintance with Dierdre, Tom basks in her absorbed attention, because he has just "left Catherine busy finishing a story and seeming to have no time for him" (51); even after she first sees Tom and Dierdre together, Catherine returns home and becomes "so absorbed" in her writing that two hours pass (112). She is basically happy in this room or text of subjectivity, in contrast to Dierdre who had hoped for poems and parties in her own room; yet she "had lost interest in the room" since it "had not fulfilled its promise" (42).[44]

Catherine, with her eclectic knowledge of story, has found her own story. Once she snatches a page of her writing from Digby, an anthropology student, and says, "It's not your kind of story" (29). With her keen ear for discourse, Catherine separates Digby from magazine romance fiction. In some respects, romance fiction is not *her* story either, though she can write it along with short nonfiction for women's magazines. She does not construct herself along the lines of the texts she offers as advice, however; she would never put her own elbows in lemon halves (194).

Catherine seeks a plurality of phrases and stories, trivial ones, different ones, that may prove useful to different people. She perceives that Tom's subjectivity is inscribed by his career as an anthropologist. The psychological and linguistic fashioning of his life belongs to prominent ("significant") symbolic structures; Tom is caught up in the grand narrative of a search for knowledge. Catherine sketches this major symbolic discourse on Tom's departure for Africa when she contrasts his "calm detachment" with the "complexity of personal relationships"—his (largely ignored) ties with his family and girlfriends (186).

Catherine, in contrast, is not written by the great, significant narratives of the West; instead, she transforms such discourses by domesticating them with the trivial and the in-significant. She has a talent for creative (linguistic) domestication. She is interested in the trivial and the incomplete rather than in arranging her life around some famous, symbolic text of success or love. As we have seen, she finds inspiration in housework (28) and enjoys the "trivial pleasures" of cooking and reading "little poems" (104). Like Pym, Catherine seeks comfort from the English poets; after Tom leaves, she reads "her favorite depressing poets, Hardy, Matthew Arnold and the lesser Victorians" (154). A domesticated literary discourse is as much a part of her life as domesticity itself. She is an everyday humanist, exercising her cultivated heart and head with spontaneity. She is a modern, female "individual" with a flat of her own (though she does not always live there in a celibate state). Her talent for story allows her to earn a living, but she does not see her own life as a big text. She renders a service (to recall Pym's remarks about journalism) with her magazine contributions, but she is not trying to write a masterpiece (or to forge the conscience of her race).

While Catherine does not usually attend church, she prays in a church after Tom's departure for Africa, and she is in continual dialogic colloquy with biblical texts as well as literary ones. Reading the wine list aloud, she finds in the phrase "very old in wood and of great delicacy" a dialogic echo of the Psalms. "Long-suffering and of great goodness, is that what I mean?" Yes, it is what she means; she is quoting the last phrase of Psalm 103:8 as the *Book of Common Prayer* renders it (which is different in every word here from the KJV).[45] Catherine has obviously been to church services often in the past, even if she does not now attend. The prayerbook Psalms have helped to construct her "self." She also marvels at the large number of people in a cafeteria: "How many souls—she thought of them in this hymn-like phrase" (108). Biblical phrases are not in opposition to her creative talent, her sex life, her sense of agency, or her relationships. Instead, religious discourse for Catherine is in dialogic apposition to several other nonprominent discourses of Western culture, including her domestic and literary discourses.

From a radical Christian point of view (and there is a hint of this in the Anglo-Catholicism of Keble and even of Pym), there is a sense in which *all* discourses are nonprominent, even trivial; both life and language are limited by mortality. Catherine acknowledges this the evening after Tom leaves her apartment. She decides not to read a "book of devotion" given her by her headmistress. She has read it before; she remembers that it says "we are strangers and pilgrims here and must endure the heart's banishment, and she felt that she knew that already" (138). So did the writers of Hebrews 11:13 and 1 Peter 2:11 (KJV), where the English phrase describes human beings as "strangers and pilgrims." Pym herself uses simply, and without irony, this classic imagery when she says in a radio interview that "we are not completely at home on this earth" but are "natives" of a "Divine" world instead.[46]

Drawing upon these ancient symbolic structures, Catherine refurbishes her pilgrim and changing self with a kind of linguistic communion. She dialogically meshes a (very patriarchal, scriptural, male-defined) symbolic language with her mundane, modern "discourse" of casual cohabitation—and the loss of her lover. For Catherine, these discourses form a hybrid, and one of them is not in oppositional, rebellious disruption to the other. There is instead an appositional congeniality in the two discourses as the religious one loses any shred of moral theology (a person is a "stranger" on earth—theologically—because of "sin") and the discourse of domesticated modern romance loses any shred of melodrama. The trivial romance, the romance that ended before the writing and never became a "text," merges subtly with the scriptural symbolic in Catherine's experimental subjectivity.

Literary and scriptural phrases never imply any great turning points in Catherine's life. Neither the style of an author nor the ring of a biblical phrase ever structures any sense of large destiny or personal conversion for her. Religious and literary phrases are as domesticated in her subjectivity as are the wine lists and her love of cooking and cleaning house. Her "self" is not constructed of great moments, great quests, great goals and endings. Instead, she thrives in a nearly meditative richness of passing discourse. She lives in a continuing textual crossroads where domestic trivia, along with literary and religious discourses, construct her flexible, caring subjectivity and her relationships. Although she is not religious, she is as attentive to the changing moments of language as Yonge's very religious Ethel was to her everyday work.

Catherine's everyday work is language. Paradoxically, her flexible consciousness as a writer is the source of stability in her life. A discourse of change is the stable center of her subjectivity. Her stories themselves privilege the varied fluctuations of trivia rather than the constrained patterns of romance or quest. She is saddened when she sees Tom with Dierdre in the restaurant, but the published story she develops out of this incident is evidently going to be related from the point of view of a peripheral, minor character—a narrator (presumably Catherine) who observes the central, developing romance. As Rowena Talbot, in *A Glass of Blessings*, describes the story (reading it under a drier at the hairdresser's), it begins "with a young man and a girl holding hands in a Greek restaurant, watched by the young man's former mistress—unknown to them, of course" (152).[47] Like Jane, preferring not to enter the legitimate author-circles, Catherine also remains outside the official, conventional structures. Although she makes a living by publishing stories, both in them and in her life she practices an eccentric, perhaps decentered, and certainly understated discourse of romance.

Even the loss of Tom does not move Catherine to perceive herself as part of a big and wonderful dramatic discourse of romance. She returns to her typewriter and the story she had started. Interrupting this ongoing story, the Tom-and-Dierdre incident has dropped like a painful digression. Catherine enters her flat and continues typing from the middle of an unfinished sentence:

so she was able to go straight on, filling in the French background of the story she was writing, where two strangers, soon to become hero and heroine, found themselves with three hours to wait between trains in the middle of a hot afternoon and wandered into the square of the little French town. They sat on a seat and looked at the pink and white oleanders, making conversation to the strains of a distant military band . . . (*LTA*, 112; original ellipsis)

Apparently, a major portion of this story happens when nothing is happening (between trains) and in a place where nothing is likely to happen. The characters must *wait* three hours in the *middle* of the afternoon and in the middle of a *little* town. There is no sense of urgent plot. The couple *wandered* at this crossroads, this trivial encounter, and sat down, making conversation; this story wanders, or this section of it does, giving background, not event. Perhaps love or even war (the military band) hover somewhere, but anything so teleological is peripheral to Catherine's understated, nonrigid text. This is the open, flexible story she is writing when Tom comes home; she is "so absorbed" when he speaks: she "smiled up at him absently, for she was still far away" (112). Catherine knows what her "kind of story" is (her text of domestic and literary pleasure), and she can return to this room of creative trivia for solace and self-affirmation.

She is willing to share this room, for hers is a relational and caring self; she is not at all an artist in an ivory tower. She enjoys giving parties, staying temporarily with the family of Mabel Swan, and providing room, board, and bed for Tom. Yet she recognizes that his story differs from hers. Even though he lost his "faith" in anthropology, he perhaps still retained a heroic sense of his profession. Miss Clovis, who envisions a kind of high-church anthropology and thus argues (with dialogic humor unperceived by herself) for "the celibacy of the anthropologist," sees Tom Mallow as "dedicated to his work" (204–5). Since Tom became disillusioned about his profession, he must once have taken it seriously; he certainly had a higher vision of it than Catherine ever had of her romance-story writing. With her more loosely structured sense of profession and story, she finds it difficult to understand what he means by "faith" in his profession.

In contrast, Alaric Lydgate is uncomfortable with expectations of greatness. If he was ever dedicated to anthropology, he has certainly lost it (this symbolic allegiance to career and fame) by the time Catherine meets him. Irritable, withdrawn (sitting sometimes behind an African mask), he has achieved neither the administrative promotion he wanted nor success in anthropology or linguistics; eleven years worth of his notes on Africa are falling to pieces in a rusty trunk (57–60). Being an anthropologist was obviously not his "kind of story," and the perceptive Catherine rather easily retextualizes him. With her ear for discourse and the person, she frees him from the manly, symbolic structures that chafed and oppressed him.

The story she is working on when they meet accidentally (some time after Tom has moved out of Catherine's flat) parallels their encounter itself in many ways. Her story concerns a "big game hunter" (in whom Alaric sees himself) who has recently returned from Africa. Catherine asks Alaric about appropriate details of an African landscape in the rain, since the plot evidently moves the game hunter's preference from Africa to England and to an English girl, the niece of an elderly visitor to the hunter. When Catherine describes her story to Alaric, he seems puzzled at the lack of action in it and the deficient sense of an ending. Catherine responds, "Oh, well, that *is* the end, really" (156). Although the story apparently has a happy ending, as her romance fiction generally does (89), there is evidently no wedding—just an optimistic meeting, a crossroads occasion that "*is* the end, really." The plot is shaped less by the action than by the subtle change in the game hunter, in his subjectivity and discourse. Catherine says that he, while walking with the young woman, "suddenly feels that there is something rather nice about the drizzly English rain" (156). His evaluative discourse changes from the heroic (and masculine) to the relational and to a very ordinary English rain.

Catherine's explication of her text deconstructs the concept of a big and wonderful text and the notion of an "ending." She rephrased or dephrased the game hunter's subjectivity; she trivialized it, feminized it, and opened it. Similarly, her response to Alaric's oppressive life-text (and trunks full of crumbling notes) deconstructs his notion of himself—the hero-anthropologist who was to write a masterpiece in the field. Again, to recall Pym's interview remarks about Cyril Connolly, Alaric obviously does not see his work in anthropology as a "service" to scholars or others but as something tied to his own definition of achievement and success. When Catherine suggests it might "be rather a bother" to write up his notes, Alaric reflects that ever "since he could remember, almost, he had been going to 'write up his material.'" This phrase, which Alaric perceives as a quote from himself to himself, is so rooted in his subjectivity that he feels "as if the ground were slipping away from under his feet" (224) when he considers not following to the letter the discourse that has written him, the script of his professional self. Yet he decides to burn his notes in his backyard, a ritual that he and Catherine are sharing when the shocked Miss Clovis arrives to protest this very undedicated gesture; Alaric exuberantly tells her it may "free" him for writing a novel (228–29).

For Alaric, turning from science to fiction implies freedom. His own newly developing subjectivity is no longer structured along the lines of bringing the notes of his experience to some ordered conclusion in a major treatise. The openness of Catherine's stories seems to have entered his discourse about himself. He no longer needs to worry whether his life ever becomes a big and wonderful text. Now that he is free from an ideology of the *important*, he can respond to the indefinite, varied possibilities of the *unimportant*—the trivia of fictional discourse.

Alaric's transition from scientific discourse to novelistic discourse is echoed in Pym's last novel, *A Few Green Leaves*, where anthropologist Emma Howick, doing research in an English village, decides to write a novel instead of working up her notes into a scientific study. Although Emma's life never becomes as restricted as Alaric's, still she recognizes in scientific discourse a certain rigidity. After preparing lunch for a former lover, Graham Pettifer, Emma reflects, "It might have been better if I'd been a novelist," since the day's material, she decides, could have been useful in fiction. As it is, a sociological study of a developing relationship with the still-married Graham (or a study of modern marriage) would "find the whole affair very commonplace and predictable."[48] Monologic, scientific discourse would only describe the predictable, and so the relationship, as sociology, would lack the subtlety, the indefiniteness, that a discourse of fiction could give it.

When Emma decides to stay in the village and in her mother's cottage there, it is a decision that weaves together dialogically several threads of discourse important in Emma's developing subjectivity. Her mother, Beatrix Howick, is a widow, a scholar, and a teacher of Victorian fiction. After the fact, Beatrix does not much regret losing her husband to the war after only a year of marriage. Like many other women in Pym's fiction, Beatrix does not perceive romance as the all-encompassing narrative of her life, yet she does not denounce it on ideological terms—as, for instance, the professionally dedicated Esther Clovis does (the anthropologist should not marry). Beatrix has fashioned a dialogic, experimental self, combining the symbolic structures of her scholarly career (including the domesticated world of Charlotte Yonge's novels) and her own relational concerns for her daughter's happiness.

Beatrix domesticates professional life and discourse, for instance, one night as she tries to fall asleep during a visit to the village. While considering her daughter's undistinguished career and uncertain relationships, Beatrix recalls the attractive young widows of Charlotte Yonge's novels (*Leaves*, 100). She obviously hopes Emma will marry, and by the end of the novel, both mother and daughter have acknowledged the eligibility of Tom Dagnall, the widowed pastor with an eccentric passion for antiquarian writings and medieval villages.

In choosing fiction and a relationship with Tom, Emma—again to recall Woolf's phrase—thinks back through her mother's discourses. In this case, however, the mother's discourses are a mix of the great and the small, the professional symbolic and the trivia of daily life and human relationships. The daughter Emma is often seen carrying a meal in her hands—through her own living room, or through the woods to Graham's cottage; like earlier Pym characters, she recalls hymns and lines of English poetry. By turning toward fiction writing (and toward Tom), Emma will perhaps domesticate the big narratives in her life; she can now renarrate, retextualize the big ones (her research on the village) as the personal story it has become for her. Like Catherine, Emma seems to have found her kind of story.

Retiring the Symbolic: *Quartet in Autumn*

Quartet in Autumn is Pym's most complex and austere study of late-twentieth-century trivia (still potentially restorative) and of nearly fossilized symbolic texts and lives. The four elderly characters, two of whom retire during the action of the novel, recall from time to time fragments of the retired discourses, we could say, or the dead languages that used to structure English culture. If Virginia Woolf's novel *The Waves* portrays a world seen "without a self," Pym's *Quartet in Autumn* gives us a contemporary urban world seen without a text. More precisely, there seems to be no *living* text or language that can dependably comfort, renew, or reconstruct the lives of the four office workers.

There are certainly languages available, but they are often fragmentary, challenging, or unfamiliar to the four workers. Letty Crowe in particular is distressed by the rough street language, the presence of dark-skinned immigrants from the former empire, and the disturbing disappearance of Britain's "pink" from world maps (*Quartet*, 58). The discourse of being British has changed for these office workers. As Michael Cotsell observes, this novel concerns to some extent the "failure of a civilization."[49] It is also about the failure of language—big languages and trivial ones as well. Even the work of the four major characters seems to be a dead language, a discourse that is no longer needed; Marcia Snow and Letty will not be replaced after they retire.

Nevertheless, the Anglo-Catholic discourse of liturgy, incense, and holy days provides the stabilizing center of Edwin's life. He is even sensitive to certain, more substantial Christian discourses. He has scruples, for instance, about his response to the Good Samaritan ethic and wonders how adequately he has been a good neighbor. When Letty's new Nigerian landlord holds a rather noisy religious celebration in her boardinghouse, Edwin exerts himself to find her a new room. Yet he is not sure whether he should visit the reclusive

Marcia, and Father Gellibrand questions his own pastoral responsibility to her; after all, she is not in his parish (157–58, 162).[50]

The discourse of Christian love and service must now compete with the more popular, glib discourses of sociological and psychological jargon in which one's neighbor becomes instead a study or "report," in the language of the social worker (187). Selves are constructed by language, and certain discourses or words (such as *neighbor*) imply community and relationship, while other modes of discourse imply only a case, a report, or an object of study. Priscilla, who lives next to Marcia, reflects on this transition in language as she considers the efforts that Janice Brabner, the social worker, has made to interest Marcia in activities. "Not only was [Marcia] a neighbor but also what Janice Brabner called 'disadvantaged' and that, whatever it might mean—Priscilla wasn't absolutely sure—was certainly something to worry about" (140).

The welfare state's "technology of the self" categorizes strictly on a materialistic and nonrelational basis; Marcia doesn't have much and is therefore a negative quality: disadvantaged. In contrast, the self that is fashioned by the word *neighbor*—as Luke's gospel uses the word at the beginning of the Good Samaritan story—is by definition (that is, by virtue of the constructing text) a relational self. Priscilla is not using Foucault's own discourse to describe the large change that she perceives in the welfare state's technology of the self, but she very precisely describes an epochal transition in the changing discourses of self-construction.

Even the three muted discourses that usually structure the actions and decisions of Pym's characters are very attenuated in *Quartet in Autumn*. Edwin's almost obsessive interest in liturgical trivia and his cautious conscience are an innervated descendant of the full parish life that so involved the Bede sisters or Mildred Lathbury. Norman has dipped into literature only enough to imagine himself as "somebody in a Noel Coward play" while he eats breakfast in pajamas and dressing gown (51). Even Norman wonders if he is recalling a psalm, "something about 'grinning like a dog,' " as he angrily observes young women playing netball; he returns to the office "dissatisfied with life" (35–36). Generally, he is held together by a resolute anger and dissatisfaction.

Norman trivializes the trivial—if that is possible. And it is possible; the process is the downside of Pym's otherwise very positive, engaging world of the ordinary: the languages of romance and housekeeping, the domesticated symbolic languages of religious faith and English literature. In *Quartet in Autumn*, Norman (mundane "norm"?) returns the trivial to its bad reputation. Usually, in Pym's novels the trivial speaks dialogically, the voice of Jane or Catherine renewing the ordinary with creative juxtapositions that evade the limiting structures of major symbolic discourses. The appositional, transforming weave of literature, faith, and domestic concerns make life "new every day." Norman's language, on the contrary, makes life old every day. His heavy proverbs pound the trivial back into triviality.

Norman's consistent fury spurs him to brief negative scenarios often captioned with a proverb. He develops "with relish" the script of an elderly person unable to open a can of food, a script that Marcia later enacts. He hears of Letty's accumulation of difficulties (her friend becomes engaged, so Letty gives up her former plan of living with the friend, and then Letty's boardinghouse gets its new owner); Norman entitles the plot of Letty's problems "It never rains but it pours." Redundantly, he offers another proverb about bad things coming in threes (58). Norman's brief, negative remarks tend to be absolute readings, totalizing conclusions, spiteful cartoon sketches of tragedy but never the casual and caring, open-ended remarks of social conversation. Norman always has "a phrase"; his discourse abruptly sums things up.

Marcia sums herself up, but in a more consistent and elaborate way than Norman does. She is starved both physically and textually. Not only is the anorexic Marcia discovered in her kitchen weak and immobilized, but her language also becomes restricted, her textual diet limited to one rigid story. Repeatedly, she elaborates to herself the romantic script of a languishing female (the surgery patient) rescued by the heroic male with his knife (Mr. Strong, her doctor). She has no sustaining acquaintance with religious discourse, literature, or domestic activities; she doesn't "read poetry now, or anything else for that matter, but sometimes she remembered the odd tag" (20).

The tags of these discourses—discourses that sustained and renewed the women in Pym's earlier fiction—are very odd ones when Marcia recalls them. She is radically and eccentrically delighted by the domestic routine of storing cans of food: there "was work to be done here and Marcia enjoyed doing it" (64). Marcia, however, restricts her domestic activity and discourse (she never cleans her house) to her obsessive preoccupation with great stories: there may be another war (so she stores milk bottles) or she may need to take one of her many packed and stored nightgowns to the hospital for an appointment with Mr. Strong (172). For Marcia, domestic trivia is not really domestic trivia; it is a preface to her big, wonderful, and fossilized text of romance.

Unlike most of Pym's women, Marcia does not want to evade the great texts of her culture. Instead, she writes herself into one of the West's most "feminine" stories. Like Leonora, Marcia writes herself as a classic feminine character in a great romantic tale. At the retirement party, Marcia talks about her mastectomy in a hushed voice, her manner and the narrator's diction implying a religious discourse. Marcia likes "to pronounce in a lowered, reverent tone the name of Mr. Strong" (103). Only the narrator, not Marcia (who cannot bring herself to say "breast"), pursues the discourse into literary territory and indulges in dialogic wit. The retirement speeches contained no "references to breast (hope springing eternal in the human) or bosom (sentiments to which every b. returns an echo)" (103).

Indeed, it is the narrator's sympathetic and amused discourse that keeps Marcia's self-destructive text graciously and benignly human. The narrator of *The Sweet Dove Died*, on the other hand, allows Leonora's selfish, manipulative discourse to judge the main character severely. In *Quartet in Autumn*, as Pym observed, she wanted to describe old age but with "comedy and irony, the problems and difficulties having been dealt with almost excessively, one might say, elsewhere."[51] The implied narrator's voice in *Quartet in Autumn* is the only voice that is consistently dialogic, the only voice that recalls the eccentric mesh of literature, faith, and domesticity that characterized Mildred's or Catherine's observations.

As Letty faces the problems and difficulties of age, however, she begins to draw upon the three alternative or muted Western discourses that so often renewed Pym's earlier characters. As Letty and her office colleagues discuss travel, she finds a Homerian reminiscence. Letty recalls having read somewhere that the Mediterranean was "the wine-dark sea—isn't that how it's described?" (*Quartet*, 37). She can remember an entire stanza of Wordsworth's "The Tables Turned," though the narrator says that Letty did not consider very closely the implications of the poem that advocates an "impulse from a vernal wood" over the teachings of "sages" (36). Letty is, however, sensitive not only to literary texts but to nature and to her own responsibilities regarding her neighbor. Once retired and part of Mrs. Pope's household, she feels "useful" as she packs clothes for the jumble sale; on the same evening, she remarks, "What a lovely evening," as she sees out the window the laburnum in flower (144).

Although she makes an effort to like it, Letty finds little in religion. Nor does she especially enjoy domestic activities; yet we see her cooking and then working on "a tapestry chair seat," a rather large sewing task that requires persistence (25). Although Letty imagines that the country life of her widow friend Marjorie is enviably "full of trivial but absorbing things," the newly engaged Marjorie has evidently been lonely (53), and Letty does not find the trivial domesticity of her own retirement to be very interesting. Letty, being her author's character, seems to know the "Pym text" of a fulfilling domestic life and discourse, but this discourse is not very enriching for her. Like Tom, who lost his faith in anthropology, Letty has lost her faith in the healing and inspiring qualities of the domestic text.

Letty is aware of her losses, and as we noted earlier, she reflects on the possible value of "not having" (25). She can still "think back through [her] mothers"; she still enacts those muted texts of domesticity, faith, and literature that have constructed the lives of the female subculture described by Pym. Perhaps because Letty is "by far the most adventurous" of the office group (38), she is the one who can grow as a result of not having. She lives more in the present (and the future) than the others do. Edwin wishes restaurants and the church had not changed (24), and Marcia is utterly imprisoned by the traditional damsel-in-distress myth; her only anticipation is to die in the arms of Dr. Strong. Letty, however, is not confined by the great stories of the West; her lack of these is part of the freedom of her "not having."

While she works on the new chair seat, she hears on the radio a play that probes "backwards into the life of an old woman." For Letty, "this kind of going back" is not congenial; she has lived "very much in the present, holding neatly and firmly on to life, coping as best she could with whatever it had to offer, little though that might be" (25). Letty realizes that she needn't follow her pattern of decades ago—always following her friend Marjorie's lead in major decisions (151). When Marjorie becomes engaged, Letty drops her plan to live with Marjorie in the village; when the engagement is broken, Letty decides she needn't retreat to the earlier plan of living with Marjorie. After Marcia's funeral, when Letty and the men are commemorating Marcia with a glass of the dead woman's sherry, Letty tries out a discourse that is new for her; she says, "Now I feel that I have a choice." She may or may not go to the country. She drinks her sherry and has "a most agreeable sensation, almost a feeling of power" (217). Letty responds to the present, exploring here one of the major discourses of her culture, not a muted one at all, as she sips the text of liberalism, freedom, and power along with her sherry.

Letty does not, however, abandon the discourses that Pym (and Western culture generally) associate with femininity. Although she is initially upset at canceling her plans to live with Marjorie, Letty can read between the lines of Marjorie's letter and find her friend's uneasy conscience. So Letty, in the best tradition of a relational and caring discourse, plans to reply in a way that will "ease [Marjorie's] conscience about the upsetting of the retirement plans"; Letty is not so trapped in the code of feminine caring as to write by return mail, however (55).

Similarly, in the last paragraph of the novel, Letty, even with her newly appropriated discourse of power and choice, reflects that the planned visit to Marjorie's village with Edwin and Norman will benefit her friend. "Any new interest that might take Marjorie's mind off her disappointment was to be encouraged," even a possible romance between Marjorie and one of the men. As the last line of the novel affirms, Letty realizes "that life held infinite possibilities for change" (218). For Letty, these possibilities include the appositional mingling of discourses; she renews her subjectivity as she acquires the more traditionally masculine texts, while retaining a relational discourse also.

The adventurous Letty has always demonstrated an ability to explore new discourses, and her dialogic creativity is occasionally as sharp as her (implied) author's. When the office coterie discuss how one should respond if an elderly person falls, Edwin allots responsibility to women: "Oh, a woman can deal with these things easily enough," and women wouldn't "make the kind of fuss" he and Norman might make in those circumstances. Norman agrees that men prefer leaving such matters "to the ladies." Yet he insists on something more specific, asking, "Anyway, what is one's responsibility in that kind of thing—answer me that." Letty's answer neatly expands to a human concern what Edwin and Norman were restricting to a woman's culture. Letty says, "Just the ordinary responsibility of one human being towards another" (79). Her diction affirms that it is not just women who must respond to the ordinary and nonheroic (while great surgeons offer heroic, professional, manly succor to distressed female patients like Marcia); men also belong to the world of everyday humanness and caring. Letty's discourse restates a traditionally female ethic of caring and ordinary relationality, but as a human ethic.

A more witty dialogic transformation of text occurs when Letty re-inscribes a phrase from a sermon, but she applies it to the seduction competition between Marjorie and Beth Doughty, the latter having managed to pry away Marjorie's fiancé. The preacher had been asking for understanding among the members of the parish who were quarreling over the removal of some pews; he asked them to recall the "humanity, in which we all share" (205). When Letty discovers that Beth will now marry the clergyman to whom Marjorie was engaged, Letty is shocked by the competition of the two women, "but the whole pattern slotted into place. Humanity in which we all share . . ." (206; original ellipsis). In Letty's dialogic consciousness here, *humanity* slides humorously from humanity in general to a specific love triangle. Further, the word (*humanity*) that in the sermon implied both human goodness and human frailty tilts in Letty's re-vision more toward frailty only.

Letty's re-textualizing here is worthy of Jane's verbal juxtapositions or Catherine's insights. In a world in which many long-standing texts have retired as well as Letty herself, she can verbally regenerate discourse and her own subjectivity. No wonder Letty courageously affirms the "infinite possibilities for change" (218). She, like the characters in the earlier novels, finds freedom in the ordinary and in-significant. In Pym's work, "not having" the big structures, not having the significant quest or romance (or even an important career), frees one for experimental discourses that make the language, as well as the complex appositional self, new every day.

4 *Christine Brooke-Rose*
S(t)imulating Origins

The ideology of the "little narrative" is thematic in Barbara Pym's novels but radically structural in the texts of Christine Brooke-Rose. Sociologically considered, Pym's characters, her women especially, are experimental in their eccentric and marginal subcultures. Many of Brooke-Rose's characters, however, are not even characters—not mimetic or realistic subjectivities. They are sometimes only a few lines of advancing text on the screen of another character's word processor; yet these sketchy subjectivities, being themselves no more than (literally) little narratives, dialogically debate the transformative potential of their fictional status.

In the fiction that she has written since *Out* was published in 1964, all of the major speakers in Brooke-Rose's texts are distinctly experimental.[1] Brooke-Rose has suggested in an interview that the experimental writer is someone who explores language itself (rather than sociological or psychological issues) and who tends to "make discoveries about language"; further, in "Illiterations," she observes that experimenting "with new forms produces new ways of looking," though new perceptions may also encourage or necessitate new forms (*Stories*, 261).[2] Like their author, Brooke-Rose's most vital characters tend to play with language. At the very least, they invent puns, fuse ideologies, and so create a double or canceled or new way of seeing heterogeneous discourses. At their most creative, the experimental selves in the novels are meditative or disoriented voices; these invent a world of loquacious alter egos or subselves. Although a Lacanian ideology of mirror opposition structures the comic linguistic and gender polarities of *Thru*, most of the voices in the novels (to the extent that such voices can claim subjectivity at all) are appositional, heterogeneously structured; they are eager to appropriate, merge, and transmutate. They would rather simulate (themselves and others) than inscribe a consistent, realistic character, ego, or gender. Except for the ill and disoriented narrator of *Out*, and maybe the traveling translator of *Between*, the voices in most of the fiction are content with the self as (mere) text, the self as a new way of seeing, or the self as a continually simulatable new word.

Like Woolf's Bernard in *The Waves*, the textualizing voices in the novels of Brooke-Rose seek phrases, and they think of identity as "story." In contrast to Bernard, however, the demanding though transitory voices afloat or dissolving in the texts of Brooke-Rose seldom balk at a "world seen without a self." Although Perry, in *Verbivore*, wishes that Mira (who has been writing him into a word processor) would continue with his story so that he could talk to her, the characters generally take textual life as it comes. They do not seek an ultimate dialogue with an ultimate creator about ultimate meaning. As a recurrent phrase in *Between* declares, "All ideas have equality before God."[3] The grand narratives, such as the emancipation of human beings, are no more important than the phrases of conference jargon that the simultaneous translator of *Between* transforms skillfully and automatically from French to German.

Yet the voices in the novels of Brooke-Rose do engage the grand narratives, the big ideologies, and the current theories of language, science, and feminism. In her thorough study, Sarah Birch examines the intellectual context of Brooke-Rose's fiction and argues that a major narrative technique of this author involves metaphor as a linking of these conceptual systems.[4] The voices in the texts of Brooke-Rose are deeply engaged with the symbolic structures of modern society. In this respect, they resemble Woolf's loquaciously meditative characters such as Bernard, Orlando, and Mrs. Ramsay. The voices in Brooke-Rose's novels, however, *play* with these grand narratives all the time. The great humanist narratives of liberation and of the unity of knowledge are very important to the professor and humanist who in *Amalgamemnon* anticipates losing her job. Yet the prospect of computer technology replacing the humanistic study of history, philosophy, and Greek generates, not discouragement, but a comic vitality as Mira imagines and writes the options of her brave new future. The voices in the texts of Brooke-Rose, like those of Woolf, speak the symbolic constantly. They do not speak from a complex but largely feminine subculture as the characters in Pym's novels often do. Instead, the characters or subcharacters, the phrasal voices, of Brooke-Rose's fiction acknowledge the (patrocentric) symbolic as the linguistic medium in which they speak. They acknowledge also, however, the ambiguities of that phallocratic medium, and they blithely and playfully deconstruct it at every opportunity.

Simulating Poetry

In the fiction of Brooke-Rose, there is little nostalgia for the ever more attenuated grand narratives that until recently defined the dominant (and male) culture of the West. There is no grieving or despair over the loss of meaning, the demise of the totalizing text, or the death of a Percival. In this, Brooke-Rose differs from Samuel Beckett (whom she acknowledges as one of several influences).[5] Her characters and voices do not collapse in despair, and they are not waiting for Godot. (Why wait? They can invent or simulate him and talk to him, and he—or she—can talk back.) Indeed the Brooke-Rose text explores the comic potential of the simulations in contemporary experience, especially the ever available simulating machine, the computer. As she writes, "*Verbivore* (and less directly all my novels) are about all our suppositions being simulations of one kind or another."[6] Her character Mira in *Amalgamemnon* indicates just how comprehensive suppositions and simulations are; she sees a world which will supply "simulating machines for opinions, arguments, loves, hates, imaginings."[7] This list includes much of what goes into constructing a self or subjectivity. The suppositions that socialize a person, the attitudes that call one into a class or a gender, a set of codes that inscribes a life—all are perhaps feignable, constructable. *Amalgamemnon* is in a sense the professor's own elaborate simulation of a multiplex and paradoxical future, one that includes a "pigfarming experiment" (46) along with other textual adventures, which this very experimental self simulates, feigns, and represents to herself. The "opinions, arguments, loves, hates, imaginings" that shape a self or voice are simulatable, flexible, in the Brooke-Rose text.

As a result, the main characters (or the prominent voices) tend to be flexible, creative, and courageous. They do not take themselves seriously enough to despair—in contrast, for instance, to the characters or voices in Samuel Beckett's fiction. In an early critical study, Brooke-Rose described the varied theories that she was using in her analysis of Pound's "Usura" Canto. She pointed to the flexibility of her approach; such a method, she emphasized, avoided a "universal grammar" and instead could "be infinitely self-subversive like the text [Pound's poetry] itself."[8] Similarly, the voices and selves in Brooke-Rose's fiction are *self-subversive* texts; that is, they are self-subversive *selves*. This capacity to self-subvert or deconstruct is also their capacity to simulate/stimulate further origin—to create additional experimental texts. Many of Brooke-Rose's characters are being created by another character, and the secondary, created, and simulated characters know this. There is a kind of poststructuralist, electronic humility in their acknowledgement of their contingent, scriptable status; they are without presence or being and are thus free to debate or advise their creator-characters about the experimental subjectivity, the simulated consciousness, in which all the voices share.

Wary of the all-encompassing answer, the totalizing grammar, Brooke-Rose agrees in general with the postmodern "incredulity" about such grand narratives, and she specifically cites Jean-François Lyotard's description of the postmodern "condition." Lyotard argues that in an increasingly technological world, only partial answers or hypotheses—in fact, "little narratives"—will predominate.[9] Though retired, Brooke-Rose taught for many years at the University of Paris VIII (Vincennes), which in its early years (founded in 1968) was experimental in its inclusion of a curriculum for retraining in the modern technologies; Lyotard refers to Paris VIII in particular in *The Postmodern Condition*, a book that he dedicates to the new polytechnic institute within this university; he also suggests that the university is perhaps "nearing what may be its end, while the

Institute may just be beginning."[10] He observes that the rising prominence of computer data banks, along with the decline of the grand narratives that sustained humanism (especially the concept of the unity of all knowledge), will sound "the knell of the age of the Professor."[11] Obviously responding to this postmodern condition, the humanist professor in *Amalgamemnon* turns with both regret and interest to the new world of little narratives—computers and language games.

Especially in the novels that are constructed from computer texts, the "characters" are preoccupied with the diverse little narratives that Lyotard sees as replacing the all-embracing ideologies that once provided "legitimation" for scientific inquiry. No longer grounded in, or backed by, a philosophical tenet of the unity of knowledge or a rationale for the liberation of human beings, science must proceed by means of little narratives, that is, by hypotheses and "imaginative invention," by less ambitious statements that generate "open systems" and additional narratives rather than final answers.[12] These little narratives can inscribe any of those "suppositions" that Brooke-Rose refers to, or the opinions, passions, and imaginings that the professor in *Amalgamemnon* anticipates deriving from computers (or "simulating machines"). Indeed, the computer-stone Xorandor misled the twins Zab and Jip into believing that he was a Martian, but Zab admits that "we all play language-games."[13] Such little narratives are the loves, imaginings, simulations that construct human supposition, and indeed human subjectivity (or a science-fiction computer's subjectivity), in the postmodern situation and in the experimental fiction of Brooke-Rose.

The most profoundly experimental quality—the really new way of seeing—that characterizes the novels of Brooke-Rose is her pervasive and playfully textual skepticism concerning grand narratives of all kinds. Although some of her characters appreciate (perhaps love) certain humanistic ideologies of the West, these characters or voices are also prepared to face a future in a world without a (traditional) self, a world without a grand narrative. The texts of Brooke-Rose (and her criticism and theory as well) challenge or play with the problematics of even the grandest narratives of all, specifically the traditional (or even postmodern and fashionable) ideologies of difference.

The grand narratives of gender difference are much older and more deeply rooted ideologies than are the recent ones of emancipation and the unity of knowledge; even the Freudian, Lacanian, and some feminist ideologies of gender difference carry a trace of their heritage. Before looking at *Amalgamemnon* (linguistically her richest, most condensed work) and more briefly at the other novels, I want to look at Brooke-Rose's critique (and playful exploitation) of certain patrocentric narratives or patterns in fiction and theory as well as her circumspect resistance to the emerging theories (have they become grand narratives?) of women's writing, or an *écriture féminine*. I will also briefly define (largely in terms she herself uses) the prominent textual strategies that render her own experimental novels self-subverting (and grand-narrative subverting) fictions, which as a result invent or s(t)imulate new ways of seeing.

Experimental fiction, as noted in my first chapter, does not inevitably involve the overturning or textual deconstruction of master ideologies. Although important contemporary fiction on both sides of the Atlantic resists interpretation and is nontotalizing, this metafiction is sometimes "regressive" in its "treatment of sex," as Brooke-Rose observed in *A Rhetoric of the Unreal*.[14] More recently, in "Which Way Did They Go? Thataways," she also notes the "regressively phallocratic" preoccupation of much science fiction (*Stories*, 176). She herself in the early novel *The Dear Deceit* has used as a structuring device the quest for (paternal) origin, the oedipal "family romance" pattern without which, Roland Barthes suggests, there would be no narrative at all.[15] This pattern is certainly a grand narrative; it is a major Western psychoanalytic ideology as well as a literary and novelistic pattern. As a pattern in fiction, it is usually a son's search for his father, and the role or voices of women are minimal or secondary.

Unlike *The Dear Deceit*, the more recent fiction of Brooke-Rose offers something like this quest pattern (a simulation of it) only in the highly modified and witty astrophysical/pseudo-Jungian quest of Larry in *Such*. Perhaps there is also a parody of the ancient grand narrative in the re-quests for origin that the subvoices make in *Amalgamemnon*, for instance, as they seek the attention of their author. She is not their father, but their mother, Mira. In *Verbivore* also, the search of the child for the parent (the search of the secondary voice for its author-character) is not a major structuring device, and the quest becomes more a matter of a computer search.

In the work of others as well as in her own fiction, Brooke-Rose appreciates the ironic or disruptive inscription of this once great narrative of difference. She praises Donald Barthelme's *The Dead Father*, for instance, because the very ironic quest for the father in this novel is not, Brooke-Rose argues, the center or source of meaning in the text.[16] In fact in her essays on theory, when Brooke-Rose discusses patterns of quest, she characteristically mutes the element of father search or father-author search. She degenderizes the pattern and instead expands the implications of this narrative structure. In "The Evil Ring: Realism and the Marvellous," reflecting on Tolkien's sagas, she parenthetically notes that a quest may be "for success, for a secret, for the conquering of evil or chaos either external or internal, for the understanding of oneself, of the world, of a situation, or even of narrative itself" (*Rhetoric*, 235). In her own fiction, the search for "narrative itself" becomes a search for a maternal or feminine origin (or a nongendered or biogendered origin) as often as a paternal or masculine origin. Indeed in *Xorandor*, one of the minor author-quests is for the disruptive author of apocalyptic narratives who is a nonhuman computer-stone; "he" is referred to as masculine, but the stone calls itself "Lady Macbeth."

In her critical prose, Brooke-Rose has perceptively examined the related ideologies of authorship and difference. She evidently accepts Lacan's description of gender as basically a rhetoric or language, and she also finds valuable his concept of the unconscious as "Other." Emphasizing Lacan's notion that to speak at all is to limit, omit, or "castrate," Brooke-Rose points to her novel *Thru* as a textual enactment of this idea ("Interview," 11–12).[17] In *Thru*, two major voices (one male and one female) seem to be authoring or deauthorizing each other, finally going through the mirror of the text, or self-deconstructing into each other's texts.

Yet Brooke-Rose has also emphasized in her essay "Id is, is Id?"

(*Stories*, 28–44) that psychoanalytic theory is distinctly text and not truth. As Verena Andermatt-Conley notes, Brooke-Rose does not subscribe to the "current terminologies of difference."[18] For instance, in her illuminating article "Woman as a Semiotic Object," Brooke-Rose recalls that Umberto Eco had difficulty understanding her perception that he was employing a socially (not linguistically) gendered example of sentence ambiguity during a seminar. Reflecting on this experience, she wonders "whether semiotics is not a peculiarly reactionary discipline, and semioticians unconsciously nostalgic for nice, deep, ancient, phallocratic, elementary structures of significance" (*Stories*, 249). If the remarks of Brooke-Rose imply that the ideology of difference may be a grand narrative that is still present, though unconsciously, Fredric Jameson makes explicit his contention that grand narratives can persist—in the "political unconscious."[19]

Certainly, the ideology or grand narrative of the author as male is one that Brooke-Rose treats with considerable "incredulity," since she is an experimental writer and also a woman. In "Illiterations," she points out that the traditions of male authorship define creative power as male (the begetting genius) yet also appropriate both of the female metaphors (passive receptor and travailing giver of birth) (*Stories*, 256–58).[20] It is a monopolistic structuring of the authorship myth. Essentially, this tradition is an androgynous narrative of the authorizing of subjectivity. Brooke-Rose herself is evidently attracted to a duo-gendered or nongendered version of the creativity myth, but she perceives this androgyny as applying to women writers as well as to men. Acknowledging that many feminists reject as reprehensibly humanist this "androgynous-great-mind stance," she nevertheless sees it as descriptive of authorship and of creativity. In addition, she argues that androgynous *readers* are needed if experimental works by women are to be read with appreciation (and read *by men* as well as women) (*Stories*, 254, 264).

The version of androgyny acceptable to Brooke-Rose may be a little different from the androgyny envisioned by Woolf (or attributed to her by readers and critics). To the extent that Woolf in *A Room of One's Own* sees the "androgynous mind" as combining masculine and feminine characteristics ("two sexes in the mind"), her view is perhaps a schematic one while that of Brooke-Rose is vehemently aschematic—to use psychologist Sandra Bem's terms. Bem's studies indicate that some participants (in questionnaires or laboratory experiences) simply do not perceive certain behaviors, attitudes, or abilities as belonging to a gender designation at all, that is, to either a male or a female schema.[21] Speaking in "A Womb of One's Own" about current theories of women's writing, Brooke-Rose observes that "the present and constant emphasis on certain structures as 'masculine' and others as 'feminine' is a gross oversimplification" (*Stories*, 231). When she argues, in the same essay, against the view that the prose of women writers consistently features disruption, nonlinearity, and "flow," she again expresses a kind of aschematic androgyny. Male experimental writers also employ these "feminine" strategies, she emphasizes. And yet a recognition of this fact "would contradict the feminist thesis of specificity, of difference" (*Stories*, 227). Indeed, the fictional texts of Brooke-Rose do not open readily to a reading that searches for opposition and difference; their dialogic complexities tend to be appositional amalgamations or constellations.

Rejecting most theories of difference (though not absolutely, as her appreciative, yet playful, response to Lacan indicates), Brooke-Rose believes that writers can be expected to speak the symbolic as well as the semiotic and flowing. The importance of Pound, Beckett, and other mentors in her own development indicates her acknowledgement of the vitality of symbolic structures. She teases this manly inheritance both respectfully and critically in her punning and disruptive essay "Self-Confrontation and the Writer." In this deconstructively evasive autobiographical essay, she calls her cultural and linguistic heritage "John" (an interior Lacanian "Other"?). She speaks of "mentors" who "are sometimes tormentors, imposing to destroy, to create only through their own pygmylion illusion of structure," and yet she appreciates the "men-towers," among whom she includes Athene, Virgil, Pound, and others.[22]

Brooke-Rose's pun in the foregoing sentence on Pygmalion/pygmylion is typical of her fiction's self-subversive strategy. The pun here makes an inventive, imaginative minor narrative out of a big narrative; it renders as a mere characteristic (small, yet like the king of beasts) a significant mythic character, a male artist whose text, a female sculpture, became real. Indeed, the most prominent experimental devices that Brooke-Rose employs have this general tendency to reduce the credibility of the big story or great (traditional and male) myth. Her frequent use of transgression of narrative levels (where a character converses with an author-narrator, for instance) also puts in doubt the myth of origin, the great narrative of authorship itself. Transgression is in some ways a prose embodiment of the Pygmalion myth, since the creation (the text or sculpture) declares a life of its own, "comes to life," and begins talking to the creator. The effect of narrative transgression is one of a floating authority, or an unnervingly insubordinate authority, as it moves here and there. Instead of a protagonist's search for origins, we find origin itself migrating from voice to voice. When all selves are thus subverted, it is hard for any one of them—even the one who has the most lines—to claim authorship or narrator-status in any mimetic, realistic sense.

In addition to transgression, the extremely voice-centered mode (a "diegetic" mode)[23] that Brooke-Rose uses for characterization also tends to reduce the solidity (and authority) of the selves or subjectivities in her novels. These speaking voices do not provide, and are not given (by a narrator outside themselves), the wealth of descriptive detail or background typical of a more realistic characterization. As Brooke-Rose has described similar characters in the experimental fiction of others, they can be merely "subthreshold sensibilities" as in the work of Natalie Sarraute, or only a neutral "emitter" as in the fiction of Maurice Roche and Philippe Sollers ("Transgressions," *Rhetoric*, 325, 326). The characters or minimal subjectivities in Brooke-Rose's fiction have likewise been slimmed down to voices and sometimes to the texts that a computer is emitting. Origin becomes a hypothesis, a little narrative, a simulation or stimulation of authorship. Origin and authorship under these textual circumstances become problematic, a game (particularly in *Thru* and *Verbivore*) of which voice can grab the "I"-microphone at any given point and declare herself or himself or itself the ad hoc narrator and source of the text.

Finally, the various strategies of wordplay in these experimental novels also contribute to the deauthorizing or liberating of the grand narrative of origin and as a result contribute to the experimental, open, flexible quality of the implied voices or selves. In "Which Way Did They Go? Thataways," Brooke-Rose echoes Walter Pater, but refers to the creative new languages of feminist theory, deconstruction, and computer technology when she says that novels now "aspire to the condition of poetry" (*Stories*, 178). She finds the techniques of poetry in many experimental novels, and such techniques are frequent in her own work as is the "poetry" of jargon (scientific, linguistic), a feature she describes, referring especially to *Between*, *Such*, and *Thru* ("Conversation," 83–84). Usually the wordplay is dialogic as are the near-repetitions of phrases; these phrases often recur, as Brooke-Rose says, "in a new context" that changes their meaning ("Interview," 3). As a result, conflicting implications and even ideologies are woven into a rich texture of apposition; sometimes the phrases deconstructively go "through" each other, confusing and complicating sources and voices.

Among the novels of Brooke-Rose, the narrator-subversion (or the subversion of the implied author-self) is the most thorough and radical in *Thru*. Surveying all of Brooke-Rose's experimental fiction to date (and at the risk of oversimplifying), one could say that the earlier experimental novels (*Out*, *Such*, and *Between*) all have a sketchy yet realistic frame in that each could be read as a near-monologue; they could each be understood and read as one person's thoughts. Yet each of the monologuists is undergoing some form of alienation from identity; each is in the process of self-subversion, though the implicit social (realistic, representational) causes vary. The cause seems to be a radiation illness in *Out*, a near-death vision in *Such*, and the dislocations of continual travel in *Between*. In the next novel, *Thru*, any frame or realistic rationale for the disjunctive and dispersed representation of subjectivity disappears completely. Although not as radically decentered and deconstructive as *Thru*, the subsequent novel *Amalgamemnon* draws on the strategies of the earlier experimental novels while at the same time envisioning the text-as-technology world of the more recent fiction. Because of its stylistic centrality in Brooke-Rose's oeuvre as well as its textual richness, my discussion will feature *Amalga-*

memnon. A brief look at the earlier novels will be useful also, since the disoriented narrator voices of *Out, Such,* and *Between* encounter with alarm or apathy the self-subversion that becomes radically more playful and wildly inventive in the later fictions.

Self-Subversive Selves

In the confused thoughts of the displaced scientist in *Out*, as he reflects achronologically on his postnuclear illness and world, there is a certain "hopelessness and gloom," as Richard Martin asserts;[24] yet there is also considerable humor in the man's inventive, perpetually revised, requests and observations. He is continually trying to find a job as gardener or groundskeeper; then he is trying to keep the job, though his illness thwarts his performance; he is frequently composing letters, trying to redress racial injustice (white people are ill and oppressed while the darker skin has protected the upper classes). The text continues to revisit these repetitive activities, but the man's thoughts about them are inventive variations on the painful textual routines that are progressively infecting his sentences.

He is often asked (or was asked in the past by an agent or employer) what his occupation is, and the narrating voice is either recounting these occasions or facing new ones, or inventing variations on the incidents. The worldwide catastrophe seems to have destroyed, or reduced to textual fragments, certain long-standing traditions; the catastrophe has destroyed the great narratives of the precrisis society. As a result, the meditating voice searches ineffectively for origins, for the person he may once have been and the person he now is. He tells a questioner that he was a "builder"; in fact he quips that he "built the tower of Pisa and it leant."[25]

His responses to this question of identity become wilder (and more comic) as he seems to realize that he will never find the story or text that is or was his. He even invents responses to his responses; he says he was a "fortune-teller," and he hears (invents?) the response: "Yes well, there's no future in that not nowadays" (*Out*, 62). His society seems to be a giant examiner, continually questioning and diagnosing his psychological, physical, and political legitimacy. He is continually being inscribed by others as this society attempts to construct or simulate its subjects. He responds that he was an electrician (24), or a welder (62); he is an odd-job man, but his previous "occupation" was that of "psychopath," and the hospital receptionist (or the narrator's imagining of this person) carefully writes and voices the syllables as though "psychopath" were a profession (127). Later, the doctor who runs the "psychoscopy" machine (which zaps the patient with a condensed dose of psychoanalysis) admits, as he reads "psychopath" on the form, "We have a sense of humour, yes?" (132). He does have a sense of humor, but he never can be sure whether anyone else really hears it (he may be only imagining scenarios of job hunting and job finding) or even acknowledges that he is speaking (if he *is* speaking and not just reminiscing).

He has almost no sense of himself as a narrator, as a functioning self, an author or source of a text. The narrative style of the *nouveau roman* contributes powerfully to this effect, and Brooke-Rose acknowledges the influence of Robbe-Grillet ("Illicitations," 102). In the novels of Robbe-Grillet, the reader hears only what impinges on the consciousness of the speaking or thinking voice in the novel; the narrator seems not to be directing or shaping what moves into the field of perception and thought. Brooke-Rose intensifies this effect with what could almost be called the "theme" of many of the repeated phrases: this man continually inquires about—or overhears remarks about—identity, story, his occupation, and what the various elaborate, diagnostic instruments might "reveal." Yet, in this very controlled society, he is never diagnosed, never sufficiently acknowledged; or rather, his urgent repetitions about his subjectivity imply that he is never certain that he has been heard, never certain who he is.

It is as though the one voice in this novel increasingly regresses, in this controlled political climate, to a nearly presymbolic state. Indeed, the man's race is now a muted culture, and he does not seem to grasp the symbolic system that rules him, rules his speech, and rules his capacity to narrate, to tell a story and write a self. If consciousness arises with the acquisition of language, as Lacan theorizes, the speaker of *Out* is undergoing a dis-acquisition of language and a deconstruction of consciousness.

In one of many dialogic distortions of biblical phrases, an agent or employer seems to be advising a better diet, but he says, "Oh I didn't mean just bread. There's consciousness too, man cannot live by bread alone. He needs his daily ration of the whole world, blessed are the conscious for they shall inherit the earth" (*Out*, 181). The old and confused hearer wonders if this is "an article of faith" (181), a phrase he uses several times. Earlier in the novel, for instance, someone advised him "to identify with the flux" (63); the voice of the puzzled narrator wonders if this is "an article of faith," and he notes that "it is difficult to tell who's talking in this type of dialogue" (63). Indeed it is. The speaker's subjectivity is dialogically acquiring (or being indoctrinated with) the postcrisis articles of faith, the legitimating narratives of the new society.

The repeated phrases are often intertextual fragments, the revisionist phrases, of a former (and biblical) grand narrative of political inversion ("the meek . . . shall inherit the earth," Mt. 5:5). The speaker's confusion about who is talking reflects his sense that more than one ideology can be "talking" as well as more than one, perhaps hallucinatory, voice inside his head. The collapsing consciousness of the narrator cannot tell when he is being fed his society's "ration of the whole world" (his society's major ideology) and when he is just trying to get a job or hear a story that is at least reminiscent of the self he thinks he once was. He senses that "the conscious" will inherit and rule; they control the symbols of the discourses that construct or simulate consciousness. In a severely restricted society, this man, who belongs already to a muted subculture, is becoming muted even to himself. He is becoming a self-subverting text and as a result is less and less conscious of *becoming* less and less conscious.

The novel can be read as a kind of dialogic elegy on the loss of the self—or of a subjectivity that is undergoing such a radical, socially imposed, and experimental rewrite that the man's consciousness is dying in the process (as his body is dying also). I suggest *elegy* because Brooke-Rose is here very successfully moving her prose towards poetry (to which, in her view, experimental novels aspire), and the repetitions, with their variations, have the quality of a refrain. The entire novel is a refrain—with no stanza, no mimetic story, no narrative between the refrains. The story, the explanation or narrative, has been lost in the worldwide catastrophe and the radiation-illness epidemic. All that remains for the speaker is a disjunctive, fragmented, but lyric response to the disaster. Although the reader has no mimetic character with which to identify, I disagree with Shirley Toulson who says that the "reader's emotions" cannot become engaged in the fiction of Brooke-Rose.[26] An elegy, and lyric poetry, may also lack characters and plot, but they can still move (in all senses) by different means. *Out* aspires to the condition of poetry, and it arrives.

In her next two novels, *Such* and *Between*, Brooke-Rose continues her experimenting with the strategies of repetition, paradox, wordplay, and again these become the narrative medium of a disoriented subjectivity. The main speaking voice in *Such*, however, gradually becomes less disoriented as he returns from the spiritual education of a near-death experience. In a way, Larry's progress in finding and connecting discourses (especially the scientific and the personal) moves in the opposite direction from the thwarted attempt by the speaker of *Out* to imagine or narrate a story and a self. Brooke-Rose has said that the "experiment" in *Such* consists of the "fusion of outer space with psychic space"; it concerns the language of astrophysics as a metaphor of human relationship ("Illicitations," 102; "Interview," 3–4). A gradual fusion of the outer and scientific (material world of objects, electrons, stars) and the inner (Larry's resurrected and more perceptive "self") results in a near-allegory of the spiritual journey.

One of the inner voices, during Larry's experience of "death," asks if he remembers anything significant about the onset of his midlife, Dantean crisis—"some final decision for or against made in the light of the person you had become midway through life in the dark wood?" Larry's midlife renewal, like Dante's, moves through cosmic imagery toward a gradual strengthening and revitalizing of subjectivity. Larry is a kind of Lazarus, and many slightly varied repetitions also link him with the rebirth imagery of Jonah emerging from the whale.[27] Unlike the speaker of *Out*, Larry arrives at a greater integration of self. Evidently quite insensitive to his family in his pre-death "life" as a psychiatrist, he achieves a kind of integration of the formerly separated texts—the personal and the scientific. His friend Stanley, who says, "I have no interest in things as such, I like people" (*Such*, 281), also insists, "People's essence, as such, bores me. We all communicate through things, superficial things mostly" (284). Yet the phrase "as such" textually links the personal (people) and the objective world, thus reinforcing the implication that Stanley's twofold denial is paradoxically a twofold affirmation; or a onefold affirmation, since the two—scientific data and the personal—seem to coalesce in his remarks, and since Larry refers to him as "Stance," the "one-stance man" (317, 319). Yet it is not clear that Stance/Stanley himself perceives and lives the unified, paradoxical vision of his statements. On the other hand, Larry does seem to acknowledge during his recovery that the scientific and physical coalesce with the personal in an integrated "such" that shapes a "presence." A voice at one point describes and advises: "That ache, and blood vessels, muscle spindles, bones flesh and such that form some sort of presence to hold on to, such as your patients. Shouldn't you perhaps start seeing a few patients again?" (305). As words begin to assume and simulate new relationships during his midlife journey, Larry also grows into a new relationship with his family and his clients.

Although the novel is distinctly experimental, it is subtly didactic (better relationships are needed). Larry's world comes together as his language does. Such a unifying movement is not the case for the disintegrating speaker of *Out* or for the perpetually traveling translator of *Between*. Like herself, her language must also continually travel. She is a simultaneous translator from French to German, and she has enough Italian, Spanish, and other European languages to talk about, and with, her lovers and colleagues, to locate left or right, to turn the cold tap or the hot (though she makes some mistakes), and to scream a rough translation of the kind of insect inevitably crawling in the hotel bathroom. Her subjectivity is a changing complex of languages and cultures, all appositionally accessible whenever the situation requires them.

She also knows the specialized language, the jargon, of many areas of scholarship, especially linguistics, anthropology, history (and she knows these in French, German, and English). She travels from discourse to discourse. Or rather, the languages themselves travel, for they are personified somewhat in this novel; the translator makes love, and the languages also "fraternise."[28] They mingle; they slide, in the same sentence, from French to German or English, and from linguistic technicalities to the jargon of sociology or the clichés of a guidebook as the narrator, between conferences, fills in time as a tourist.

In this novel that never employs a form of the verb "to be," the narrator is always between; with the traveler's St. Christopher medal between her breasts, she moves between conferences, between countries, between languages, lovers, and ideas. Acknowledging, as we noted earlier, that all ideas are equal before God, she merely translates those of other people. As she says to her friend Siegfried: "No one requires us to have any [ideas] of our own. We live between ideas, nicht wahr, Siegfried?" (*Between*, 143). She lives in effect between discourses, between any given society's languages and myths that might define or hail into a steady subjectivity this continually experimenting consciousness and so give her a local habitation and a name. As Brooke-Rose has suggested, speaking of her own "trilingual family," which delighted in multilanguage puns and jokes, there is a "loss of identity through language" in such an experience and in her novel *Between* ("Conversation," 84). Like the distressed speaker of *Out*, the translator in *Between* also contemplates a world seen without a self, yet for her the uprooted, fragmentary scraps of various discourses are the medium of her professional life. Although her profession casts her as the passive translator, a subject "constituted in the signifying chain of language," as Karen Lawrence argues, yet the woman's discursive variations imply a different, less restrictive language than those of her male-dominated culture.[29] The creative, ever simulating voice of *Between* lives the loss of one identity and contrives the gaining of another, as nonchalantly as Woolf's Orlando.

If she is not quite between grand narratives (emancipation? the unity of knowledge?), she certainly travels only the periphery of these. As a modern divorced woman with a career, she perhaps could be considered the product of the West's technology and its ideology of "emancipation." Yet she is not by any means thoroughly inscribed into an ideology of liberation. One of the repeated phrases reminds us (and reminds her) that the "Lord Mayor" wants her to "commit" herself "to one single idea" (*Between*, 413, 457, and elsewhere). Yet the translator's itinerant subjectivity is not wholly the product of a postmodern disintegration of meaning, the collapse of the large legitimizing and explanatory narratives. She is *between* her betweenness and her still nagging commitment to a "single idea."

Paradoxically, she did make one very serious commitment—to her husband, to the idea and life of a marriage. Although divorced and thus free in a secular sense to respond to the persistent Siegfried, she either does not want to marry again at all or she is delaying while the church processes her annulment request. She seems to take seriously her nonbelief or perhaps her belief—her remnant loyalty to her former faith. Many of the repeated phrases, the refrains that move through several languages in the same sentence, concern this almost endlessly processed and reprocessed annulment case. She reflects with frustration at one point that after seven years' processing in England and then in Germany, the subsequent reorganizing of witnesses and interviews in France has taken three more years, and "all this for four years of marriage, after seventeen years one can't remember exactly" (*Between*, 459). Obviously, she takes this one single "idea" very seriously, seriously enough to wait for an official, legitimate emancipation from it.

This translator's ever experimenting consciousness for most of the novel (and most of her life) is in transit between her freefloating postmodern condition and her residual commitment to a life that was not so "between." The only plot in this novel (where plot or action or psychological direction derives from the repeated surflike collisions of language) seems to be a gradual chipping away at the notion of committing to "one single idea," to one loyalty, and—by implication—to one authority or authorizing source for one's life. And some of this tendency is her own persistent chipping; she insists on officially peeling away, on documenting—with the annulment declaration—her "between" status, her liberation from loyalties. Much of the dialogic mingling of discourse (conferences, tourist idiom, theological language) plays with the juxtaposition of phrases that imply loyalty or belief and those that suggest freedom from loyalties (and so from the oppressive, possessive quality that can accompany dedication to a single idea).

For instance, Coleridge's phrase, the "willing suspension of disbelief," sometimes merges with the mechanical requests of customs agents; these very long sentences also move into the imagery of planes, large wings, and a sense of the suspension of the body and of consciousness in space. With such meshed voices, the narrator reflects, "Have you anything to declare such as love desire ambition or a glimpse that in this air-conditioning and other circumstantial emptiness freedom has its sudden attractions as the body floats in willing suspension of responsibility to anyone" (*Between*, 422).

This complex of discourse regenerates itself often, the subtle variations indicating another stage of the traveler's ongoing translation of herself to herself and perhaps a kind of de-authorizing or liberating of herself. The varied phrase passes through her mind with "Have you anything to declare such as love desire ambition nothing at all just personal effects," and this time there is a "willing suspension of loyalty to anyone" as the plane moves from conference to conference: narcotics, timber, immigration (461–62). For the traveling consciousness of *Between*, declarations of responsibility, love, or loyalty have proved costly. The airport phrase assembles and simulates the implications: "Please declare if you have any love loyalty lust intellect belief of any kind or even simple enthusiasm for which you must pay duty to the Customs and Excise" (444). This sentence, traveling through at least two discourses (as though the customs phraseology were managing the ethic of commitment) parallels or "writes" the traveling ideologies of the narrator. In dialogue and in her silent, multifold reflections, she moves toward a greater freedom from the ideologies that have cost her something while they also authorized her life.

The most costly authorization, cultural writing, of her life seems to have been her marriage and the long arm of the church's annulment process. Her subsequent refusals of marriage may be costing her something also. Sometimes the rising and subsiding repetitions imply her judgment on others, especially men; then again the surfacing or disappearing refrain-language indicts the translator herself. In dialogue with Siegfried, she says that he has tried "to undermine what little faith remained," but to this accusation she adds, "Everyone. And life. And Rome more than anyone" (514). When the annulment finally is granted, the words of a very long sentence at last reach this event but only after traveling through references to "buttons" (on both clothes and elevators), the translator's "lilt of the heart" (in the elevator and then as she begins translating into the mouthpiece), and a conference on sociology, which merges into the official letter:

This our masculine-dominated civilisation which has turned vital lies into fragile truths such as Madam, I have just received the notification of the Nullity decision in your favour at the Last Judgment and enclose it with great joy and felicitation at the happy outcome just in time for the menopause. (570)

The cruel humor in this wonderful chain of discourse suggests that the woman perhaps wanted a new marriage and even children. Yet she clung to her hope of an official release, the *legitimate delegitimating* of her commitments. Was the oppressively high price of loyalty (and belief, love, responsibility, etc.) set by the church and a "masculine-dominated" society or by herself? The woman's subjectivity travels between the two convictions.

As another refrain-repetition often suggests, she may have injured her own heart; the end of a long, layered sentence often asks: "Where when and to whose heart did one do that?" (464; similarly, 500). The third-person disjunction between acknowledgment and pain (the gap between knowing and feeling) is more prominent when her questioning reflection varies: "Where when and to whose heart did one make anything matter?" (465). For this traveler, the highest price of loyalty (especially an ill-advised one? an oppressively restrictive one?) is an eventual *loyal disloyalty* to any "one single idea." To put it another way, this speaker is loyal to her disloyalty; she is disloyal on principle and is not just a postmodern consciousness adrift in meaninglessness.

She has fought hard for the costly meaninglessness, or betweenness, of her life. She resists origin as though she has had enough of one civilization's discourses about it. She travels light—much lighter than Forster's Cyril Fielding, who also was between loyalties and ideologies. Among her many appositional languages (and her ideas that are equal before God), the experimental subjectivity of the translator lives her willing suspension of belief, disbelief, love; she is quite willing, indeed persistently willing, to suspend these things. The paradoxical, multifaceted refrains tease her about what she has lost as they perpetually translate and imaginatively revise her playful, if disorienting, freedom.

Even though the translator's continual movement (geographically and psychologically) results in (or parallels) a disorienting array of discourses in the same sentence, there is still one narrating consciousness who willingly, voluntarily suspends these discourses that temporarily shape themselves into her life. There is no single narrating subjectivity in *Thru*, however. Here it is every discourse for itself, every upstart voice for itself, whether it's the intertextual voice of Diderot's Jacques arguing with his master or the voice of a creative-writing student discussing with the instructor and other students the characterization of Larissa and Armel—characters who in other sections seem to be the major authors or narrating authorities of this very experimental novel. Transgression is pervasive, and the narrative space is shared by almost everyone. Even Larissa and Armel, the two major voices, discover they are writing, authorizing each other.

In a sense, the narrative is, for this quarreling couple, the Pygmalion myth in double. It is as though Galatea, in her stone world, had all along been writing the story of Pygmalion and is incredulous to realize that he imagines that *he* has been creating *her*. Larissa and Armel sense each other's presence. They mirror each other, while the lines on the page are slanted upward as the driver (the conscious "mind") adjusts a rearview mirror in an effort to glimpse the suspected presence of the (Lacanian) unconscious. Indeed, in this "Lacanian love story," as Hanjo Berressem describes the novel,[30] texts flirt with texts and quarrel with texts.

Here difference is all; there is no transcendent, authorizing subject or self among these linguistic segments, all clamoring for subject status in a comic jamboree of intertextual fraternization (an intertextuality that includes Shakespeare, Diderot, Coleridge, T. S. Eliot, Joyce, and others). The novel enacts poststructuralist theories about the disappearance of the author and indeed the self; here the multiple transgressions keep translating the presumption of narratorship into mere textual illusion. The full subtlety of this witty fictional adventure can be appreciated best by narratologists. The book is "a private joke," Brooke-Rose says, for the linguistically sophisticated ("Illicitations," 103).[31] Yet even the common reader can, with some willing suspension of traditional expectation, enjoy this highly self-subversive text. It offers a kind of linguistic asceticism where the poststructuralist gist and jest is, not that all flesh is grass, but that all self is text.

Thru is tense, intellectual poetry; in this linguistic apocalypse there is no "loitering into prose." As a poetic gesture, *Thru* is indeed similar to Pope's cerebral wit in the *Dunciad*, except that in Brooke-Rose's twentieth-century untuning of the sky, everything disappears, not with a yawn and the "uncreating word" of Chaos, but with the uncreating words of clever voices, their mutual usurpations deconstructing a *text* that becomes anagrammatically the *exit* into and through itself (*Thru*, 742).[32]

S(t)imulating Origins

If *Thru* enacts a linguistically collapsing universe of subjectivity, *Amalgamemnon* inscribes a hypothetical future of new selves and texts. Written in future tense (with some passages in the subjunctive), this novel populates the subjectivity of a female professor with the loquacious vitality of many experimental voices. Anticipating that the incursions of "high technology" (5) will mean the loss of her job (and she will go the way of all humanist professors, as Lyotard has predicted), the redundant woman professor begins inventing possible futures. She imagines characters in apposition (and sometimes, opposition) to herself; to these subsensibilities she gives names, ambitions, actions, and the transgressive capacity to interact with their author. In Mira's speech, the discourses mingle and reproduce themselves with variations, refrainlike repetitions, as they did in the traveling translator's monologue in *Between*. The professor's language, however, is more dense with wordplay, yet the dialogic puns never impede the flow of the text as it aspires to the poetic inscribings of apprehension and hope.

The humanist professor is obviously appreciative of the several patrocentric symbolic structures that have largely constituted her life's work. Like Brooke-Rose, who acknowledged certain mentors as "men-towers," the narrator anticipates that she will still read Herodotus after losing her job—especially when bored with her lover Willy (*Amalgamemnon*, 15). Yet the punning and the rapid juxtapositions of discourses within the same (often very long) sentence also suggest a semiotic play or an *écriture féminine*. The narrator's experimental consciousness (as she invents possible choices, relationships, characters) is a rich reservoir of language and cannot be categorized as strictly either patrocentric or feminine and revolutionary. Along with the qualities often linked to the experimental (and which could be linked to the feminine), her reflections also include several "little narratives." Some of these are hypotheses about her own future—the experimental pig farm and her life with Willy (then Wally, her next Amalgamemnon). Other hypothetical stories or little narratives are closer to the imaginative scientific narratives that Lyotard sees as replacing the former grand narratives. Several times the narrator's voice speaks of instructing "all X and Y chromosomes" within her; one punning instruction is a revisionary narrative of difference, as the voice tries out, "Let sex equal why" (82).

A few of the little narratives could be classed as feminine or domestic, especially perhaps the recipes; with two egg yolks, the narrator will combine "salt and pepper and a cupful of fresh modifiers finely chopped" (29; another recipe, 43). Yet the dialogic presence of the academic ("cupful of fresh modifiers finely chopped") thoroughly deconstructs any effort to distinguish the feminine and the masculine in this very intellectual (and angry and passionate) subjectivity. Unlike most of Pym's characters, Mira does not evade or ignore masculine discourses and ideologies in favor of a widespread muted culture and language of women. Like Jacob (and like Woolf and Brooke-Rose), Mira is an "inheritor," and she delights in the discourses of her civilization (she perceives them as *hers*), male-authorized though they may be.

She retains a certain nostalgia for the great myths or narratives of Western humanistic (and especially academic) culture. The emancipation story is the rationale for many of the feminist arguments that occupy Sandra (Cassandra) and Willy on the envisioned pig farm, and the narrator as a teacher is so much defined by the humanistic culture that she sees the loss of her job as a death. The first sentence of the novel is a near-quotation of the first sentence in Samuel Beckett's *Malone Dies*. The narrator says, "I shall soon be quite redundant at last despite of all" (*Amalgamemnon*, 5), while Malone says, "I shall soon be quite dead."[33] Perhaps it should be emphasized that the professor's subjectivity is very centrally constituted by her work. Hers is a late-twentieth-century voice and inscription. In contrast to Woolf's Lily, who had to contend with the verbal "infection" that "women can't paint," Mira and Cassandra have apparently never doubted that women could think.

The narrator regrets losing her career as thinker and teacher, but she then thinks the possible futures she may invent and live. Her profession is central to her identity; it is her life, as the replacing of Beckett's *dead* with her own *redundant* indicates. Richard Martin has argued that the notion of redundancy generates the text of *Amalgamemnon*, its repetitions, issues, solutions, and deconstructions.[34] But Mira's redundancy is very different from Malone's death. After many a sentence, Malone dies, but Mira lives. She keeps on inventing sentences; she simulates and resimulates her own experimental text and subjectivity. Death is for Malone the ultimate confirmation of meaninglessness, but redundancy (the death of her identity as a humanistic scholar) is for Mira a crisis of rebirth, of textual and experimental rebirth.

The experimental, hypothetical hope of Mira's creative discourse is ambivalently imaged in the persistent future tense and in the subjunctive speculations. As Brooke-Rose has said, *Amalgamemnon* explores "the sort of predictability of discourse, particularly political discourse, but also of much ordinary human discourse in private situations" ("Conversation," 85). Indeed, it is the political element of her private and domestic discourse, in arguments with Willy, that the redundant professor sees as most irritatingly predictable. Like Cassandra (whose name the narrating voice appropriates along with the unheeded quality of the Trojan's prophecies), the professor predicts that a version of Agamemnon will try to take her captive. Her own amalgamation of middle-class male heroism, Willy, will impose his version of the feminine mystique on her; he will suggest a celebration—"when you'll be rid of the university, when thanks to me you will accept, and face, being only a woman" (15; similarly, 136). The predictabilities of the ideology of difference recur often, and the responses of Cassandra/Sandra are just as predictable as those of Willy/Amalgamemnon. A change in climate or weather (a "polar low," 15, 136) inscribes the narrator's predictable coolness here in response to Willy's vision of her professorial identity degenerating into "only" a woman. The grand narrative of sexual difference will produce the expected patterns, the stereotypical responses, over and over for millennia, from Agamemnon and earlier, and into the twentieth century.

Yet the meditating consciousness also utters prophecies that have a more revolutionary and even biblical tone. Brooke-Rose had suggested, in "Metafiction and Surfiction," that apocalyptic "prophets can be pessimistic (total destruction) or optimistic (death and renewal)" (*Rhetoric*, 387). The predictable destruction of the narrator's identity (its redundancy, its capture by Willy, and its death) is woven into stories of escape and guerilla warfare. In addition, the continuing chorus of punning, comic, dialogic phrases implies a kind of linguistic birth or revolution, a renewal of the language and consequently of subjectivity.

The narrating voice may sometimes "mimagree" (45, 138) with male culture and male acquaintances, but the musing consciousness asks:

Wouldn't it be better to mimage myself as an Abyssinian maid, striking two small hammers on the cords of her dulcimer and singing of Mount Abora? Or a Cambodgean child? Or a New York streetsweeper or myself as foetus or as constellation, Perseus, Orion, Andromeda, Cygnus, Cetus, Draco? (14)

Eventually the experimenting, prophesying voice tries out each of these selves and more. The voice of the black streetsweeper (as he travels, cleaning the whole world) has the ring of a biblical prophet; the streetsweeper harangues a lethargic community of "rightists," calling them "whited sepulchers" and declaring a new future for Africa, the "promised land" (57). Orion, another male projection, seems to be Mira's closest linguistic relative; he talks with her often and acknowledges her as his author and creator. Somewhat like the captive Cassandra voice, Orion has been "siberianized," imprisoned "for flagrant delight of opinion" (17). The streetsweeper, Orion, and the Abyssinian maid all develop into radical voices; the Abyssinian maid, as Fatima, slides out of an ornate fairy-tale text to speak, now as a "sad Somali girl," some comic "smattered Arabic" (127) with a young terrorist, Roland, who seems to become a revolutionary amalgamation: "Rolandrover streetsweeper Anon" (137). The language and images of a radical, reborn future are throughout the novel engaged in a creative dialogue with those that imply a self-entrapping "mimagreement" (14).

The text's manipulation of tense, the de-authorizing strategy of transgression, and the vigorous wordplay all shape the narrator's ambivalent and experimental simulation of her own future. The coy future tense, for instance, acts very much like the narrator herself; the future tense pretends to a reality.[35] A voice describes the nonexistent future while yet manipulating the text into rebellious scenarios. Mira imagines reading Herodotus at night but then acknowledges that in the morning she will have to pretend, for Willy's sake, that she has no intellectual interests; she enjoys reading history, which, as she says, "I'll have carefully to deconstruct tomorrow by letting him abolish all these other discourses into an acceptance of his although sooner or later the future will explode into the present despite the double standard at breaking points" (15–16). The professor will have to mime or mimic her agreement with Willy's vision of her as merely a woman.

Even though the narrator imagines having to accommodate her discourse to the male voice, and even though this "double standard" may limit her life with any Amalgamemnon, yet there are breaking points. At these points, the narrator's future-tense constructions may explode into the present. And indeed they do explode. There are extended sections of direct nonnarrated dialogue, and these move along in a quite realistic manner as though in *present* tense. Although other dialogue passages in the book are indirectly narrated and in future tense ("she will say" and "he will say" and "I will say"), there are a number of quite bare passages in which no narratorial voice directs the traffic. We know who is speaking only because the speakers allude to material that we've heard them mention earlier or because the two speakers mention each other's names.

Most of the dialogue between the kidnapping conspirators, who use Mira's farm for a cover, is presented directly. There is an occasional framing "I'll ask" (79), but these characters then argue at length without benefit of narrator as they discuss what to feed the hostage (84) and whether they will remain on the farm or not (108–9, 118–19). Some of their dialogue is indeed in future tense, because they are discussing plans, but the unnarrated exchanges move by with an immediacy that mimes a present tense. Certain other dialogue sections (Jean-Luc, Lizvieta, and Bea, for instance, 114–17) also give a sense of the present, simply because no narratorial voice moves the scene into the future with a "he will say" or "I will say."

Similarly, the present-tense conversations on the radio talk shows or interviews move directly across the silent narrator-perceiver's consciousness and into the reader's. These sections, too, contribute to a sense of narrative presentness or immediacy; they "explode into the present." Finally, all of the dialogue between Roland and Fatima is given without a narratorial "he will say" or "she will say" and thus moves along with an immediacy that suggests present tense. When Fatima steps out of her future-tense, parodically narrated fairy tale of dragon capture and heroic rescue, she enters the textual arena of Middle Eastern guerilla warfare. It is one of the breaking points (of gender role and of politics) in her narrative, and appropriately at this time, her story seems to explode into the present.

The future tense not only structures most of the sentences, but it structures the narrator's ambivalent expectations. The narrator expects that the future may explode into the present, something that happens during dialogues when the characters (in heated arguments, and so at "breaking points"?) communicate with each other and the confrontations are unsoftened by any explicit narratorial control. The Mira voice in particular experiences a breakthrough of the present when her character Orion accuses her of imprisoning him in her "forgetfulness to be now made present by my existence" (70–71). Mira cuts this direct dialogue short by telling Orion he "can go back to the future and other negative capabilities" (71). And he does.

This altercation between Mira and one of her characters is not unusual in *Amalgamemnon*, where transgression of narrative levels is a major contributor to the rebellious undercutting of authority and of origin. Each character wants to claim a little textual territory. When Hans (at one time identified by Mira as her student) and his kidnapping conspirators take over her farm, they take over the text as well, even though Mira is their narrator; she is making them up. They order her around and tell her to shut up (79–81, 99). She, their narrator-creator admits that she is unpopular among her own characters (79, 95, 102).

These conspirators, kidnappers, are trying to kidnap the text, and in so doing, they are echoing one of the reiterated verbal motifs of the book: words, ideas, and women may be "kidnapped" or "plagiarized" and held for ransom (16, 22, 29, 30). Indeed, the narrating consciousness takes a lot of lines hostage from "Kubla Khan" and from *Hamlet*. Orion, in a scene of narrated dialogue, rages at Anna, since he fears that he is becoming one of her "assimilations" or "amalgamations" (41–43); he perceives such verbal kidnapping as a terrorist act (41). And a computer ("Your alter ego, Gigo"—Garbage In Garbage Out) sends a note to "Dear Uncle Ego" asking Ego to give up his hostages (83). These hostages seem to be characters; Gigo lists "Hans and Co," the kidnappers and invaders of Mira's farm and the transgressors of her text. In this novel, characters are continually amalgamating or "cassandring" (136) each other, creating and simulating, or muting and deconstructing each other. Those who are the objects of such textual control are nervous, rebellious, or manipulative.

One of the most rebellious and manipulative voices is that of Sandra/Cassandra. Addressing this subsensibility, the narrator admonishes: "Keep quiet, Cassandra, forecastor of your own pollux, keep your castrations in perpetual cassation" (30). The motive for warning Cassandra to keep her deconstructive/castrating language, and her sexual politics, under control is that the future seldom turns out as anticipated; "time," as a similar voice warns later, is "the great corrector and corrupter of meaning" (120). But many narrator-voices usurp these powers of time; casting their language into the future, they corrupt and correct by means of puns.

Having lost her voice and her language, Cassandra (and other conquered figures like her) has disappeared into the discourse of the male heroes. As a prophetic voice says, and as a narrator reiterates later, applying it to her relationship with Wally (Willy's replacement): "Similarly the young Scythians will be unable to learn the language of the Amazons but the women will succeed in picking up theirs, and therefore disappear" (11, 141). In order to speak at all, the brooding, prophesying consciousness realizes that she will, like the conquered mythic Amazons, have to play the part assigned to her. Her language and her subjectivity will have to appear yet disappear at the same time, like a pun. She reflects, "Perhaps it'll be the very redundancy of this or that ancient cultural guilt that will make me try so hard to want to be pygmalioned although for that it will be essential to go on seeming idiotic to prop the pigmylion and thus to disappear" (13; similarly, 129). The notion of the man creating the woman in an ideal image designed by him is, in the quoted sentence, made literally and linguistically to disappear into a punning disguise. The woman's voice masks and mimics the word, and the same voice mocks this hubristic grand narrative of the (male) creative imagination. The voice turns "Pygmalion" into a "pigmylion"—but at the cost of disappearing herself because of her proximity to the syllables of the male word that she was forced to use even while deconstructing (cassandring, castrating) it.

Under the cassandring language of the narrator, the ideology of competition also suffers a punning deconstruction. Instead of being "only" a woman and playing cheerleader to male ambition with "Let the best man win," the narrating voice offers a sabotaging parody: "Let the beast man wane" (57) and "Let the boast man whine" (52, 57). These experimental vowels transform the grand narrative of quest or success into a petty, defensive failure; competition becomes a declining story, the amalgamation of a once legitimizing ideology that is on the wane.

In this novel, the punning, and the varied reweaving of phrases, function narratively as a kind of syllabic guerilla warfare. The masked words and many recurring phrases change disguises and meaning each time they come on stage; the words and phrases mimic themselves, simulate themselves, or subvert themselves, like a chorus crossing and recrossing the text and each time providing another nuance of opinion. The narrator's verbal mimicry of the language that has amalgamated her is a silenced speaking not unlike the hysterical miming that Luce Irigaray identifies in *The Speculum of the Other Woman* as the only language available to a woman who tries to enter male discourse; this indirect (silent, miming) speech of the hysteric can, as Hélène Cixous has argued, be a political act.[36]

The almost continuous punning, however, does not always drag a narrator into a trap that she identifies as male and oppressive. In the first few pages of the book, the narrator, already succumbing to the portly official, mocks the transformation of discourse that this relationship will bring: "Mimecstasy and mimagreement will always go together, like sexcommunication." Fake ecstasy, fake agreement will yield a sex communication that puns on excommunication, noncommunication, severe outsiderhood. The very next sentence is the one I quoted previously, in which a narrator asks if it might not be better to "mimage" herself as, among other things, an Abyssinian maid, a "foetus," Orion, and Cetus, the constellation of the Whale (14). The puns and allusions concerning "foetus," the Whale, and rebirth become a prominent refrain in the novel. The intermittent series of puns on "foetus" (14, 28, 47, 82, 83), "profoetus" (18, 137), and "prophetus"/"prophetic" (83, 102) intermingle with other phrases about leviathan (102), whales enclosing or disgorging prophets, as in the Jonah story (20) and as implied by Mira's name: Mira Enketei or Mira in the Whale. Mira, like Jonah, wants to get out, and get her experimental language out.

As Mira says of Orion, one of the voices she authorizes, "I must get himself out" (21). The slipping of the pronoun (female "I") into "himself" degenders origin and simulates it as inclusive. The language also stimulates an experimental, prophetic rebirth of subjectivity. Similarly, in the future-tense speculations and in the transgressive takeovers of the text, the narrating subjectivity, who expects to lose her (professional) identity, her "self," prophesies a multi-voiced future. She envisions texts that playfully de-authorize and de-originate authority, allowing it to travel experimentally from voice to voice.

In the later novels of Brooke-Rose, authority and legitimation become ever more problematic and subjectivity ever more experimental. When living computer-stones can make or become texts, all humanistic subjectivity, or perhaps even human subjectivity, begins to be a peripheral tradition, a little story, a muted mode, just one option of textual generation among others. Although the narrator's early reflections about her retirement in *Amalgamemnon* could constitute an overheard, inner monologue, she seems to be typing this into a computer (as the letter from Gigo suggests), and she does anticipate that technology will take the place of the humanist scholar. In the subsequent novels, however, the computer text is almost a character; the conversations are not so much a tête-à-tête as a text-à-text.

Although the language, the scientific jargon, in *Xorandor*, *Verbivore*, and *Textermination* is poetry (as Brooke-Rose uses the word), these novels are less lyrical than *Amalgamemnon*; the sentences are not as elaborate with echoing phrases, and the prose generally is less thick with wordplay. The very dense, rich language of *Amalgamemnon*, and of *Between* and *Out*, drew the reader in and encouraged the reader (at least, this reader) to "identify" with the music and emotion of the narrating voice. Yet the more scientific language of the later novels gains in comedy, and the sparer style encourages a focus on the slipping, erasing, transgressing, and retrieval of (temporary) authority.

In *Xorandor*, which can be read as science fiction, there is no (technical) transgression of narrative levels. Yet the computer whiz kids, the twins Jip (John Ivor Paul) and Zab (Isabel), each record distinctive responses to the ongoing story, the threat or problem posed by radiation-eating computer-stones. There is not just one (authoritative, legitimating) story of events. Xorandor offers two stories about his own origin (an alien from the planet Mars, or perhaps merely a long-term resident species on planet Earth). As Lincoln Konkle emphasizes, both origin and gender are (like some computer operations) "undecidable" in this novel.[37] One result (or cause) of this undecidability is a persistent disjunction between narrative and narrator. In fact, when the twins are sent to Germany (so that adult scientists can presumably attend to the supposed invasion of aliens), Jip and Zab feel cheated of their text; Jip notes that "we've dropped out of our own story" (159). Although the remark has a geographic and realistic basis, it also has a transgressive quality—as though a narrative could do without its narrator and muddle along on its own, unauthorized.

Jip's comment also affirms a futuristic world in which the self is understood as text. When text and self are a matter of lighting up a sequence of electrical impulses on a screen, even the grand narrative of "difference" becomes experimental, muted, problematic, and certainly garbled. One of Xorandor's children takes the name Lady Macbeth; he or it is intertextual and (mistakenly) assumed to be interplanetary as well. The gender of this stone is not the concern of the police and the scientists, who instead focus on the fact that Lady Macbeth managed to become a very destructive text. It "got himself out" (to paraphrase Mira) and is threatening to destroy a nuclear waste storage depot. If Jip and Zab feel alienated from their own story, Lady Macbeth—the product of a "syntax error" (*Xorandor*, 137)—is rolling around loose in "his" story. In both cases, there is a disjunction between text and authority. In *Xorandor*, though it is accessible science fiction and has a plot, the presence of a nonhuman, highly intelligent species (whose origin remains persistently obscure) seems to short out, fuse, threaten to explode (as Lady Macbeth threatens) the traditional human narrative circuitry of authorial agency and the generating of texts.

In the sequel, *Verbivore*, this disjunction of text and origin achieves even further degeneration, or liberation. *Verbivore* is virtually a high-tech epistolary novel as human voices, along with characters from a play and characters from novels written by characters, all write to each other. Most use word processors (or *are* the texts within word processors), but some resort to pen and paper, since Xorandor's species has started to feed on electricity (thus, on computer texts and programs).

The device or "machinery" of this novel is the unexplained attack, the feeding frenzy, of the electricity-consuming verbivores. In her remarks, quoted earlier, Brooke-Rose defined a central concern of her novels, and especially *Verbivore*, as the simulations that constitute most suppositions. Like all of her experimental fiction, *Verbivore* "produces new ways of looking," and this new way gives to simulation (in the largest sense, texts and talking and selves) a very high value. As the threat or anticipation of death may enhance the value of life, so the threatened demise of all texts (including financial markets and the broadcast of Dame Paula in the role of Lady Macbeth) makes the text in itself absolutely valuable. In a world where the simulation or stimulation of origin is threatened, it is important to simulate: to invent, to inscribe (oneself and others), to get everyone out ("out," that is, textualized, enselved in language). One must speak, speak out, or at least get spoken, perhaps get *acted*, simulated by somebody; the actress who *plays* the role of Decibel (a character in a play by the "sublime" Perry Hupsos) evidently *becomes* Decibel (112–13).

Origin is elusive in *Verbivore*, and the sense-of-an-ending comes and goes with the power blackouts that shut down the texts. Textual children and "real" children do seek origin. Yet any quest pattern is a threadbare remnant of its formerly great tradition. The only crucial quest or search now (as Zab and Jip—in middle age—peruse old discs and meet with experts and ministers) is for the origin of the ending, the imminent ending of all texts. Zab's grown child Hanjo, questing for identity and origin, is furious when his "bachelor mother" defends the norm of her generation—motherhood and career but not necessarily marriage (47–51). He goes to China to look for his father. And the writer Perry, a textual character, asks Mira to return to narrating his story (but all the characters are textual, and Mira is narrating the Zab text as well [110–11]). Giving up on his quest for his author, Perry decides no one can get him out of "the mess of wordprocessing a novel, except my own authorial authority" (188). The text is all—the final value; the textual play's the thing wherein a textualized and textualizing author catches the consciousness of words crossing a screen. At least, the text *thinks* it's conscious, assumes it is an authorizing and simulating subjectivity. This assumption that one can authorize or simulate is—in *Textermination*—viewed from the inside out. That is, it is seen largely from the point of view of authorized (already written) characters. The frame of the novel's action purports to be certain already extant literary texts, generally canonical texts. We begin in Jane Austen's text (her sentences) and in Emma's thoughts as she finds herself in the carriage with Mr. Elton just before he begins his unwelcome marriage proposal. At the end of *Textermination*, we are returned precisely to the same text, that is, to the passage in Austen's novel. In between, participating in a carnivalized allegory of reader-response theory, Emma and many other characters travel by coach, train, and "aerobrain" to San Francisco, where they attend "the annual Convention of Prayer for Being."[38] The convention is an international literary conference (the meeting of friends, the hearing of papers on literary works, lunching in Sausalito, sight-seeing). And yet the conference is experienced by the characters themselves. Personifications of their own texts, these characters gather to petition "interpretive communities" to read the texts; they perceive their "Creator" as the "Implied Reader" who is, in recent times, more interested in television than in written texts (26). These gathered texts revive when they hear a paper read about themselves. Indeed, the entire convention is, as the narrator suggests, an "international ritual for the revival of the fittest" (8).

The punning phrase suggests that the professor of *Amalgamemnon* is probably narrating much of the text, and in fact she shows up in typical transgressive dialogue with her created character, Orion, who tells Mira to stop punning (*Textermination*, 65). She is a little bit surprised to be at the convention, since hers is not a canonical text. As she tells Orion during lunch, she has reason to be here: "I mean I appear in two books, though I invented four. But I'm amazed anyone took any notice of them, enough for me to be here I mean" (66). Indeed, Mira's textual existence is somewhat precarious. She has been merely seen (but hardly acknowledged) earlier, by an "Interpreter," Jack Knowles, one of the conference organizers. She had been sitting with Emma Woodhouse, Emma Bovary, Dorothea Brooke, and Mr. Casaubon; the reader-interpreter recognized the famous characters but couldn't place the "nondescript" (49) professor-narrator-character.

Origin is in the eye of the beholder. *Textermination* plays with the concept that being read, being accepted as "literature," is almost as important as being initially written or invented. In contrast to Larissa and Armel of *Thru*, who seem worried that they are being written (and thus fear that they are not autonomous, authorizing selves), the characters in *Textermination* are eager to be acknowledged as texts. Even characters who are prominent in this novel disappear when they find their own names written in the enormous "Index of names Forbidden by the Canon" (92). Kelly McFadgeon, another "Interpreter," and a major character during the first half of the novel, finds that she herself is only a character in "Textermination, by Mira Enketei" (92), but Mira also succumbs to textermination when she too finds her name in the index (105).

So the "author" alone, after providing an intricate explanation of narrative theory (106–7), remains to invent (or sort of de-invent) the international literary conference. Everything is anxious to become text, preferably canonical text. Television characters (Columbo, MacGyver, others) disrupt the convention as they proclaim their legitimacy as texts. Even the hotel staff seem to be turning into fictional characters; a maid turns out to be Jenny Gerhardt, for instance (164–65). When an earthquake destroys most of California, the fictional characters, stranded on a narrow strip of land, eventually find conveyances appropriate to their own classic texts and take these vehicles back into the fictional passages from which they had emerged at the beginning of the book.

Text is home. For the characters in *Textermination*, origin and authority mean finding one's writtenness—and hearing this discussed occasionally by interested readers (who themselves are not "outside the text" either). In this near-allegory of intertextuality, written readers mingle with written characters, both the classic ones and the "forbidden" characters. The political presence of the "Index" indicates a large, wild literary subculture, much of it muted by the dominance of a canon. Yet the literary conference brings the vitality of both the experimental and the canonized voices into dialogic play. Simulation in this novel thinks back (through fathers, mothers) but thinks widely and radically also, the style and the quotations drawing upon many contemporary and experimental modes of authorizing.

The experimental fiction of Brooke-Rose is playful above all—or almost above all. If there is a subject matter or content, it is the utter value of words (surely, puns are appropriate in critical prose about this author). More words, more utterances, are needed (the texts of this author declare), playful, flexible, and exploratory words, words that get themselves out—escapees from the "siberianized" phrases of totalitarian grand narratives and the pygmalionizing texts of difference. The characters or voices in the novels of Brooke-Rose explore the relative freedom of the linguistic "wild"; they are often outside, between, redundant, or indexed among the minor and the unknown. Yet they dialogically and appositionally engage traditions of all kinds. The somewhat alienated speaker of *Between*, though acknowledging a distance from her own heart, is not disengaged from words.

A contemporary, disoriented self, but a courageous one, the creative subjectivity of *Between* travels on words through the continually revised translations of her life, "between" after "between." Similarly, the redundant professor, sensing an ending but without Malone's despair, explores and simulates future after future. She can live without her professional identity, but her experimental, self-inventive wordplay does not cease. Indeed, even the computer humanoids (or electroids?) declare themselves, construct agency and value; they s(t)imulate origin. The brave new poststructuralist worlds of these novels imply that if the self did not exist, words would invent it.

5   *Conclusion*
The Implied Critic

The dialogic remark that concludes the preceding chapter surely applies to the critic as well. If words can invent the self, they also invent the critic. We are our discourses, each of us being an implied critic whose subjectivity and writing are to some extent inscribed by the dominant literary theories of our time. Fortunately for those who are writing near the end of the twentieth century, most of the currently canonized theories are themselves anticanonical; that is, they "read" all texts, including theory texts, as problematic, with the theory text of deconstruction being perhaps the most acrobatically self-conscious among these. The result for literary critics has on the whole been salutary, since we now have a variety of complex and subtle strategies by which to "imply" criticism, or (to be appositional in my statements) by which to negotiate significantly among signs. Many readers and scholars construct a varied mesh or hybrid of theory (psychoanalytic, marxist, poststructuralist) around the fiction they are examining. The implied critic in our time is often an experimental self, a dialogically complex theory-persona or teacher-persona.

    We still need to extend this rich variety of critical discourses to the concept of subjectivity in the novel. As I have argued in this study, a more complex and appositional concept of the self is appropriate and critically helpful when we are talking about the voices in twentieth-century fiction. Although the opposing self is still present and politically significant in literature, there are as well characters and voices constructed of various but not necessarily polarized discourses. What we might call "the sense of an opposi-

Conclusion 159

tion" has developed a vigorous tradition in philosophy, political theory, and literary criticism. Theories of opposition, subversion, and difference, however, can lead to difficulty in perceiving (or reading or inscribing) a more integrated, though still variegated, hybrid of discourse and subjectivity.

John McGowan, in his *Postmodernism and Its Critics*, calls attention to such typically "oppositional strategies" of liberal Western thought. He notes that "modernist freedom" (with precedents among the Romantics) is constructed "oppositionally, as the negation of everything bourgeois," including the concepts of a state and a unified self. Extending this modern and liberal tendency, most varieties of postmodernism (understandably wary of essentialism) carry even further the attack on "reason" (it dominates and oppresses), on agency, and on the "autonomous" self. While such conceptual strategies may lead, McGowan suggests, to despair and inaction politically, Gerald Graff has argued that for literary critics, a deconstructive zeal sometimes sets up false oppositions and polarities that misrepresent traditional theories. As he observes, critics who wish "to liberate the reader from the determinacy of the text" sometimes write as if the only alternatives were creativity and free play on the one hand, but a narrow "monolithic criticism" on the other.[1] Focusing particularly on feminists who develop theories of subjectivity, Jane Flax argues against a simplistic opposition of the self as autonomous and the self as "being-in-relations"; the two concepts are not mutually exclusive.[2] As I have indicated in the preceding chapters, the two concepts, along with other discourses, do indeed mesh into creative transformation and hybridization in the dialogic subjectivities that speak in the texts of Woolf, Pym, and Brooke-Rose.

Using a variety of discourses, these texts elaborate three distinctive strategies for the construction of a dialogic appositional self. Woolf's narrative modes are experimental, her politics liberal, and her feminism radical. Yet her strategy of feminizing the symbolic can be seen as belonging to a great tradition. That is, there are precedents for the major uprooting or transforming of the symbolic, which much of Woolf's fiction implies and enacts. The last great transforming of the symbolic, however, seems to have moved in the other direction—towards a masculinizing of a (feminine) symbolic. Some scholars find evidence of such a trend in certain transformed, ancient words for deities when a more "masculine" myth and culture appropriated "feminine" ones.[3] The effect of such a transforming of the symbolic is to critique, appropriate, and change an acknowledged tradition or complex of texts and ideologies. As Rachel Blau DuPlessis phrases it in "For the Etruscans" (a deconstructive, playful essay), some feminists have a "revolutionary desire" for a "nonpatriarchal order, in the symbolic realm and in the realms of productive, personal, and political relations."[4]

This mode of "revolutionary desire" seems to have characterized much of Woolf's appositional discourse about "experimentation" and women's subjectivity. She never ceased to think back through the fathers (as well as the mothers) of the English traditions. The point, in feminizing the symbolic, is to alter or erase its arrogance and exclusiveness and to open the once patriarchal discourses to relationality. Many of Woolf's characters and voices are engaged in this long-term, evolutionary project of *changing the definition of the (British) symbolic*. When Lily translates "his work" (Tansley's dissertation) into "her work," then her painting (and its relational vision) can develop as a dialogic discourse about herself and the action of the text; Lily has feminized the symbolic category of (serious, male) quest or work. She has rendered less patriarchal a discourse of the symbolic order.

Similarly, Bernard feminizes the symbolic as this traditionally schooled male becomes the gossipy, Marlovian talker and, in a real sense, a woman writing (the sense is real enough to awe and disturb him). The appositional voices of Lily, Bernard, Mrs. Ramsay, Orlando, and others appropriate the *sermo* and make it a little less paternal, a little more maternal. Their voices can be heard as part of a hybridizing tradition among English writers and thinkers, a tradition to which the feminine individual, described by Armstrong, contributed as did certain Nonconformist groups—perhaps Mill, Arnold, and (in Woolf's view) the "experiment" of the women's movement.

In contrast to Woolf's strategies, the appositional discourses of subjectivity employed by Barbara Pym draw upon the trivial, the

Conclusion 161

in-significant, and they thus often elude any hint of the grand narrative, of the monomythic quest, the "Great Code," or indeed, plot. Her texts are to this extent outside the reality of literary culture and of permissible discourse. Edward Said has suggested that critics need to examine "the degree to which texts are made permissible"; he asks: "What is it that maintains texts inside reality? What keeps some of them current while others disappear? How do authors imagine for themselves the 'archive' of their time, into which they propose to put their text?"[5] By employing a discourse that deliberately eschewed the significant, Pym may have rendered her texts less permissible (less legitimate), and indeed her novels did not maintain themselves inside (published) "reality." They went out of print, and publishers rejected her new manuscripts year after year.

As her interview responses indicated, she did not write for the great-literature archive of her time; nor did she see herself in the role of the thwarted genius, the artist-as-oppositional-hero. She declared, "I am not a professional writer," as we saw earlier. Instead, she textualizes the nonprofessional life, the everyday, the trivial. She does, however, transform or hybridize the ordinary into a text (that is, she makes the muted subculture speak), but the discourses she employs in doing this are the nonarchival ones. By textualizing the trivial, Pym relies on the less "permissible" discourses of feminine domesticity or a nineteenth-century faith discourse. The appositional discourse of her major women characters appropriates and transforms a humanism in which "great literature" becomes the simple produce of the common day. The poets are quoted in the kitchen, and intertextuality descends into cafeterias and jumble sales.

Although the narrative strategies of textualizing the everyday and the ordinary (and often this means the feminine) all effect a retrieval of a muted and usually nonvalorized subculture, each such strategy is probably distinctive. The complex of dialogic trivia in Pym's novels is not the same as the quotidian focus of, for instance, Margaret Drabble's fiction or the fiction of Anita Brookner. These writers also circumvent the literary grand narratives, and they tend to write beyond the ending (or before it or on the margins of it). Yet the discourses of the everyday are somewhat like Tolstoy's unhappy families; each was unhappy in its own way. The "Great Code" is, by definition, one code. There is not just one way, however, of textualizing a marginal ideology. The wild discourses of the trivial are each distinctive.

Frances Wingate, in Drabble's *The Realms of Gold*, for instance, is sensitive to the delights of ordinary life. Going to dinner at the home of her lawyer and his wife, Frances appreciates their "comfortable" home. She "shivered on the edge of perfectly enjoying a perfectly ordinary experience, a perfectly ordinary encounter, an event so rare, as she walked down the wide stairs."[6] Nothing is ever made of this moment; it does not rise to epiphany, and it is somewhat similar to the acknowledgments made by Pym's Catherine as she responds to the trivia of sad poems, of wine lists, of cooking, and of writing her romance stories. Yet Drabble's characters do occasionally rise to full-blown "modernist" epiphanies, while Pym's do not.

If Drabble heightens the pitch of the ordinary a bit (as compared with Pym), Anita Brookner mutes or dulls it. Brookner's women are never surprised by joy; they are instead surprised by banality. Edith Hope (who is sometimes mistaken by new acquaintants for Virginia Woolf) in *Hotel du lac* reluctantly decides she can marry an apparently sensitive and perceptive man but then sees him emerge at 6:00 A.M. from another woman's hotel room.[7] Brookner's retrieval of the ordinary inscribes a text very different from the narratives of Pym. The trivial or the (feminine) ordinary does not constitute just one discourse. It is very likely constructed of many subcultures, as varied as those to which the eccentric female (and male) diarists and letter writers belonged whose rich dialogic discourse Woolf explored in her essays.

In the experimental fiction of Brooke-Rose, variety and heterogeneity become moot issues, since the text is virtually confiscated by textuality itself. Among the continually eliding voices in her novels, all selves are dialogic—when they are selves at all. It would be more accurate to say that some dialogic texts are indeed selves, that is, human. But many are blithely content with their primal textual condition, their written or electronic or pop-text status (a phrase in someone's computer, an electricity-eating stone, a television character). Here discourses write discourses that write discourses. Yet such a complex, dialogic world is not entirely decentered. Entering into the multiplicity of voices in these novels is an implied author (indeed, an implied critic) who speaks for a humanistic generosity and delight in words and intellectual play—whether the language game is a canonized *sermo*, a child's computer slang, or (literally) a sermon in stone.

One could argue that in Brooke-Rose's fiction the experimental self is more experimental than self, yet her books simply demonstrate with greater textual extravagance the richness discovered by Pym's characters in the trivia of the everyday, the in-significant, the not-yet-signalized, small-letter texts that have nearly escaped the archive of official reality. All three writers circumvent the symbolic archive or tradition, Woolf by transforming and feminizing it, Pym by giving various nonvalorized discourses a chance to speak, and Brooke-Rose by creatively deconstructing the symbolic. Yet the major characters, the implied selves, in the fiction of these writers also construct an experimental relationship with the dominant discourses of Western tradition and in so doing offer several models for a more complex understanding of a subjectivity that is dialogic, appositional, creative, and transformative of its own developing text.

Notes
Works Cited
Index

Notes

1. Subjectivity and Appositional Discourse

1. Fredric Jameson describes this "more radical poststructuralist position," but he prefers the "historicist" formulation of a once-centered self, which modern bureaucracy has destroyed; see "Postmodernism: The Cultural Logic of Late Capitalism," *New Left Review* 146 (July/Aug. 1984): 63. Drawing upon Enlightenment concepts of the self, Vincent Pecora sees the writers of modernist fiction as abandoning irony (crucial to the narrative self) under pressure of social "commodification" and manipulation; see *Self and Form in Modern Narrative* (Baltimore: Johns Hopkins Univ. Press, 1989), 1–114.

2. D. H. Lawrence to Edward Garnett, 5 June 1914, *The Letters of D. H. Lawrence*, ed. George J. Zytaruk and James T. Boulton (Cambridge: Cambridge Univ. Press, 1981), 2:183; E. M. Forster, "What I Believe," in *Two Cheers for Democracy* (New York: Harcourt, Brace and World, 1951), 67–68; Virginia Woolf, *Collected Essays* (London: Hogarth Press, 1966–67), 1:320–21 (hereafter cited as *CE* parenthetically in the text).

3. Caryl Emerson argues that Bakhtin formulated the notion of "inner speech" (though others claim the idea is part of the Bakhtinian school); see "The Outer Word and Inner Speech: Bakhtin, Vygotsky, and the Internalization of Language," in *Bakhtin: Essays and Dialogues on His Work*, ed. Gary Morson (Chicago: Univ. of Chicago Press, 1986), 25. Bakhtin does note the experimentation resulting from the external and internal play and the formation of hybrid discourses; see *The Dialogic Imagination*, ed. Michael Holquist, trans. Caryl Emerson and Michael Holquist (Austin: Univ. of Texas Press, 1981), 37, 303–7 (hereafter cited as *DI* parenthetically in the text). Note also that Bakhtin's experimentation refers to the *discourses* that construct the self, and this is how I will use the idea of experimentation. For a broad survey, not of discourse but of the experimental lives of women writers (British, American, American-ethnic) working in all genres from 1900 to 1945, see Mary Loeffelholz, *Experimental Lives: Women and Literature, 1900–1945* (New York: Twayne, 1992). For Loeffelholz, the word *experimental* has the very general reference of modernism and the social issues

167

(suffrage, paid work, and birth control) facing women early in the century; see especially 1–20.

4. Lionel Trilling, preface to *The Opposing Self* (New York: Viking Press, 1955), xi–x.

5. Harold Bloom, *The Anxiety of Influence* (New York: Oxford Univ. Press, 1973); Sandra Gilbert and Susan Gubar, *No Man's Land*, vol. 1, *The War of the Words* (New Haven: Yale Univ. Press, 1988), 125–56, 232–57.

6. See especially Jacques Lacan, "The Subversion of the Subject and the Dialectic of Desire in the Freudian Unconscious," in *Écrits: A Selection*, trans. Alan Sheridan (New York: Norton, 1977), 292–325.

7. Nancy Chodorow, "Gender, Relation, and Difference in Psychoanalytic Perspective," in Eisenstein and Jardine, 8–10. See also Chodorow's classic study of the differing socialization given to boys and girls and its consequences—girls becoming more relational, boys requiring a greater assurance of separateness: *The Reproduction of Mothering: Psychoanalysis and the Sociology of Gender* (Berkeley: Univ. of California Press, 1978).

8. Julia Kristeva, "From One Identity to Another," in *Desire in Language*, ed. Leon S. Roudiez, trans. Thomas Gora, Alice Jardine, and Leon S. Roudiez (New York: Columbia Univ. Press, 1980), 125–47; Hélène Cixous, "The Laugh of the Medusa," trans. Keith Cohen and Paula Cohen, *Signs* 1 (summer 1976): 875–93; Luce Irigaray, *This Sex Which Is Not One*, trans. Catherine Porter and Carolyn Burke (Ithaca, N.Y.: Cornell Univ. Press, 1985).

9. Susan Friedman, "Lyric Subversion of Narrative in Women's Writing: Virginia Woolf and the Tyranny of Plot," in *Reading Narrative*, ed. James Phelan (Columbus: Ohio State Univ. Press, 1989), 162–85; Makiko Minow-Pinkney, *Virginia Woolf and the Problem of the Subject* (New Brunswick, N.J.: Rutgers Univ. Press, 1987), 14–15; Ellen G. Friedman and Miriam Fuchs, "Context and Continuities: An Introduction to Women's Experimental Fiction in English," in Friedman and Fuchs, *Breaking the Sequence*, 4.

10. Christine Brooke-Rose, "A Womb of One's Own?" in *Stories, Theories and Things* (Cambridge: Cambridge Univ. Press, 1991), 223–34 (hereafter cited parenthetically in the text).

11. Alice Jardine, *Gynesis: Configurations of Woman in Modernity* (Ithaca, N.Y.: Cornell Univ. Press, 1985), 18–26; Gabriele Schwab, *Subjects Without Selves: Transitional Texts in Modern Fiction* (Cambridge: Harvard Univ. Press, 1994), 1–48. Jardine and Schwab are talking about texts, about literary selves, and this also is my focus; for a thorough (Foucauldian) argument on the *political* construction of gender (and of such concepts as a feminine semiotic, for instance), see Judith Butler, *Gender Trouble: Feminism and the Subversion of Identity* (New York: Routledge, 1990), 79–149.

12. Rita Felski, *Beyond Feminist Aesthetics: Feminist Literature and Social*

Change (Cambridge: Harvard Univ. Press, 1989), 63–64; Christine Brooke-Rose, "The Dissolution of Character in the Novel," in *Reconstructing Individualism: Autonomy, Individuality, and the Self in Western Thought*, ed. Thomas C. Heller et al. (Stanford: Stanford Univ. Press, 1986), 193; Marianne DeKoven, "Male Signature, Female Aesthetic: The Gender Politics of Experimental Writing," in Friedman and Fuchs, *Breaking the Sequence*, 76. Molly Hite's articulation of the problem is similar: "[It] would seem that in the contemporary period, fictional experimentation has everything to do with feminism and nothing to do with women—and emphatically nothing to do with women as points of origin, as authors." See *The Other Side of the Story: Structures and Strategies of Contemporary Feminist Narrative* (Ithaca, N.Y.: Cornell Univ. Press, 1989), 17.

13. Rachel Blau DuPlessis, *Writing Beyond the Ending: Narrative Strategies of Twentieth-Century Women Writers* (Bloomington: Indiana Univ. Press, 1985), 84–85.

14. Patricia S. Yaeger, " 'Because a Fire Was in My Head': Eudora Welty and the Dialogic Imagination," *PMLA* 99 (Oct. 1984): 955–73; Dale M. Bauer, *Feminist Dialogics: A Theory of Failed Community* (Albany: State Univ. of New York Press, 1988), 1–15.

15. Anne Herrmann, *The Dialogic and Difference: "An/Other Woman" in Virginia Woolf and Christa Wolf* (New York: Columbia Univ. Press, 1989), 6–7, 146–47; Beth Carole Rosenberg, *Virginia Woolf and Samuel Johnson: Common Readers* (New York: St. Martin's Press, 1995), 1–68 (Rosenberg's fine study of the essays and selected novels appeared while my book was in press); Peter Hitchcock, *Dialogics of the Oppressed* (Minneapolis: Univ. of Minnesota Press, 1993), 9–12, 61–62.

16. Margaret Homans, *Bearing the Word: Language and Female Experience in Nineteenth-Century Women's Writing* (Chicago: Univ. of Chicago Press, 1986), 8, 11, 13.

17. Virginia Woolf, *A Room of One's Own* (New York: Harcourt Brace Jovanovich, 1957), 79, 101 (hereafter cited parenthetically in the text).

18. Homans, *Bearing the Word*, 33.

19. Edwin Ardener defines the concept of a "muted" culture existing in a "wild" substructure of the dominant society; see "Belief and the Problem of Woman," 1–17, and "The 'Problem' Revisited," 19–27, in Shirley Ardener. Elaine Showalter argues that such a wilderness is the site of women's writing and feminist criticism; see "Feminist Criticism in the Wilderness," in Showalter, *New Feminist Criticism*, 261–65.

20. Carol Gilligan, *In a Different Voice* (Cambridge: Harvard Univ. Press, 1982), 29–31, 62–63, 104–5.

21. Patricia Meyer Spacks, *Gossip* (New York: Knopf, 1985), 5–9, 43–46. For Bernard's "little language," see Virginia Woolf, *The Waves* (New York: Harcourt Brace Jovanovich, Harvest Books, 1978), 295 (hereafter cited parenthetically in the text).

22. Kathy E. Ferguson, *The Feminist Case Against Bureaucracy* (Philadelphia: Temple Univ. Press, 1984), 186–89. Homans speculates that her own distinctions between a literal feminine language and a more figurative masculine one may someday not be pertinent—if childrearing, for instance, ceases to be exclusively the mother's province; see *Bearing the Word*, 29.

23. Lillian Robinson, "Who's Afraid of a Room of One's Own?" in Robinson, *Sex*, 144–46.

24. Mikhail Bakhtin, *Problems of Dostoevsky's Poetics*, ed. and trans. Caryl Emerson (Minneapolis: Univ. of Minnesota Press, 1984), 127, 164–67, 182–83.

25. For Foucault's discussion of the Greek "self-mastery" paradigm, see *The History of Sexuality*, vol. 2, *The Use of Pleasure*, trans. Robert Hurley (New York: Random House, Vintage Books, 1986), 63–93. For his argument that modern people perceive sexual identity as the substance of the self, see *The History of Sexuality*, vol. 1, *An Introduction*, trans. Robert Hurley (New York: Random House, Vintage Books, 1980), 20–21, 112–20, 155–56.

In his analysis of the written documents about a society's notion of the self (or its ethic of the self's behavior and structure), Foucault employs a four-part strategy or instrument that resembles Aristotle's four-part system for defining something. Foucault's first category is "substance" or "subject matter." He then asks why the individual accepts a given self-structure (the "mode of subjection"). Third, he looks at the means (discipline, practice) by which the person seeks to fit the society's expectation regarding the self. The fourth question or category is teleological: What does the person finally hope for by becoming a certain kind of self? See *The Use of Pleasure*, 35–37, and the interview of Foucault, "On the Genealogy of Ethics: An Overview of Work in Progress," in *Michel Foucault: Beyond Structuralism and Hermeneutics*, ed. Hubert L. Dreyfus and Paul Rainbow (Chicago: Univ. of Chicago Press, 1983), 237–44. In my discussion, I am collapsing Foucault's second and fourth categories into one, a category that I call the *rationale* for accepting a given self-structure. His third category I will call the *means, discipline,* or *practice*, using Foucault's words.

26. Virginia Woolf, *Three Guineas* (New York: Harcourt, Brace and World, Harbinger, 1963), 115–16 (hereafter cited parenthetically in the text).

27. Marianne DeKoven, *Rich and Strange: Gender, History, Modernism* (Princeton, N.J.: Princeton Univ. Press, 1991), 21–25.

28. Teresa DeLauretis, *Technologies of Gender: Essays on Theory, Film, and Fiction* (Bloomington: Indiana Univ. Press, 1987), 16; Marianne Hirsch, *The Mother/Daughter Plot: Narrative, Psychoanalysis, Feminism* (Bloomington: Indiana Univ. Press, 1989), 194.

29. William J. Goode, *World Revolution and Family Patterns* (New York: Macmillan, Free Press, 1963), 380.

30. Jeremy Hawthorn, "Individuality and Characterization in the Mod-

ernist Novel," in *The Uses of Fiction*, ed. Douglas Jefferson and Graham Martin. (Stony Stratford, Milton Keynes: Open Univ. Press, 1982), 54.

31. Sondra Farganis, *The Social Reconstruction of the Feminine Character* (Totowa, N.J.: Rowman and Littlefield, 1986), 6–7.

32. Grace Baruch, Rosalind Barnett, and Caryl Rivers, *Lifeprints: New Patterns of Love and Work for Today's Women* (New York: McGraw-Hill, 1983), 5, 210–12; Starr Roxanne Hilz, "Widowhood: A Roleless Role," in *Single Life: Unmarried Adults in Social Context*, ed. Peter J. Stein (New York: St. Martin's Press, 1981), 79–97.

33. Muriel Spark, *The Prime of Miss Jean Brodie* (New York: New American Library, Plume, 1984), 17.

34. Peter L. Berger and Thomas Luckmann, *The Social Construction of Reality* (Garden City, N.Y.: Doubleday, Anchor Books, 1967), 168–73.

35. Elizabeth A. Meese, *Crossing the Double-Cross: The Practice of Feminist Criticism* (Chapel Hill: Univ. of North Carolina Press, 1986), 12, 147; Elizabeth Janeway, "Women and the Uses of Power," in Eisenstein and Jardine, 330.

36. Christine van Boheemen, *The Novel as Family Romance: Language, Gender, and Authority from Fielding to Joyce* (Ithaca, N.Y.: Cornell Univ. Press, 1987), 32.

37. For discussion of the sexual ideology of the early feminists and activists, see Sheila Jeffreys, *The Spinster and Her Enemies: Feminism and Sexuality, 1880–1930* (London: Pandora Press, 1985), 27–85. The vocational conversion of a feminine ideology from the home to the workplace is detailed by Martha Vicinus, *Independent Women: Work and Community for Single Women, 1850–1920* (Chicago: Univ. of Chicago Press, 1985), 15–16, 37–42.

38. Ashis Nandy, *The Intimate Enemy: Loss and Recovery of Self under Colonialism* (Delhi: Oxford Univ. Press, 1983), pp. xiii–xiv, 12.

39. Jean-François Lyotard, *The Postmodern Condition*, trans. Geoff Bennington and Brian Massumi (Minneapolis: Univ. of Minnesota Press, 1984), xxiv, 34, 60.

40. Lillian Robinson and Lise Vogel, "Modernism and History," 43, and Lillian Robinson, "Working/Women/Writing," 223–53, in Robinson, *Sex*; Gayatri Spivak, "Three Women's Texts and a Critique of Imperialism," *Critical Inquiry* 12 (fall 1985): 244–49.

41. Trilling, "The Poet as Hero: Keats in His Letters," in *The Opposing Self*, 3–49.

42. Jessica Benjamin, "The Bonds of Love: Rational Violence and Erotic Domination," in Eisenstein and Jardine, 46–47.

43. Hans Walter Wolff discerns in very early Hebrew scriptures a gradual detachment of the individual person from the group (particularly during the period of the Hebrew exile when communal religious observance was

difficult); see *Anthropology of the Old Testament*, trans. Margaret Kohl (Philadelphia: Fortress Press, 1974), 220–22. Joseph Campbell perceives in Greek mythic and cultic stories a "shift of loyalty from the impersonal to the personal," and he notes that women and slaves were not recipients of this new sense of a personal, individual destiny available to men; see *The Masks of God: Occidental Mythology* (New York: Viking Press, 1964), 236. For a broad discussion of the philosophical sources, ancient and modern, of the concept of "inwardness," see Charles Taylor, *Sources of the Self: The Making of the Modern Identity* (Cambridge: Harvard Univ. Press, 1989), 111–207.

44. Linda Georgianna, *The Solitary Self: Individuality in the* Ancrene Wisse. (Cambridge: Harvard Univ. Press, 1981), 1–7, 140–41. For a focus on the religious sources of modern individualism, see also Daniel Shanahan, *Toward a Genealogy of Individualism* (Amherst: Univ. of Massachusetts Press, 1992), 23–95.

45. See Kenneth Slack, *The British Churches Today* (London: SCM Press, 1970), 45–46.

46. David Martin, *A Sociology of English Religion* (New York: Basic Books, 1967), 84.

47. C. B. MacPherson, *The Political Theory of Possessive Individualism: Hobbes to Locke*. Oxford: Clarendon Press, 1962), 3–56, 139–266.

48. Elizabeth Fox-Genovese, "Placing Women's History in History," *New Left Review* 133 (May–June 1982): 5–29. In her book, Fox-Genovese attacks what she sees as individualism in Western culture and in feminist theory itself. See *Feminism Without Illusions: A Critique of Individualism* (Chapel Hill: Univ. of North Carolina Press, 1991).

49. Martin Green, *The English Novel in the Twentieth Century* [*The Doom of Empire*] (London: Routledge, 1984), xv, 2–57.

50. Forster, "The Challenge of Our Time," in *Two Cheers for Democracy*, 56–57.

51. Edward Engelbert, *Elegiac Fictions: The Motif of the Unlived Life* (University Park: Pennsylvania State Univ. Press, 1989), 1–22, 250; Charles I. Glicksberg, *The Self in Modern Literature* (University Park: Pennsylvania State Univ. Press, 1963), 1–91.

52. Nancy Armstrong, *Desire and Domestic Fiction: A Political History of the Novel* (Oxford: Oxford Univ. Press, 1987), 3–27, 253–54. See also Ian Watt, *The Rise of the Novel: Studies in Defoe, Richardson and Fielding* (Berkeley: Univ. of California Press, 1962), 95–96.

53. John Stuart Mill, *Autobiography and Other Writings*, ed. Jack Stillinger (Boston: Houghton Mifflin, 1969), 86.

54. Matthew Arnold, *Culture and Anarchy*, ed. J. Dover Wilson (Cambridge: Cambridge Univ. Press, 1966), 145–64.

55. Patricia Waugh, *Feminine Fictions: Revisiting the Postmodern* (London: Routledge, 1989), 10, 12–14, 85–86. Perhaps an experimental self, a

narrated experimental character, should consistently be called a "subject." Waugh (along with other critics) uses the two terms interchangeably, and I will continue to employ both words also, appositionally, though each has a distinct heritage. *Subject* (from Lacan and the marxists) implies the linguistic and political construction and even subjection of consciousness, while *self*—its critics protest—is still trailing clouds of glory, implying agency, unity, something transcendent and real. For Jacques Derrida's critique of the notion of self and consciousness as "presence," see "Differance," in *Speech and Phenomena and Other Essays on Husserl's Theory of Signs*, trans. David B. Allison (Evanston: Northwestern Univ. Press, 1973), 145–47. In their introduction to *The Book of the Self*, editors Polly Young-Eisendrath and James A. Hall emphasize and try to classify the variety of discourses about subjectivity that scholars and physicians employ in their research on the self; see *The Book of the Self*, (New York: New York Univ. Press, 1987), 1–9.

2. Virginia Woolf: Feminizing the Symbolic

1. *The Letters of Virginia Woolf*, ed. Nigel Nicolson and Joanne Trautmann (New York: Harcourt Brace Jovanovich, 1975–80), 6:379 (hereafter cited parenthetically in the text).

2. Joan Lidoff, "Virginia Woolf's Feminine Sentence: The Mother-Daughter World of *To the Lighthouse*," *Literature and Psychology* 32 (1986): 43–59; Patricia Ondek Laurence, *The Reading of Silence: Virginia Woolf in the English Tradition* (Stanford: Stanford Univ. Press, 1991), 1–12, 89–213; Minow-Pinkney, *Virginia Woolf and the Problem of the Subject*, 17–23, 187–94; Ellen Rosenman, *The Invisible Presence: Virginia Woolf and the Mother-Daughter Relationship* (Baton Rouge: Louisiana State Univ. Press, 1986), 134–68. Bonnie Kime Scott notes images of waves and seeds (linked to Ceres) as indicating Woolf's outsider fluidity impinging on rigid structure; see "The Word Split Its Husk: Woolf's Double Vision of Modernist Language," *Modern Fiction Studies* 34 (autumn 1988): 371–85.

3. Gillian Beer, *Arguing with the Past: Essays in Narrative from Woolf to Sidney* (London: Routledge, 1989), 138–82; Richard Pearce, *The Politics of Narration: James Joyce, William Faulkner, and Virginia Woolf* (New Brunswick, N.J.: Rutgers Univ. Press, 1991), 7–9, 164–66; Herrmann, *The Dialogic and Difference*, 1–6, 45, 148–50; M. Keith Booker, *Techniques of Subversion in Modern Literature: Transgression, Abjection, and the Carnivalesque* (Gainesville: Univ. of Florida Press, 1991), 164–75. For an argument that Woolf virtually deconstructs the self, see Ruth Porritt, "Surpassing Derrida's Deconstructed Self: Virginia Woolf's Poetic Disarticulation of the Self," *Women's Studies* 21 (1992): 323–38. On Woolf's development of a dialogic style, see Rosenberg, *Virginia Woolf and Samuel Johnson*, 1–68.

4. Joanne S. Frye, *Living Stories, Telling Lives: Women and the Novel in Contemporary Experience* (Ann Arbor: Univ. of Michigan Press, 1986), 55–56.

5. Virginia Woolf, *The Diary of Virginia Woolf*, ed. Anne Olivier Bell (New York: Harcourt Brace Jovanovich, 1976–1984), 2:285 (hereafter cited as *D* parenthetically in the text).

6. Mark Hussey, *The Singing of the Real World: The Philosophy of Virginia Woolf's Fiction* (Columbus: Ohio State Univ. Press, 1986), 121.

7. Michael Levenson describes Eliot's theory and sees it at work in the "plurality of consciousness" in *The Wasteland*; see *A Genealogy of Modernism* (Cambridge: Cambridge Univ. Press, 1984), 184–93; Avrom Fleishman, "Woolf and McTaggart," in *Fiction and the Ways of Knowing: Essays on British Novels* (Austin: Univ. of Texas Press, 1978), 170–71.

8. Carol Gilligan, "Remapping the Moral Domain: New Images of the Self in Relationship," in *Reconstructing Individualism: Autonomy, Individuality, and the Self in Western Thought*, ed. Thomas C. Heller et al. (Stanford: Stanford Univ. Press, 1986), 248–50.

9. David Cecil, in a selection from a BBC interview, in *Recollections of Virginia Woolf by Her Contemporaries*, ed. Joan Russell Noble (New York: William Morrow, 1972), 125.

10. Bette London affirms that Woolf was indeed preoccupied with the ambition of finding her own voice (for instance, Woolf declaring that she had found her "own voice" with *Jacob's Room* [*D*, 2:186]); London then argues that Woolf's narrative strategies end by undercutting Woolf's ambition and do so by "exploding the very concept of voice." See *The Appropriated Voice: Narrative Authority in Conrad, Forster, and Woolf* (Ann Arbor: Univ. of Michigan Press, 1990), 132–42.

11. George Edward Moore, *Principia Ethica* (Cambridge: Cambridge Univ. Press, 1959), 120, 177–78, 186–200.

12. Moore, *Principia Ethica*, 188.

13. See S. P. Rosenbaum's discussion of the responses of the Bloomsbury members to Moore in "Virginia Woolf and the Intellectual Origins of Bloomsbury," in Ginsberg and Gottlieb, 11–26. For a structuralist reading of Moore as someone who in his earliest drafts, at least, argued that only the concept exists, see Tom Regan, *Bloomsbury's Prophet: G. E. Moore, and the Development of His Moral Philosophy* (Philadelphia: Temple Univ. Press, 1986), 104–9, 192–93.

14. Luce Irigaray, *The Speculum of the Other Woman*, trans. Gillian C. Gill (Ithaca, N.Y.: Cornell Univ. Press, 1985), 133.

15. Virginia Woolf, *Orlando* (New York: Harcourt Brace Jovanovich, 1928), 219–20 (hereafter cited parenthetically in the text).

16. Spacks, *Gossip*, 13–15, 170.

17. Jennifer Coates, "Gossip Revisited: Language in All-Female

Groups," in *Women in Their Speech Communities*, ed. Jennifer Coates and Deborah Cameron (London: Longman, 1988), 113–19.

18. Virginia Woolf, *Mrs. Dalloway* (New York: Harcourt Brace Jovanovich, 1925), 160 (hereafter cited parenthetically in the text).

19. Spacks, *Gossip*, 3–4, 170.

20. Gilligan, *In a Different Voice*, 27–33.

21. James Joyce, *A Portrait of the Artist as a Young Man* (New York: Viking Press, 1956), 240.

22. Waugh, *Feminine Fictions*, 8.

23. Virginia Woolf, *Jacob's Room* (New York: Harcourt Brace Jovanovich, 1960), 94–95 (hereafter cited parenthetically in the text).

24. Louis Althusser describes the social apparatus as "interpellating" (calling or hailing) the subjects, i.e., subjecting the person to the cultural and political structures; see "Ideology and Ideological State Apparatuses," in *Lenin and Philosophy and Other Essays*, trans. Ben Brewster (New York: Monthly Review Press, 1971), 127–86.

25. William R. Handley, "War and the Politics of Narration in *Jacob's Room*," in Hussey, *Woolf and War*, 110–33; Jane Archer, "The Characterization of Gender-Malaise: Gazing Up at the Windows of *Jacob's Room*," in *Gender Studies: New Directions in Feminist Criticism*, ed. Judith Spector (Bowling Green, Ohio: Bowling Green State Univ. Popular Press, 1986), 36–37; Virginia Blain, "Narrative Voice and the Female Perspective in Virginia Woolf's Early Novels," in *Virginia Woolf: New Critical Essays*, ed. Patricia Clements and Isobel Grundy (New York: Barnes and Noble, 1983), 134–35; Rachel Bowlby, *Virginia Woolf: Feminist Destinations* (Oxford: Basil Blackwell, 1988), 103–6; and see *Jacob's Room*, 27–28.

26. Judy Little, "*Jacob's Room* as Comedy: Woolf's Parodic Bildungsroman," in *New Feminist Essays on Virginia Woolf*, ed. Jane Marcus (Lincoln: Univ. of Nebraska Press, 1981), 105–24.

27. Minow-Pinkney, *Virginia Woolf and the Problem of the Subject*, 79.

28. Elizabeth Abel, " 'Cam the Wicked': Woolf's Portrait of the Artist as Her Father's Daughter," in *Virginia Woolf and Bloomsbury*, ed. Jane Marcus (Bloomington: Indiana Univ. Press, 1987), 170–94. For a discussion of semiotic discourse (Mrs. Ramsay and Lily), see Minow-Pinkney, *Virginia Woolf and the Problem of the Subject*, 97–112.

29. Virginia Woolf, *To the Lighthouse* (New York: Harcourt Brace Jovanovich, 1927), 95 (hereafter cited parenthetically in the text).

30. DuPlessis, *Writing Beyond the Ending*, 60–61; Homans, *Bearing the Word*, 284–86.

31. Pamela Caughie, *Virginia Woolf and Postmodernism* (Urbana: Univ. of Illinois Press, 1991), 28–29. Marianne Hirsch also sees Lily's vision as the process of her art and the process itself as satisfying and valuable to Lily; see *The Mother/Daughter Plot*, 113–15.

32. Minow-Pinkney, *Virginia Woolf and the Problem of the Subject*, 183–85, 158; Schwab, *Subjects Without Selves*, 79–92; Patrick McGee, "The Politics of Modernist Form: Or, Who Rules *The Waves*," *Modern Fiction Studies* 38 (autumn 1992): 641–42; Miriam L. Wallace, "Imagining the Body: Gender Trouble and Bodily Limits in *The Waves*," in *Virginia Woolf: Emerging Perspectives, Selected Papers from the Third Annual Conference on Virginia Woolf*, ed. Mark Hussey and Vara Neverow (New York: Pace Univ. Press, 1994), 132–39; Tony E. Jackson, *The Subject of Modernism: Narrative Alterations in the Fiction of Eliot, Conrad, Woolf, and Joyce* (Ann Arbor: Univ. of Michigan Press, 1994), 139–61.

33. Eric Warner, *Virginia Woolf: The Waves* (Cambridge: Cambridge Univ. Press, 1987), 2–3, 40–41; Eileen B. Sypher, "*The Waves*: A Utopia of Androgyny?" in Ginsberg and Gottlieb, 204–10.

34. Roland Barthes, *Writing Degree Zero*, trans. Annette Lavers and Colin Smith (London: Jonathan Cape, 1977), 38.

35. J. W. Graham, "Point of View in *The Waves*: Some Services of the Style," in *Virginia Woolf: A Collection of Criticism*, ed. Thomas S. W. Lewis (New York: McGraw-Hill, 1975), 96.

36. Bakhtin, *Problems of Dostoevsky's Poetics*, 58–59.

37. Randy Malamud, *The Language of Modernism* (Ann Arbor: U.M.I. Research Press, 1989), 152; Waugh, *Feminine Fictions*, 122. M. Keith Booker also emphasizes the "interrelatedness" of Bernard; see "Tradition, Authority, and Subjectivity: Narrative Constitution of the Self in *The Waves*," *LIT* 3 (1991): 46–49.

38. Maria DiBattista, *Virginia Woolf's Major Novels* (New Haven: Yale Univ. Press, 1980), 115–17.

39. For Woolf's reviews of Yeats's poetry and her citations of him, see Elizabeth Steele, *Virginia Woolf's Rediscovered Essays: Sources and Allusions* (New York: Garland, 1987), 45, 134, 150–51, 160.

40. For the listing of *Ideas of Good and Evil*, see *Catalogue of Books from the Library of Leonard and Virginia Woolf* (Brighton, Eng.: Holleyman and Treacher, 1975), section 5 of Victoria Square library, 56; and for the library listing of *The Tower* and *Autobiographies* (1926), see Elizabeth Steele, "An Addendum to Holleyman," in *Virginia Woolf's Literary Sources and Allusions: A Guide to the Essays* (New York: Garland, 1983), 339.

41. William Butler Yeats, "The Tower," line 85; see *The Poems*, ed. Richard J. Finneran (New York: Macmillan, 1983), 196.

42. William Butler Yeats, "The Trembling of the Veil: Book III, Hodos Chameliontos," in *The Autobiography* (New York: Macmillan, Collier Books, 1967), 176, and *Ideas of Good and Evil* (New York: Russell and Russell, 1967), 55.

43. Yeats, *Autobiography*, 182–83.

44. Yeats, *Autobiography*, 174.

45. Booker, "Tradition, Authority, and Subjectivity," 36–38; Jane Mar-

cus, "Britannia Rules *The Waves*," in *Decolonizing Tradition: New Views of Twentieth-Century "British" Literary Canons*, ed. Karen R. Lawrence (Urbana: Univ. of Illinois Press, 1992), 136–62. Kathy J. Phillips discusses Woolf's critique of empire, politics, marriage, and education in all the novels; for her discussion of *The Waves*, see *Virginia Woolf Against Empire* (Knoxville: Univ. of Tennessee Press, 1994), 153–83. Richard Pearce also suggests that Bernard is linked to a Conradian discourse of dominance and colonizing; see *Politics of Narration*, 163. On the contrary, I argue below that Woolf's reading of Conrad's (Marlovian) discourse inscribes it as relational.

46. Beverly Schlack, *Continuing Presences: Virginia Woolf's Use of Literary Allusion* (University Park: Pennsylvania State Univ. Press, 1979), 105–10.

47. Virginia Woolf, *The Waves: The Two Holograph Drafts*, ed. J. W. Graham (Toronto: Univ. of Toronto Press, 1976), 202.

48. Note in Wordsworth's sonnet the parallel words or images: majesty, domes, temples, asleep, and a personification of London as apparently a sleeping woman who wears the "beauty of the morning" like a "garment." See "Composed upon Westminster Bridge, September 3, 1802," in William Wordsworth, *Selected Poems and Prefaces*, ed. Jack Stillinger (Boston: Houghton Mifflin, 1965), 170.

49. Gilbert and Gubar, *War of the Words*, 193–94. Consistent with her very radical reading of *The Waves*, Jane Marcus sees the lady as an image of the ruling-class writer, in fact of "the gentleman artist," Bernard; see "Britannia Rules *The Waves*," 139.

50. Woolf also writes that Marlow "sometimes lets fall a few words of epitaph which remind us . . . of the darkness of the background" ("Joseph Conrad," *CE*, 1:305). Compare Bernard at the beginning of section 7: "And time . . . lets fall its drop" (*Waves*, 184). At the second dinner, Bernard says, "Drop upon drop . . . silence falls," and similar phrases are repeated immediately following, Louis noting that their "separate drops," and civilization itself, are lost "in the darkness" (224–25).

51. Booker, "Tradition, Authority, and Subjectivity," 51; Judith Lee, " 'This Hideous Shaping and Moulding': War and *The Waves*," in Hussey, *Woolf and War*, 196–98. J. W. Graham argues that although Woolf intended a heroic theme of effort and personality, the final draft does not present Bernard (and his death) as heroic; see "Manuscript Revision and the Heroic Theme of *The Waves*," *Twentieth-Century Literature* 29 (fall 1983): 312–32. Judith Wilt reads Bernard's entire "summing up" as a "male modality" and emphasizes that his early consolation of Susan represents their mutual sense of exclusion, so they become spies; see "God's Spies: The Knower in *The Waves*," *Journal of English and Germanic Philology* 92 (Apr. 1993): 198. In contrast, I see this early narrative gesture as identifying Bernard's relational and caring mode.

52. Sandra Kemp, " 'But How Describe the World Seen Without a Self?'

Feminism, Fiction and Modernism," *Critical Quarterly* 32 (spring 1990): 99–118; Patrick McGee, *Telling the Other: The Question of Value in Modern and Postcolonial Writing* (Ithaca, N.Y.: Cornell Univ. Press, 1992), 94–115. Daniel Ferrer, employing Lacan's "Real," argues that the voices in the novel screen a reality (of early trauma) that can, however, be identified in Woolf's own life; see *Virginia Woolf and the Madness of Language*, trans. Geoffrey Bennington and Rachel Bowlby (London: Routledge, 1990), 65–96.

3. Barbara Pym: Textualizing the Trivial

1. Jacques Derrida, *Of Grammatology*, trans. Gayatri Chakravorty Spivak (Baltimore: Johns Hopkins Univ. Press, 1976), 155.

2. Barbara Griffin, "Private Space and Self-Definition in Barbara Pym's *Excellent Women*," *Essays in Literature* 19 (spring 1992): 132–43; Laura L. Doan, "Pym's Singular Interest: The Self as Spinster," in *Old Maids to Radical Spinsters: Unmarried Women in the Twentieth-Century Novel*, ed. Laura L. Doan (Urbana: Univ. of Illinois Press, 1991), 147–51; Orphia Jane Allen, *Barbara Pym: Writing a Life* (Metuchen, N.J.: Scarecrow Press, 1994), xiv–xv.

3. Among several good studies of the transition from the moderns to the (postwar) "contemporaries," see Rubin Rabinovitz, *The Reaction Against Experiment in the English Novel: 1950–1960*, rev. ed. (New York: Columbia Univ. Press, 1967), 3–36. Barbara Everett suggests that Pym's provincial and suburban focus links her not only to Amis and Larkin but to earlier writers such as Leigh Hunt; see "The Pleasures of Poverty," in Rossen, *Independent Women*, 19. Pym's "microscopic detailing" of the social world also places her fiction in the broad tradition of the novel of manners, as Annette Weld asserts; see *Barbara Pym and the Novel of Manners* (New York: St. Martin's Press, 1992), 6–17. Pym's late work, however, can perhaps be read as modernist. Margaret Diane Stetz finds parallels with Woolf; see "*Quartet in Autumn*: New Light on Barbara Pym as Modernist," *Arizona Quarterly* 41 (spring 1985): 24–37.

4. Robert Emmet Long, *Barbara Pym* (New York: Ungar, 1986), 99; Michael Cotsell, *Barbara Pym* (New York: St. Martin's Press, 1989), 33.

5. Barbara Pym, *Jane and Prudence* (New York: Harper & Row, 1981), 21, 217 (hereafter cited as *JP* parenthetically in the text).

6. Edith S. Larson, "The Celebration of the Ordinary in Barbara Pym's Novels," *San Jose Studies* 9 (spring 1983): 17–18; William Greenway, " 'The Trivial Round, the Common Task': Barbara Pym's Working Girls," *Barbara Pym Newsletter* 4 (Mar. 1992): 4–6; Robert J. Graham, "The Narrative

Sense of Barbara Pym," in Salwak, *Life and Work*, 142–47; Allen, *Barbara Pym: Writing a Life*, xvi.

7. Barbara Pym, *Less Than Angels* (New York: Harper & Row, 1982), 23 (hereafter cited as *LTA* parenthetically in the text).

8. See Weld, *Barbara Pym and the Novel of Manners*, 117. Weld is quoting from an unpublished manuscript.

9. For a note on the influence of Woolf on Pym, see Judy Little, "Influential Anxieties: Woolf and Pym," *Virginia Woolf Miscellany*, no. 39 (fall 1992), 5–6. For some modernist parallels, see Stetz, "New Light on Barbara Pym," 24–37.

10. Woolf herself places quotes around *important* and *trivial*. She makes a fuller distinction between the values of the sexes (each trivializing the other's) in "Women and Fiction" (*CE*, 2:146). For Pym's journal entry, see *A Very Private Eye: An Autobiography in Diaries and Letters*, ed. Hazel Holt and Hilary Pym (New York: Dutton, 1984), 159 (hereafter cited as *VPE* parenthetically in the text).

11. Barbara Pym, *Excellent Women* (New York: Harper & Row, 1980), 255 (hereafter cited as *EW* parenthetically in the text). Jane Nardin argues that many of Pym's women, even Marcia Snow, have a fuller life (expressed in observation and imagination) than first appears; see *Barbara Pym* (Boston: Twayne, 1985), 17–19.

12. Barbara Pym, *Quartet in Autumn* (New York: Harper & Row, 1980), 25 (hereafter cited parenthetically in the text).

13. Barbara Pym, *No Fond Return of Love* (New York: Dutton, 1982), 46 (hereafter cited as *NFR* parenthetically in the text).

14. See Penelope Lively, "The World of Barbara Pym," in Salwak, *Life and Work*, 48–49; Robert Liddell, *A Mind at Ease: Barbara Pym and Her Novels* (London: Peter Owen, 1989), 60, 81, 104–5.

15. Nardin, *Barbara Pym*, 24–25, 31–32. Similarly, Mason Cooley finds Pym clear about "logical connections, but comfortably indefinite about motives and meanings." See *The Comic Art of Barbara Pym* (New York: AMS Press, 1990), 275.

16. Long, *Barbara Pym*, 205–6.

17. Spark, *Prime of Miss Jean Brodie*, 186.

18. DuPlessis, *Writing Beyond the Ending*, 1–19, 31–46; Jean E. Kennard, "Barbara Pym and Romantic Love," *Contemporary Literature* 34 (spring 1993): 44–60.

19. Barbara Pym, "An Interview with Barbara Pym," by Iain Finlayson, *Literary Review*, no. 10 (23 Feb. 1980): 3 (hereafter cited parenthetically in the text).

20. Lionel Trilling described the concept or myth of "The Poet as Hero: Keats in His Letters," in *The Opposing Self*, 3–49; also see my discussion in chapter 1 of this study.

21. Barbara Pym, *Some Tame Gazelle* (New York: Dutton, 1983), 68, and *An Academic Question* (New York: New American Library, Plume 1987), 2, 6 (hereafter cited, respectively, as *STG* and *AQ* parenthetically in the text).

22. Logan Pearsall Smith, *Trivia* (London: Constable, 1918), 9. Pym's quotation of Pearsall Smith's second paragraph is exact except for punctuation.

23. Nardin, *Barbara Pym*, 29–30; Janice Rossen, *The World of Barbara Pym* (New York: St. Martin's Press, 1987), 80, 88–90. On Pym's understated Anglicanism, see also Cotsell, *Barbara Pym*, 119; Robert Smith, "Remembering Barbara Pym," in Rossen, *Independent Women*, 161–63; Eleanor B. Wymard, "Barbara Pym on Organized Religion: A Case of Folly," *The Month: A Review of Christian Thought and World Affairs* 248 (Aug./Sept. 1987): 318–20.

24. W. S. F. Pickering, *Anglo-Catholicism: A Study in Religious Ambiguity* (New York: Routledge, 1989), 17–21, 121–31. The distinctive Anglo-Catholic vocabulary is also prominent in Pym's novels. Pickering notes the use of "Mass" and "saying Mass" (instead of receiving "holy communion") and the emergence of a "clergy house" (for celibate clergy) instead of the more usual "vicarage" or "rectory" for the married pastor of the Church of England; see 166–67.

25. W. J. A. M. Beek, *John Keble's Literary and Religious Contribution to the Oxford Movement* (Nijmegen, Neth.: Centrale Druckkery n.v., 1959), 11–22, 124–25, 137–49.

26. Pickering, *Anglo-Catholicism*, 171; for the spread of Marian devotion, see 39 and elsewhere.

27. Pickering describes the importance of the *Church Times* as an organ of Anglo-Catholicism; see *Anglo-Catholicism*, 54. Pym notes in 1977 that the *Church Times* will review her book because she has given the magazine so many "splendid free commercials" (*VPE*, 307). For some of these "commercials," see *JP*, 12; *EW*, 108, 157; *LTA*, 90; *Quartet*, 45.

28. Barbara Pym, *An Unsuitable Attachment* (London: Macmillan, 1982), 128 (hereafter cited parenthetically in the text). Rupert cites lines 37–38 of Keble's hymn for the Annunciation; see Keble, *The Christian Year, Lyra Innocentium, and Other Poems* (London: Oxford Univ. Press, 1914), 161 (hereafter cited parenthetically in the text by line number).

29. Charlotte M. Yonge writes that her novel "is an overgrown book of a nondescript class"; for "those who may deem the story too long, and the characters too numerous, the Author can only beg their pardon for any tedium that they may have undergone before giving it up." See *The Daisy Chain* (1856; reprint, London: Macmillan, 1908), vii–viii (hereafter cited parenthetically in the text). Beek's bibliography lists Yonge's *Musings over the Christian Year and Lyra Innocentium . . .* (Oxford, 1871), 180.

Notes to Pages 94–104

30. Barbara Pym, *Crampton Hodnet* (New York: New American Library, Plume, 1985), 157 (hereafter cited as *CH* parenthetically in the text).
31. Pickering, *Anglo-Catholicism*, 77.
32. Barbara Pym, *A Glass of Blessings* (New York: Dutton, 1989), 148, 226–33 (hereafter cited parenthetically in the text). Robert Smith has observed that there is "no dark night of the soul" in Pym's work; see "How Pleasant to Know Miss Pym," in Salwak, *Life and Work*, 61. Others who have commented on the very noticeable lack of interiorized religious reflection in Pym's novels include Charles Burkhart, *The Pleasure of Miss Pym* (Austin: Univ. of Texas Press, 1987), 106–10; Liddell, *A Mind at Ease*, 75.
33. Vineta Colby discusses Yonge as part of a popular tradition of domestic fiction in the early nineteenth century; see *Yesterday's Woman: Domestic Realism in the English Novel* (Princeton: Princeton Univ. Press, 1974), 185–201.
34. Anne M. Wyatt-Brown, *Barbara Pym: A Critical Biography* (Columbia: Univ. of Missouri Press, 1992), 3–6, 18, 36–39.
35. Foucault, *An Introduction*, 20–21, 112–20, 155–56. Also see my discussion in chapter 1. For Roland Barthes's discussion of mythic speech as the political way of calling something "natural," see *Mythologies*, trans. Annette Lavers (New York: Hill and Wang, 1972), 143.
36. Jeffreys, *The Spinster and Her Enemies*, 93–99, 129–45, 166–96.
37. Although Belinda here is an instance of Mary, Robert J. Graham rightly observes that Pym's spinsters are usually hard-working Marthas; see "Cumbered with Much Serving: Barbara Pym's 'Excellent Women,'" *Mosaic* 17 (spring 1984): 141–60.
38. Nancy Armstrong, *Desire and Domestic Fiction*, 3–27, 253–54. Among those who have given some attention to Pym's use of literature, Lotus Snow offers a detailed identification of the literary allusions; see *One Little Room an Everywhere: Barbara Pym's Novels* (Orono, Maine: Puckerbrush Press, 1987), 31–54. Katherine Anne Ackley argues that literature, in the experience of Pym's characters, gives them greater freedom for the exercise of imagination and compassion; see "But What Does It Lead To?" *Barbara Pym Newsletter* 3 (Dec. 1988): 3–5.
39. Matthew Arnold, "The Study of Poetry," in *The Complete Prose Works of Matthew Arnold*, vol. 9, *English Literature and Irish Politics*, ed. R. H. Super (Ann Arbor: Univ. of Michigan Press, 1973), 161.
40. Beek, *John Keble's Literary and Religious Contribution*, xi; for Beek's discussion of Keble and Wordsworth, see 10–11, 73–86.
41. "Women of Character," anonymous review, *Times Literary Supplement*, 7 July 1950, 417. Briefly quoted by Dale Salwak, *Barbara Pym: A Reference Guide* (Boston: G. K. Hall, 1991), 1.
42. Barbara Pym, *The Sweet Dove Died* (New York: Dutton, 1988), 91 (hereafter cited parenthetically in the text).

43. Robert Long insists that the "rejected woman," the "isolation of women," and "women's loneliness" prevail in *Less Than Angels* and Pym's other novels; see *Barbara Pym*, 102–3, 107.

44. Dierdre's symbolic conception of her room is probably a reflection of Pym's reading of Woolf's *A Room of One's Own*; in 1943, she calls it "delightful and profound" (*VPE*, 159).

45. See *The Book of Common Prayer* (New York: Thomas Nelson and Sons, 1935), 466. Contrast Catherine's prayer book version with: "slow to anger, and plenteous in mercy" ([KJV] Ps. 103:8b).

46. For Pym's statement (from an unpublished manuscript), see Weld, *Barbara Pym and the Novel of Manners*, 93.

47. I disagree with critics who see in Catherine's decision to write about herself and Tom a change from her romantic fiction to a more realistic and authentic mode. See, for instance, Weld, *Barbara Pym and the Novel of Manners*, 129; Barbara Brothers, "Women Victimized by Fiction: Living and Loving in the Novels of Barbara Pym," in *Twentieth-Century Women Novelists*, ed. Thomas F. Staley (Totowa, N.J.: Barnes & Noble, 1982), 69. As I argue here, Catherine's style has always been subtle, avoiding a closed form and meaning.

48. Barbara Pym, *A Few Green Leaves* (New York: Harper & Row, 1981), 37 (hereafter cited parenthetically in the text).

49. Cotsell, *Barbara Pym*, 122–23.

50. Diana Benet discusses in detail the conflict between Luke's Good Samaritan ethic and the sterile world of the welfare state along with the prevailing "catchphrases" of privacy and independence; see *Something to Love: Barbara Pym's Novels* (Columbia: Univ. of Missouri Press, 1986), 134–45, 160.

51. Barbara Pym, "Finding a Voice," in *Civil to Strangers and Other Writings*, ed. Hazel Holt (New York: New American Library, 1989), 385–86.

4. Christine Brooke-Rose: S(t)imulating Origins

1. The novels preceding *Out* are: *The Languages of Love* (1957), *The Sycamore Tree* (1959), *The Dear Deceit* (1961), and *The Middlemen: A Satire* (1961). For a brief description of these novels, see Richard Martin, " 'Just Words on a Page': The Novels of Christine Brooke-Rose," *Review of Contemporary Fiction* 9 (fall 1989): 110–14.

2. Christine Brooke-Rose, "A Conversation with Christine Brooke-Rose," interview by Ellen G. Friedman and Miriam Fuchs, *Review of Contemporary Fiction* 9 (fall 1989): 84 (hereafter cited parenthetically in the text).

3. Christine Brooke-Rose, *Between*, in *The Christine Brooke-Rose Omnibus* (Manchester, Eng.: Carcanet Press, 1986), 424, 426; similarly, 462

(hereafter cited parenthetically in the text). For Perry's request that Mira continue with his story, see Brooke-Rose, *Verbivore* (Manchester, Eng.: Carcanet Press, 1990), 188 (hereafter cited parenthetically in the text).

4. Sarah Birch, *Christine Brooke-Rose and Contemporary Fiction* (Oxford: Clarendon Press, 1994), 3–16, 46–54.

5. Brooke-Rose says her "big influences" are Pound and Beckett; see "An Interview with Christine Brooke-Rose," by David Hayman and Keith Cohen, *Contemporary Literature* 17 (winter 1976): 10 (hereafter cited parenthetically in the text).

6. Christine Brooke-Rose, "Illicitations," *Review of Contemporary Fiction* 9 (fall 1989): 108 (hereafter cited parenthetically in the text). For a detailed discussion of Brooke-Rose in relation to Jean Baudrillard's analysis of the simulations in a media-dominated world, see Birch, *Christine Brooke-Rose and Contemporary Fiction*, 113–17, 130–34.

7. Christine Brooke-Rose, *Amalgamemnon* (Manchester, Eng.: Carcanet Press, 1984), 52 (hereafter cited parenthetically in the text).

8. Christine Brooke-Rose, *A Structural Analysis of Pound's Usura Canto* (The Hague: Mouton, 1976), 9.

9. Brooke-Rose quotes and paraphrases *The Postmodern Condition* in "Whatever Happened to Narratology?" in *Stories*, 18. Also see chapter 1 of the present study for a discussion of Lyotard.

10. Lyotard, *Postmodern Condition*, xxv; on the gap between humanistic and technological studies, see 41, 48–49; also 95 n. 133, 98 n. 170.

11. Lyotard, *Postmodern Condition*, 53.

12. Lyotard, *Postmodern Condition*, 60–67.

13. Christine Brooke-Rose, *Xorandor* (Manchester, Eng.: Carcanet Press, 1986), 190 (hereafter cited parenthetically in the text).

14. Christine Brooke-Rose, *A Rhetoric of the Unreal* (Cambridge: Cambridge Univ. Press, 1981), 387 (hereafter cited parenthetically in the text). Brooke-Rose examines several terms for experimental fiction, including "metafiction" and "surfiction"; see "Metafiction and Surfiction: A Simpler Formal Approach," in *Rhetoric*, 364–89. I will continue to use the term "experimental" in the sense in which she uses it (in the interview quoted above) as textual discovery that also means a new way of seeing.

15. Roland Barthes argues that the quest for the father is central to narrative "pleasure," but he implies that the radically disruptive textual *jouissance* would violate this pattern; see *The Pleasure of the Text*, trans. Richard Miller (New York: Hill and Wang, 1975), 10–14, 47, 53.

16. Other critics have perceived the psychoanalytic quest myth as the key to *The Dead Father*, but Brooke-Rose takes issue with such a reading; see "Metafiction and Surfiction," in *Rhetoric*, 377–78.

17. Brooke-Rose offers an in-depth Lacanian analysis of *The Turn of the Screw*; see *Rhetoric*, 47, 158–87.

18. Verena Andermatt-Conley's remarks occur in her overview of state-

ments by writers on writing; see her headnote, *New Literary History* 9 (autumn 1977): 186.

19. Fredric Jameson, foreword to *The Postmodern Condition* by Jean-François Lyotard, trans. Geoff Bennington and Brian Massumi (Minneapolis: Univ. of Minnesota Press, 1984) xii.

20. Brooke-Rose also observes that the presence of her knowledge and intelligence in her fiction is often criticized as a flaw, although she has not seen knowledge criticized as an impediment in the work of male authors; see "Palimpest History," in *Stories*, 188.

21. Sandra Lipsitz Bem, "Gender Schema Theory and Its Implication for Child Development: Raising Gender-Aschematic Children in a Gender-Schematic Society," *Signs* 8 (summer 1983): 598–616. Virginia Woolf suggests that the androgynous mind may be one that "is resonant and porous" (aschematic?) or perhaps it is "man-womanly" ("schematic"?) like Shakespeare's; see *Room*, 102.

22. Christine Brooke-Rose, "Self-Confrontation and the Writer," *New Literary History* 9 (autumn 1977): 132. The Pygmalion myth (as an image of presumptuous, manipulative male creativity) is evidently a favorite for Brooke-Rose; in *The Dear Deceit*, Laura wonders at the "Pygmalion's pleasure" her husband must have enjoyed, converting her to Roman Catholicism, which he didn't really believe himself; see *The Dear Deceit* (Garden City, N.Y.: Doubleday, 1961), 125–26. The Pygmalion/pygmylion pun and myth is also prominent in *Amalgamemnon*.

23. Linda Hutcheon describes the so-called experimentalist's favoring of storytelling (that is, use of a diegetic mode), as an emphasis on "process mimesis" rather than on the "product," the goal of conventional realism. See *Narcissistic Narrative: The Metafictional Paradox* (Waterloo, Ont.: Wilfrid Laurier Univ. Press, 1980), 1–6.

24. Richard Martin, " 'Just Words on a Page,' " 115.

25. Christine Brooke-Rose, *Out*, in *The Christine Brooke-Rose Omnibus*, 19, 20 (hereafter cited parenthetically in the text).

26. Shirley Toulson, "Christine Brooke-Rose," in *Contemporary Novelists*, 4th ed., ed. D. L. Kirkpatrick (London: St. James Press, 1986), 141.

27. Christine Brooke-Rose, *Such*, in *The Christine Brooke-Rose Omnibus*, 303; for the refrain of Jonah imagery, see 205, 271, 290, 313, 371, 344 (hereafter cited parenthetically in the text).

28. The word or concept is one of the refrains; see *Between*, 449, 517, 544–45, 548, 549, and elsewhere.

29. Karen R. Lawrence, " 'Floating on a Pinpoint': Travel and Place in Brooke-Rose's *Between*," in Friedman and Martin, 87–91.

30. Hanjo Berressem, "*Thru* the Looking Glass: A Journey into the Universe of Discourse," *Review of Contemporary Fiction* 9 (fall 1989): 131. For the typographically slanted mirror, see Christine Brooke-Rose, *Thru*,

in *The Christine Brooke-Rose Omnibus*, 610 (hereafter cited parenthetically in the text).

31. For an extensive discussion of Brooke-Rose's witty explorations of theories of Lacan, Griemas, and Derrida along with the implicit feminist critique (of narrative theory), a critique deriving from references to Irigaray and Kristeva, see Birch, *Christine Brooke-Rose and Contemporary Fiction*, 89–102.

32. On the final page of *Thru* (742), "TEXT" and "EXIT" intersect and the *I* becomes merely parenthetical. Independently of my reading, Damian Grant has also called attention to *The Dunciad*, citing the last two lines (4.655–56) and noting especially similar moments of "cultural crisis" in Shakespeare, Kafka, and others; see "The Emperor's New Clothes: Narrative Anxiety in *Thru*," in Friedman and Martin, 119, 127–28. For "loit'ring into prose" and the "uncreating word," see *The Dunciad*, 1.274 and 4.654. I slightly alter John Dryden's "music shall untune the sky"; see the last line of "A Song for St. Cecilia's Day, 1687."

33. Samuel Beckett, *Malone Dies* (New York: Grove Press, 1970), 1.

34. Richard Martin, "'Stepping-Stones into the Dark': Redundancy and Generation in Christine Brooke-Rose's *Amalgamemnon*," in Friedman and Fuchs, *Breaking the Sequence*, 177–87.

35. Roland Barthes argues that the narrative past (preterit) is an image of order (something has happened) that the reader expects; use of the future tense suggests that nothing has happened and so breaks the implied agreement between reader and author; see *Writing Degree Zero*, 38. Gerard Genette also analyzes the strategies and effects of tense or voice, including the use of future tense; see *Narrative Discourse*, trans. Jane E. Lewin (Ithaca, N.Y.: Cornell Univ. Press, 1980), 212–27.

36. Irigaray, *Speculum of the Other Woman*, 124. Hélène Cixous and Catherine Clement, *The Newly Born Woman*, trans. Betsy Wing (Minneapolis: Univ. of Minnesota Press, 1986), 154–57.

37. Lincoln Konkle, "'Histrionic' vs. 'Hysterical': Deconstructing Gender as Genre in *Xorandor* and *Verbivore*," in Friedman and Martin, 179–82.

38. Christine Brooke-Rose, *Textermination* (Manchester, Eng.: Carcanet Press, 1991), 9, 8 (hereafter cited parenthetically in the text). For a discussion of reader theorists (Ingarden, Iser, and others) as conceptual sources of *Textermination*, see Birch, *Christine Brooke-Rose and Contemporary Fiction*, 135–44.

5. Conclusion: The Implied Critic

1. John McGowan, *Postmodernism and Its Critics* (Ithaca, N.Y.: Cornell Univ. Press, 1991), x, 1–15. Gerald Graff uses Verena Conley's phrase,

"monolithic criticism"; see Graff, *Literature Against Itself: Literary Ideas in Modern Society* (Chicago: Univ. of Chicago Press, 1979), 80–82.

2. Jane Flax, "Postmodernism and Gender Relations in Feminist Theory," *Signs* 12 (1987): 641. Michael Levenson examines with a more general focus the tensions between individualism and a more communal norm; see *Modernism and the Fate of Individuality: Character and Novelistic Form from Conrad to Woolf* (Cambridge: Cambridge Univ. Press, 1991), xi–xiii, 78–89. From a clinical viewpoint, a "unitary" self is not the rigid ego that postmodernists imply, and a firm identity is necessary for health, James M. Glass argues; truly "shattered selves" suffer from childhood trauma and are very different from "selves deconstructed in texts." See *Shattered Selves: Multiple Personality in a Postmodern World* (Ithaca, N.Y.: Cornell Univ. Press, 1993), 1–23.

3. Frank Moore Cross, for instance, points out that "El Saddai," a Hebrew designation for (a masculine) God, indicated not only a "Mountain One," but in its linguistic roots suggested "breast" as well (a female mountain god); see *Canaanite Myth and Hebrew Epic* (Cambridge: Harvard Univ. Press, 1973), 55–56. Annotated Bibles will indicate the link (or dialogic appropriation?) between Christ as "the image of the invisible God, the first-born of all creation" (Col. 1:15) and the very similar language of a hymn to the earlier (feminine) "Sophia" figure of Wisdom 7:26. For a discussion of the linguistic and cultural changes in the Wisdom tradition, see Susan Cady, Marian Ronan, and Hal Taussig, *Sophia: The Future of Feminist Spirituality* (New York: Harper & Row, 1986). Among classicists, Joan V. O'Brien argues that the Hera of the *Iliad* is a much-diminished figure, although a close study of language and imagery suggests that Hera was once a powerful goddess of the seasons; see *The Transformation of Hera: A Study of Ritual, Hero, and the Goddess in the* Iliad (Lanham, Md: Rowman & Littlefield, 1993).

4. Rachel Blau DuPlessis, "For the Etruscans," in Showalter, *New Feminist Criticism*, 288.

5. Edward W. Said, *The World, the Text, and the Critic* (Cambridge: Harvard Univ. Press, 1983), 175, 152–53.

6. Margaret Drabble, *The Realms of Gold* (New York: Knopf, 1975), 308.

7. Anita Brookner, *Hotel du lac* (New York: Pantheon Books, 1984), 27, 75–76, 170–83.

Works Cited

Virginia Woolf

Collected Essays. 4 vols. London: Hogarth Press, 1966–67.
The Diary of Virginia Woolf. Edited by Anne Olivier Bell. 5 vols. New York: Harcourt Brace Jovanovich, 1976–84.
Jacob's Room. New York: Harcourt Brace Jovanovich, 1960.
The Letters of Virginia Woolf. Edited by Nigel Nicolson and Joanne Trautmann. 6 vols. New York: Harcourt Brace Jovanovich, 1975–80.
Mrs. Dalloway. New York: Harcourt Brace Jovanovich, 1925.
Orlando. New York: Harcourt Brace Jovanovich, 1928.
A Room of One's Own. New York: Harcourt Brace Jovanovich, 1957.
Three Guineas. New York: Harcourt, Brace and World, Harbinger, 1963.
To the Lighthouse. New York: Harcourt Brace Jovanovich, 1927.
The Waves. New York: Harcourt Brace Jovanovich, Harvest Books, 1978.
The Waves: The Two Holograph Drafts. Edited by J. W. Graham. Toronto: Univ. of Toronto Press, 1976.

Barbara Pym

An Academic Question. New York: New American Library, Plume, 1987.
Crampton Hodnet. New York: New American Library, Plume, 1985.
Excellent Women. New York: Harper & Row, 1980.
A Few Green Leaves. New York: Harper & Row, 1981.
"Finding a Voice." In *Civil to Strangers and Other Writings,* edited by Hazel Holt, 381–88. New York: New American Library, 1989.
A Glass of Blessings. New York: Dutton, 1988.
"An Interview with Barbara Pym." By Iain Finlayson. *Literary Review,* no. 10 (23 Feb. 1980): 2–5.
Jane and Prudence. New York: Harper & Row, 1981.
Less Than Angels. New York: Harper & Row, 1982.
No Fond Return of Love. New York: Dutton, 1982.
Quartet in Autumn. New York: Harper & Row, 1980.

Some Tame Gazelle. New York: Dutton, 1983.
The Sweet Dove Died. New York: Dutton, 1988.
An Unsuitable Attachment. London: Macmillan, 1982.
A Very Private Eye: An Autobiography in Diaries and Letters. Edited by Hazel Holt and Hilary Pym. New York: Dutton, 1984.

Christine Brooke-Rose

Amalgamemnon. Manchester, Eng.: Carcanet Press, 1984.
The Christine Brooke-Rose Omnibus: Four Novels: Out, Such, Between, Thru. Manchester, Eng.: Carcanet Press, 1986.
"A Conversation with Christine Brooke-Rose." Interview by Ellen G. Friedman and Miriam Fuchs. *Review of Contemporary Fiction* 9 (fall 1989): 81–90.
The Dear Deceit. Garden City, N.Y.: Doubleday, 1961.
"The Dissolution of Character in the Novel." In *Reconstructing Individualism: Autonomy, Individuality, and the Self in Western Thought,* edited by Thomas C. Heller et al., 184–96. Stanford: Stanford Univ. Press, 1986.
"Illicitations." *Review of Contemporary Fiction* 9 (fall 1989): 101–9.
"An Interview with Christine Brooke-Rose." By David Hayman and Keith Cohen. *Contemporary Literature* 17 (winter 1976): 1–23.
A Rhetoric of the Unreal. Cambridge: Cambridge Univ. Press, 1981.
"Self-Confrontation and the Writer." *New Literary History* 9 (autumn 1977): 129–36.
Stories, Theories and Things. Cambridge: Cambridge Univ. Press, 1991.
A Structural Analysis of Pound's Usura Canto. The Hague: Mouton, 1976.
Textermination. Manchester, Eng.: Carcanet Press, 1991.
Verbivore. Manchester, Eng.: Carcanet Press, 1990.
Xorandor. Manchester, Eng.: Carcanet Press, 1986.

Other Writers

Beckett, Samuel. *Malone Dies.* New York: Grove Press, 1970.
Brookner, Anita. *Hotel du lac.* New York: Pantheon Books, 1984.
Drabble, Margaret. *The Realms of Gold.* New York: Knopf, 1975.
Forster, E. M. *Two Cheers for Democracy.* New York: Harcourt, Brace and World, 1951.
Joyce, James. *A Portrait of the Artist as a Young Man.* New York: Viking Press, 1956.
Keble, John. *The Christian Year, Lyra Innocentium, and Other Poems.* London: Oxford Univ. Press, 1914.
Lawrence, D. H. *The Letters of D. H. Lawrence.* 7 vols. Edited by George

J. Zytaruk and James T. Boulton. Cambridge: Cambridge Univ. Press, 1981–93.
Mill, John Stuart. *Autobiography and Other Writings*. Edited by Jack Stillinger. Boston: Houghton Mifflin, 1969.
Pearsall Smith, Logan. *Trivia*. London: Constable, 1918.
Spark, Muriel. *The Prime of Miss Jean Brodie*. New York: New American Library, Plume, 1984.
Wordsworth, William. *Selected Poems and Prefaces*. Edited by Jack Stillinger. Boston: Houghton Mifflin, 1965.
Yeats, William Butler. *The Autobiography*. New York: Macmillan, Collier Books, 1967.
———. *Ideas of Good and Evil*. New York: Russell and Russell, 1967.
———. *The Poems*. Edited by Richard J. Finneran. New York: Macmillan, 1983.
Yonge, Charlotte M. *The Daisy Chain*. 1856. Reprint, London: Macmillan, 1908.

Theory and Criticism

Abel, Elizabeth. " 'Cam the Wicked': Woolf's Portrait of the Artist as Her Father's Daughter." In *Virginia Woolf and Bloomsbury*, edited by Jane Marcus, 170–94. Bloomington: Indiana Univ. Press, 1987.
Ackley, Katherine Anne. "But What Does it Lead To?" *Barbara Pym Newsletter* 3 (Dec. 1988): 3–5.
Allen, Orphia Jane. *Barbara Pym: Writing a Life*. Metuchen, N.J.: Scarecrow Press, 1994.
Althusser, Louis. "Ideology and Ideological State Apparatuses." In *Lenin and Philosophy and Other Essays*, translated by Ben Brewster, 127–86. New York: Monthly Review Press, 1971.
Andermatt-Conley, Verena. Headnote. *New Literary History* 9 (autumn 1977): 186.
Archer, Jane. "The Characterization of Gender-Malaise: Gazing Up at the Windows of *Jacob's Room*." In *Gender Studies: New Directions in Feminist Criticism*, edited by Judith Spector, 30–42. Bowling Green, Ohio: Bowling Green State Univ. Popular Press, 1986.
Ardener, Edwin. "Belief and the Problem of Woman." In Shirley Ardener, 1–17.
———. "The 'Problem' Revisited." In Shirley Ardener, 19–27.
Ardener, Shirley, ed. *Perceiving Women*. London: J. M. Dent and Sons, 1977.
Armstrong, Nancy. *Desire and Domestic Fiction: A Political History of the Novel*. Oxford: Oxford Univ. Press, 1987.

Arnold, Matthew. *Culture and Anarchy*. Edited by J. Dover Wilson. Cambridge: Cambridge Univ. Press, 1966.
———. "The Study of Poetry." In *The Complete Prose Works of Matthew Arnold*, Vol. 9, *English Literature and Irish Politics*, edited by R. H. Super, 161–88. Ann Arbor: Univ. of Michigan Press, 1973.
Bakhtin, Mikhail. *The Dialogic Imagination*. Edited by Michael Holquist. Translated by Caryl Emerson and Michael Holquist. Austin: Univ. of Texas Press, 1981.
———. *Problems of Dostoevsky's Poetics*. Edited and translated by Caryl Emerson. Minneapolis: Univ. of Minnesota Press, 1984.
Barthes, Roland. *Mythologies*. Translated by Annette Lavers. New York: Hill and Wang, 1972.
———. *The Pleasure of the Text*. Translated by Richard Miller. New York: Hill and Wang, 1975.
———. *Writing Degree Zero*. Translated by Annette Lavers and Colin Smith. London: Jonathan Cape, 1977.
Baruch, Grace, Rosalind Barnett, and Caryl Rivers. *Lifeprints: New Patterns of Love and Work for Today's Women*. New York: McGraw-Hill, 1983.
Bauer, Dale M. *Feminist Dialogics: A Theory of Failed Community*. Albany: State Univ. of New York Press, 1988.
Beek, W. J. A. M. *John Keble's Literary and Religious Contribution to the Oxford Movement*. Nijmegen, Neth.: Centrale Druckkery n.v., 1959.
Beer, Gillian. *Arguing with the Past: Essays in Narrative from Woolf to Sidney*. London: Routledge, 1989.
Bem, Sandra Lipsitz. "Gender Schema Theory and Its Implications for Child-Development: Raising Gender-Aschematic Children in a Gender-Schematic Society." *Signs* 8 (summer 1983): 598–616.
Benet, Diana. *Something to Love: Barbara Pym's Novels*. Columbia: Univ. of Missouri Press, 1986.
Benjamin, Jessica. "The Bonds of Love: Rational Violence and Erotic Domination." In Eisenstein and Jardine, 41–70.
Berger, Peter, and Thomas Luckmann. *The Social Construction of Reality*. Garden City, N.Y.: Doubleday, Anchor Books, 1967.
Berressem, Hanjo. "*Thru* the Looking Glass: A Journey into the Universe of Discourse." *Review of Contemporary Fiction* 9 (fall 1989): 130–33.
Birch, Sarah. *Christine Brooke-Rose and Contemporary Fiction*. Oxford: Clarendon Press, 1994.
Blain, Virginia. "Narrative Voice and the Female Perspective in Virginia Woolf's Early Novels." In *Virginia Woolf: New Critical Essays*, edited by Patricia Clements and Isobel Grundy, 115–36. New York: Barnes and Noble, 1983.
Bloom, Harold. *The Anxiety of Influence*. New York: Oxford Univ. Press, 1973.
Boheemen, Christine van. *The Novel as Family Romance: Language, Gen-*

der, and Authority from Fielding to Joyce. Ithaca, N.Y.: Cornell Univ. Press, 1987.

Booker, M. Keith. *Techniques of Subversion in Modern Literature: Transgression, Abjection, and the Carnivalesque*. Gainesville: Univ. of Florida Press, 1991.

———. "Tradition, Authority, and Subjectivity: Narrative Constitution of the Self in *The Waves*." *LIT* 3 (1991): 33–55.

The Book of Common Prayer. New York: Thomas Nelson and Sons, 1935.

Bowlby, Rachel. *Virginia Woolf: Feminist Destinations*. Oxford: Basil Blackwell, 1988.

Brothers, Barbara. "Women Victimized by Fiction: Living and Loving in the Novels of Barbara Pym." In *Twentieth-Century Women Novelists*, edited by Thomas F. Staley, 61–80. Totowa, N.J.: Barnes & Noble, 1982.

Burkhart, Charles. *The Pleasure of Miss Pym*. Austin: Univ. of Texas Press, 1987.

Butler, Judith. *Gender Trouble: Feminism and the Subversion of Identity*. New York: Routledge, 1990.

Cady, Susan, Marian Ronan, and Hal Taussig. *Sophia: The Future of Feminist Spirituality*. New York: Harper & Row, 1986.

Campbell, Joseph. *The Masks of God: Occidental Mythology*. New York: Viking Press, 1964.

Catalogue of Books from the Library of Leonard and Virginia Woolf. Brighton, Eng.: Holleyman and Treacher, 1975.

Caughie, Pamela. *Virgina Woolf and Postmodernism*. Urbana: Univ. of Illinois Press, 1991.

Cecil, David. BBC interview. In *Recollections of Virginia Woolf by Her Contemporaries*, edited by Jane Russell Noble, 123–26. New York: William Morrow, 1972.

Chodorow, Nancy. "Gender, Relation, and Difference in Psychoanalytic Perspective." In Eisenstein and Jardine, 3–19.

———. *The Reproduction of Mothering: Psychoanalysis and the Sociology of Gender*. Berkeley: Univ. of California Press, 1978.

Cixous, Hélène. "The Laugh of the Medusa." Translated by Keith Cohen and Paula Cohen. *Signs* 1 (summer 1976): 875–93.

Cixous, Hélène, and Catherine Clement. *The Newly Born Woman*. Translated by Betsy Wing. Minneapolis: Univ. of Minnesota Press, 1986.

Coates, Jennifer. "Gossip Revisited: Language in All-Female Groups." In *Women in Their Speech Communities*, edited by Jennifer Coates and Deborah Cameron, 94–122. London: Longman, 1988.

Colby, Vineta. *Yesterday's Woman: Domestic Realism in the English Novel*. Princeton: Princeton Univ. Press, 1974.

Cooley, Mason. *The Comic Art of Barbara Pym*. New York: AMS Press, 1990.

Cotsell, Michael. *Barbara Pym*. New York: St. Martin's Press, 1989.

Cross, Frank Moore. *Canaanite Myth and Hebrew Epic.* Cambridge: Harvard Univ. Press, 1973.
DeKoven, Marianne. "Male Signature, Female Aesthetic: The Gender Politics of Experimental Writing." In Friedman and Fuchs, *Breaking the Sequence,* 72–81.
———. *Rich and Strange: Gender, History, Modernism.* Princeton, N.J.: Princeton Univ. Press, 1991.
DeLauretis, Teresa. *Technologies of Gender: Essays on Theory, Film, and Fiction.* Bloomington: Indiana Univ. Press, 1987.
Derrida, Jacques. "Differance." In *Speech and Phenomena and Other Essays on Husserl's Theory of Signs,* translated by David B. Allison, 129–60. Evanston: Northwestern Univ. Press, 1973.
———. *Of Grammatology.* Translated by Gayatri Chakravorty Spivak. Baltimore: Johns Hopkins Univ. Press, 1976.
DiBattista, Maria. *Virginia Woolf's Major Novels.* New Haven: Yale Univ. Press, 1980.
Doan, Laura L. "Pym's Singular Interest: The Self as Spinster." In *Old Maids to Radical Spinsters: Unmarried Women in the Twentieth-Century Novel,* edited by Laura L. Doan, 139–54. Urbana: Univ. of Illinois Press, 1991.
DuPlessis, Rachel Blau. "For the Etruscans." In Showalter, *New Feminist Criticism,* 271–91.
———. *Writing Beyond the Ending: Narrative Strategies of Twentieth-Century Women Writers.* Bloomington: Indiana Univ. Press, 1985.
Eisenstein, Hester, and Alice Jardine, eds. *The Future of Difference.* Boston: G. K. Hall, 1980.
Emerson, Caryl. "The Outer Word and Inner Speech: Bakhtin, Vygotsky, and the Internalization of Language." In *Bakhtin: Essays and Dialogues on His Work,* edited by Gary Morson, 21–40. Chicago: Univ. of Chicago Press, 1986.
Engelbert, Edward. *Elegiac Fictions: The Motif of the Unlived Life.* University Park: Pennsylvania State Univ. Press, 1989.
Everett, Barbara. "The Pleasures of Poverty." In Rossen, *Independent Women,* 9–20.
Farganis, Sondra. *The Social Reconstruction of the Feminine Character.* Totowa, N.J.: Rowman and Littlefield, 1986.
Felski, Rita. *Beyond Feminist Aesthetics: Feminist Literature and Social Change.* Cambridge: Harvard Univ. Press, 1989.
Ferguson, Kathy E. *The Feminist Case Against Bureaucracy.* Philadelphia: Temple Univ. Press, 1984.
Ferrer, Daniel. *Virginia Woolf and the Madness of Language.* Translated by Geoffrey Bennington and Rachel Bowlby. New York: Routledge, 1990.
Flax, Jane. "Postmodernism and Gender Relations in Feminist Theory." *Signs* 12 (1987): 621–43.

Fleishman, Avrom. "Woolf and McTaggart." In *Fiction and the Ways of Knowing: Essays on British Novels*, 163–78. Austin: Univ. of Texas Press, 1978.

Foucault, Michel. "On the Genealogy of Ethics: An Overview of Work in Progress." Interview by Hubert L. Dreyfus and Paul Rainbow. In *Michel Foucault: Beyond Structuralism and Hermeneutics*, edited by Hubert L. Dreyfus and Paul Rainbow, 229–52. Chicago: Univ. of Chicago Press, 1983.

———. *The History of Sexuality.* Vol. 1, *An Introduction.* Translated by Robert Hurley. New York: Random House, Vintage Books, 1980.

———. *The History of Sexuality.* Vol. 2, *The Use of Pleasure.* Translated by Robert Hurley. New York: Random House, Vintage Books, 1986.

Fox-Genovese, Elizabeth. *Feminism Without Illusions: A Critique of Individualism.* Chapel Hill: Univ. of North Carolina Press, 1991.

———. "Placing Women's History in History." *New Left Review* 133 (May/June 1982): 5–29.

Friedman, Ellen G., and Miriam Fuchs, "Context and Continuities: An Introduction to Women's Experimental Fiction in English." In Friedman and Fuchs, *Breaking the Sequence*, 3–51.

Friedman, Ellen G., and Miriam Fuchs, eds. *Breaking the Sequence: Women's Experimental Fiction.* Princeton, N.J.: Princeton Univ. Press, 1989.

Friedman, Ellen G., and Richard Martin, eds. *Utterly Other Discourse: The Texts of Christine Brooke-Rose.* Normal, Ill.: Dalkey Archive Press, 1995.

Friedman, Susan. "Lyric Subversion of Narrative in Women's Writing: Virginia Woolf and the Tyranny of Plot." In *Reading Narrative*, edited by James Phelan, 162–85. Columbus: Ohio State Univ. Press, 1989.

Frye, Joanne S. *Living Stories, Telling Lives: Women and the Novel in Contemporary Experience.* Ann Arbor: Univ. of Michigan Press, 1986.

Genette, Gerard. *Narrative Discourse.* Translated by Jane E. Lewin. Ithaca, N.Y.: Cornell Univ. Press, 1980.

Georgianna, Linda. *The Solitary Self: Individuality in the* Ancrene Wisse. Cambridge: Harvard Univ. Press, 1981.

Gilbert, Sandra, and Susan Gubar. *No Man's Land.* Vol. 1, *The War of the Words.* New Haven: Yale Univ. Press, 1988.

Gilligan, Carol. *In a Different Voice.* Cambridge: Harvard Univ. Press, 1982.

———. "Remapping the Moral Domain: New Images of Self in Relationship." In *Reconstructing Individualism: Autonomy, Individuality, and the Self in Western Thought*, edited by Thomas C. Heller et al., 237–52. Stanford: Stanford Univ. Press, 1986.

Ginsberg, Elaine, and Laura Gottlieb, eds. *Virginia Woolf: Centennial Essays.* Troy, N.Y.: Whitson, 1983.

Glass, James M. *Shattered Selves: Multiple Personality in a Postmodern World.* Ithaca, N.Y.: Cornell Univ. Press, 1993.

Glicksberg, Charles I. *The Self in Modern Literature*. University Park: Pennsylvania State Univ. Press, 1963.
Goode, William J. *World Revolution and Family Patterns*. New York: Macmillan, Free Press, 1963.
Graff, Gerald. *Literature Against Itself: Literary Ideas in Modern Society*. Chicago: Univ. of Chicago Press, 1979.
Graham, J. W. "Manuscript Revision and the Heroic Theme of *The Waves*." *Twentieth-Century Literature* 29 (fall 1983): 312–32.
———. "Point of View in *The Waves*: Some Services of the Style." In *Virginia Woolf: A Collection of Criticism*, edited by Thomas S. W. Lewis, 94–112. New York: McGraw-Hill, 1975.
Graham, Robert J. "Cumbered with Much Serving: Barbara Pym's 'Excellent Women.'" *Mosaic* 17 (spring): 141–60.
———. "The Narrative Sense of Barbara Pym." In Salwak, *Life and Work*, 142–55.
Grant, Damian. "The Emperor's New Clothes: Narrative Anxiety in *Thru*." In Friedman and Martin, 117–29.
Green, Martin. *The English Novel in the Twentieth Century [The Doom of Empire]*. London: Routledge, 1984.
Greenway, William. "'The Trivial Round, the Common Task': Barbara Pym's Working Girls." *Barbara Pym Newsletter* 4 (Mar. 1992): 4–6.
Griffin, Barbara. "Private Space and Self-Definition in Barbara Pym's *Excellent Women*." *Essays in Literature* 19 (spring 1992): 132–43.
Handley, William R. "War and the Politics of Narration in *Jacob's Room*." In Hussey, *Woolf and War*, 110–33.
Hawthorn, Jeremy. "Individuality and Characterization in the Modernist Novel." In *The Uses of Fiction*, edited by Douglas Jefferson and Graham Martin, 41–58. Stony Stratford, Milton Keynes: Open Univ. Press, 1982.
Herrmann, Anne. *The Dialogic and Difference: "An/Other Woman" in Virginia Woolf and Christa Wolf*. New York: Columbia Univ. Press, 1989.
Hilz, Starr Roxanne. "Widowhood: A Roleless Role." In *Single Life: Unmarried Adults in Social Context*, edited by Peter J. Stein, 79–97. New York: St. Martin's Press, 1981.
Hirsch, Marianne. *The Mother/Daughter Plot: Narrative, Psychoanalysis, Feminism*. Bloomington: Indiana Univ. Press, 1989.
Hitchcock, Peter. *Dialogics of the Oppressed*. Minneapolis: Univ. of Minnesota Press, 1993.
Hite, Molly. *The Other Side of the Story: Structures and Strategies of Contemporary Feminist Narrative*. Ithaca, N.Y.: Cornell Univ. Press, 1989.
Homans, Margaret. *Bearing the Word: Language and Female Experience in Nineteenth-Century Women's Writing*. Chicago: Univ. of Chicago Press, 1986.
Hussey, Mark. *The Singing of the Real World: The Philosophy of Virginia Woolf's Fiction*. Columbus: Ohio State Univ. Press, 1986.

Hussey, Mark, ed., *Virginia Woolf and War: Fiction, Reality, and Myth.* Syracuse, N.Y.: Syracuse Univ. Press, 1991.
Hutcheon, Linda. *Narcissistic Narrative: The Metafictional Paradox.* Waterloo, Ont.: Wilfrid Laurier Univ. Press, 1980.
Irigaray, Luce. *The Speculum of the Other Woman.* Translated by Gillian C. Gill. Ithaca, N.Y.: Cornell Univ. Press, 1985.
———. *This Sex Which Is Not One.* Translated by Catherine Porter and Carolyn Burke. Ithaca, N.Y.: Cornell University Press, 1985.
Jackson, Tony E. *The Subject of Modernism: Narrative Alterations in the Fiction of Eliot, Conrad, Woolf, and Joyce.* Ann Arbor: Univ. of Michigan Press, 1994.
Jameson, Fredric. Foreword to *The Postmodern Condition*, by Jean-François Lyotard, translated by Geoff Bennington and Brian Massumi, vii–xxi. Minneapolis: Univ. of Minnesota Press, 1984.
———. "Postmodernism: The Cultural Logic of Late Capitalism." *New Left Review* 146 (July/Aug. 1984): 53–92.
Janeway, Elizabeth. "Women and the Uses of Power." In Eisenstein and Jardine, 327–44.
Jardine, Alice. *Gynesis: Configurations of Woman and Modernity.* Ithaca, N.Y.: Cornell Univ. Press, 1985.
Jeffreys, Sheila. *The Spinster and Her Enemies: Feminism and Sexuality, 1880–1930.* London: Pandora Press, 1985.
Kemp, Sandra. "'But How Describe the World Seen Without a Self?' Feminism, Fiction and Modernism." *Critical Quarterly* 32 (spring 1990): 99–118.
Kennard, Jean E. "Barbara Pym and Romantic Love." *Contemporary Literature* 34 (spring 1993): 44–60.
Konkle, Lincoln. "'Histrionic' vs. 'Hysterical': Deconstructing Gender as Genre in *Xorandor* and *Verbivore*." In Friedman and Martin, 176–91.
Kristeva, Julia. "From One Identity to Another." In *Desire in Language*, edited by Leon S. Roudiez, translated by Thomas Gora, Alice Jardine, and Leon S. Roudiez. New York: Columbia Univ. Press, 1980.
Lacan, Jacques. "The Subversion of the Subject and the Dialectic of Desire in the Freudian Unconscious." In *Écrits: A Selection*, translated by Alan Sheridan, 292–325. New York: Norton, 1977.
Larson, Edith S. "The Celebration of the Ordinary in Barbara Pym's Novels." *San Jose Studies* 9 (spring 1983): 17–22.
Laurence, Patricia Ondek. *The Reading of Silence: Virginia Woolf in the English Tradition.* Stanford: Stanford Univ. Press, 1991.
Lawrence, Karen R. "'Floating on a Pinpoint': Travel and Place in Brooke-Rose's *Between*." In Friedman and Martin, 76–96.
Lee, Judith. "'This Hideous Shaping and Moulding': War and *The Waves*." In Hussey, *Woolf and War*, 180–202.

Levenson, Michael. *A Genealogy of Modernism.* Cambridge: Cambridge Univ. Press, 1984.

———. *Modernism and the Fate of Individuality: Character and Novelistic Form from Conrad to Woolf.* Cambridge: Cambridge Univ. Press, 1991.

Liddell, Robert. *A Mind at Ease: Barbara Pym and Her Novels.* London: Peter Owen, 1989.

Lidoff, Joan. "Virginia Woolf's Feminine Sentence: The Mother-Daughter World of *To the Lighthouse*." *Literature and Psychology* 32 (1986): 43–59.

Little, Judy. "Influential Anxieties: Woolf and Pym." *Virginia Woolf Miscellany*, no. 39 (fall 1992): 5–6.

———. "*Jacob's Room* as Comedy: Woolf's Parodic Bildungsroman." In *New Feminist Essays on Virginia Woolf*, edited by Jane Marcus, 105–24. Lincoln: Univ. of Nebraska Press, 1981.

Lively, Penelope. "The World of Barbara Pym." In Salwak, *Life and Work*, 45–49.

Loeffelholz, Mary. *Experimental Lives: Women and Literature, 1900–1945.* New York: Twayne, 1992.

London, Bette. *The Appropriated Voice: Narrative Authority in Conrad, Forster, and Woolf.* Ann Arbor: Univ. of Michigan Press, 1990.

Long, Robert Emmet. *Barbara Pym.* New York: Ungar, 1986.

Lyotard, Jean-François. *The Postmodern Condition.* Translated by Geoff Bennington and Brian Massumi. Minneapolis: Univ. of Minnesota Press, 1984.

MacPherson, C. B. *The Political Theory of Possessive Individualism: Hobbes to Locke.* Oxford: Clarendon Press, 1962.

Malamud, Randy. *The Language of Modernism.* Ann Arbor: U.M.I. Research Press, 1989.

Marcus, Jane. "Britannia Rules *The Waves*." In *Decolonizing Tradition: New Views of Twentieth-Century "British" Literary Canons*, edited by Karen R. Lawrence, 136–62. Urbana: Univ. of Illinois Press, 1992.

———. *Virginia Woolf and the Languages of Patriarchy.* Bloomington: Indiana Univ. Press, 1987.

Martin, David. *A Sociology of English Religion.* New York: Basic Books, 1967.

Martin, Richard. " 'Just Words on a Page': The Novels of Christine Brooke-Rose." *Review of Contemporary Fiction* 9 (fall 1989): 110–23.

———. " 'Stepping-Stones into the Dark': Redundancy and Generation in Christine Brooke-Rose's *Amalgamemnon*." In Friedman and Fuchs, *Breaking the Sequence*, 177–87.

McGee, Patrick. "The Politics of Modernist Form: Or, Who Rules *The Waves*." *Modern Fiction Studies* 38 (autumn 1992): 631–50.

———. *Telling the Other: The Question of Value in Modern and Postcolonial Writing.* Ithaca, N.Y.: Cornell Univ. Press, 1992.

———. "Woolf's Other: The University in Her Eye." *Novel* 23 (spring 1990): 229–46.
McGowan, John. *Postmodernism and Its Critics*. Ithaca, N.Y.: Cornell Univ. Press, 1991.
Meese, Elizabeth A. *Crossing the Double-Cross: The Practice of Feminist Criticism*. Chapel Hill: Univ. of North Carolina Press, 1986.
Minow-Pinkney, Makiko. *Virginia Woolf and the Problem of the Subject*. New Brunswick, N.J.: Rutgers Univ. Press, 1987.
Moore, George Edward. *Principia Ethica*. Cambridge: Cambridge Univ. Press, 1959.
Nandy, Ashis. *The Intimate Enemy: Loss and Recovery of Self under Colonialism*. Delhi: Oxford Univ. Press, 1983.
Nardin, Jane. *Barbara Pym*. Boston: Twayne, 1985.
O'Brien, Joan V. *The Transformation of Hera: A Study of Ritual, Hero, and the Goddess in the* Iliad. Lanham, Md.: Rowman & Littlefield, 1993.
Pearce, Richard. *The Politics of Narration: James Joyce, William Faulkner, and Virginia Woolf*. New Brunswick, N.J.: Rutgers Univ. Press, 1991.
Pecora, Vincent. *Self and Form in Modern Narrative*. Baltimore: Johns Hopkins Univ. Press, 1989.
Phillips, Kathy J. *Virginia Woolf Against Empire*. Knoxville: Univ. of Tennessee Press, 1994.
Pickering, W. S. F. *Anglo-Catholicism: A Study in Religious Ambiguity*. New York: Routledge, 1989.
Porritt, Ruth. "Surpassing Derrida's Deconstructed Self: Virginia Woolf's Poetic Disarticulation of the Self." *Women's Studies* 21 (1992): 323–38.
Rabinovitz, Rubin. *The Reaction Against Experiment in the English Novel: 1950–1960*. Rev. ed. New York: Columbia Univ. Press, 1967.
Regan, Tom. *Bloomsbury's Prophet: G. E. Moore and the Development of His Moral Philosophy*. Philadelphia: Temple Univ. Press, 1986.
Robinson, Lillian. *Sex, Class and Culture*. Bloomington: Indiana Univ. Press, 1978.
———. "Who's Afraid of a Room of One's Own?" in Robinson, *Sex*, 97–149.
———. "Working/Women/Writing." In Robinson, *Sex*, 223–53.
Robinson, Lillian, and Lise Vogel. "Modernism and History." In Robinson, *Sex*, 22–46.
Rosenbaum, S. P. "Virginia Woolf and the Intellectual Origins of Bloomsbury." In Ginsberg and Gottlieb, 11–26.
Rosenberg, Beth Carole. *Virginia Woolf and Samuel Johnson: Common Readers*. New York: St. Martin's Press, 1995.
Rosenman, Ellen. *The Invisible Presence: Virginia Woolf and the Mother-Daughter Relationship*. Baton Rouge: Louisiana State Univ. Press, 1986.

Rossen, Janice. *The World of Barbara Pym*. New York: St. Martin's Press, 1987.
Rossen, Janice, ed. *Independent Women: The Function of Gender in the Novels of Barbara Pym*. Sussex, Eng.: Harvester Press, 1988.
Said, Edward W. *The World, the Text, and the Critic*. Cambridge: Harvard Univ. Press, 1983.
Salwak, Dale. *Barbara Pym: A Reference Guide*. Boston: G. K. Hall, 1991.
Salwak, Dale, ed. *The Life and Work of Barbara Pym*. Iowa City: Univ. of Iowa Press, 1987.
Schlack, Beverly. *Continuing Presences: Virginia Woolf's Use of Literary Allusion*. University Park: Pennsylvania State Univ. Press, 1979.
Schwab, Gabriele. *Subjects Without Selves: Transitional Texts in Modern Fiction*. Cambridge: Harvard Univ. Press, 1994.
Scott, Bonnie Kime. "The Word Split Its Husk: Woolf's Double Vision of Modernist Language." *Modern Fiction Studies* 34 (autumn 1988): 371–85.
Shanahan, Daniel. *Toward a Genealogy of Individualism*. Amherst: Univ. of Massachusetts Press, 1992.
Showalter, Elaine. "Feminist Criticism in the Wilderness." In Showalter, *New Feminist Criticism*, 243–70.
Showalter, Elaine, ed. *New Feminist Criticism*. New York: Pantheon Books, 1985.
Slack, Kenneth. *The British Churches Today*. London: SCM Press, 1970.
Smith, Robert. "How Pleasant to Know Miss Pym." In Salwak, *Life and Work*, 58–63.
———. "Remembering Barbara Pym." In Rossen, *Independent Women*, 159–63.
Snow, Lotus. *One Little Room an Everywhere: Barbara Pym's Novels*. Orono, Maine: Puckerbrush Press, 1987.
Spacks, Patricia Meyer. *Gossip*. New York: Knopf, 1985.
Spivak, Gayatri. "Three Women's Texts and a Critique of Imperialism." *Critical Inquiry* 12 (fall 1985): 244–49.
Steele, Elizabeth. "An Addendum to Holleyman." In *Virginia Woolf's Literary Sources and Allusions: A Guide to the Essays*, 281–341. New York: Garland, 1983.
———. *Virginia Woolf's Rediscovered Essays: Sources and Allusions*. New York: Garland, 1987.
Stetz, Margaret Diane. "*Quartet in Autumn*: New Light on Barbara Pym as Modernist." *Arizona Quarterly* 41 (spring 1985): 24–37.
Sypher, Eileen B. "*The Waves*: A Utopia of Androgyny?" In Ginsberg and Gottlieb, 204–10.
Taylor, Charles. *Sources of the Self: The Making of the Modern Identity*. Cambridge: Harvard Univ. Press, 1989.
Toulson, Shirley. "Christine Brooke-Rose." In *Contemporary Novelists*, 4th ed., edited by D. L. Kirkpatrick, 141–42. London: St. James Press, 1986.

Trilling, Lionel. "The Poet as Hero: Keats in His Letters." In *The Opposing Self*, 3–49. New York: Viking Press, 1955.

———. Preface to *The Opposing Self*. New York: Viking Press, 1955.

Vicinus, Martha. *Independent Women: Work and Community for Single Women, 1850–1920*. Chicago: Univ. of Chicago Press, 1985.

Wallace, Miriam L. "Imagining the Body: Gender Trouble and Bodily Limits in *The Waves*." In *Virginia Woolf: Emerging Perspectives, Selected Papers from the Third Annual Conference on Virginia Woolf*, edited by Mark Hussey and Vara Neverow, 132–39. New York: Pace Univ. Press, 1994.

Warner, Eric. *Virginia Woolf: The Waves*. Cambridge: Cambridge Univ. Press, 1987.

Watt, Ian. *The Rise of the Novel: Studies in Defoe, Richardson and Fielding*. Berkeley: Univ. of California Press, 1962.

Waugh, Patricia. *Feminine Fictions: Revisiting the Postmodern*. London: Routledge, 1989.

Weld, Annette. *Barbara Pym and the Novel of Manners*. New York: St. Martin's Press, 1992.

Wilt, Judith. "God's Spies: The Knower in *The Waves*." *Journal of English and Germanic Philology* 92 (Apr. 1993): 179–99.

Wolff, Hans Walter. *Anthropology of the Old Testament*. Translated by Margaret Kohl. Philadelphia: Fortress Press, 1974.

Wyatt-Brown, Anne M. *Barbara Pym: A Critical Biography*. Columbia: Univ. of Missouri Press, 1992.

Wymard, Eleanor B. "Barbara Pym on Organized Religion: A Case of Folly." *The Month: A Review of Christian Thought and World Affairs* 248 (Aug./Sept. 1987): 318–20.

Yaeger, Patricia S. " 'Because a Fire Was in My Head': Eudora Welty and the Dialogic Imagination." *PMLA* 99 (Oct. 1984): 955–73.

Young-Eisendrath, Polly, and James A. Hall, eds. *The Book of the Self*. New York: New York Univ. Press, 1987.

Index

Abel, Elizabeth, 49
Academic Question, An (Pym), 89
Ackley, Katherine Anne, 181n. 38
Allen, Orphia Jane, 77, 79
Althusser, Louis, 40
Amalgamemnon (Brooke-Rose), 123, 124–25, 128, 132–33, 143–52, 155
Andermatt-Conley, Verena, 129
appositional discourse, 2–3, 6–7; as dialogic discourse, 2, 15–16, 20, 23
Archer, Jane, 40
Ardener, Edwin, 8, 84
Armstrong, Nancy, 21, 22
Arnold, Matthew, 21–22, 81, 100

Bakhtin, Mikhail, 2, 10–11, 15, 29, 40, 56–58, 63, 82
Barthes, Roland, 56, 97, 127
Baruch, Grace, 13
Bauer, Dale, 7
Beckett, Samuel, 124, 125, 130, 145
Beek, W. J. A. M., 92, 100
Beer, Gillian, 26
Bem, Sandra, 130
Benet, Diana, 182n. 50
Benjamin, Jessica, 18
Berger, Peter, 14
Berressem, Hanjo, 142
Between (Brooke-Rose), 123, 132, 133, 137–42, 144, 152
Birch, Sarah, 123, 183n. 6, 185n. 31
Blain, Virginia, 40
Bloom, Harold, 3–4
Boheemen, Christine, 14–15
Booker, Keith, 26, 61, 73
Bowlby, Rachel, 40–41
Brooke-Rose, Christine, 1, 2, 5–7, 22, 122–57; and experimental writing, 5–6, 122–23, 130–32. See also names of individual works

Brookner, Anita, 161–62
Brothers, Barbara, 182n. 47
Burkhart, Charles, 181n. 32
Butler, Judith, 168n. 11

Cady, Susan, 186n. 3
Campbell, Joseph, 172n. 43
Caughie, Pamela, 51
Cecil, David, 31
Chodorow, Nancy, 4, 18
Cixous, Hélène, 5, 151
Coates, Jennifer, 35, 41
Colby, Vineta, 181n. 33
Connolly, Cyril, 88–89, 98
Conrad, Joseph, 9, 56, 61, 73; Woolf's remarks on, 30, 71–72
Cooley, Mason, 179n. 15
Cotsell, Michael, 78, 114
Crampton Hodnet (Pym), 93–94
Cross, Frank Moore, 186n. 3

Daisy Chain, The (Yonge), 93, 96–97
Dear Deceit, The (Brooke-Rose), 127
DeKoven, Marianne, 6, 12
DeLauretis, Teresa, 12
Derrida, Jacques, 76, 173n. 55
dialogic discourse, 2–3, 15, 22–24, 82, 117, 120, 158, 162–63; and Brooke-Rose, 122, 132, 135, 140, 144, 146, 157; and Pym, 107–8, 110, 113, 120; and the trivial, 77, 78, 82, 101–2; and Woolf, 25–26, 34–38, 40, 70–75
DiBattista, Maria, 58
difference: Brooke-Rose evaluates, 126–30; and feminist theory, 4–7
Doan, Laura, 77
Dostoevsky, Fyodor: Woolf on, 57–58
Drabble, Margaret, 161–62
DuPlessis, Rachel Blau, 6, 50, 86, 160

Index

Eliot, T. S., 4, 32, 101–2
Emerson, Caryl, 167n. 3
Engelbert, Edward, 20
Everett, Barbara, 178n. 3
Excellent Women (Pym), 81–82, 87, 97
experiment, Woolf's remarks on, 12, 25, 28–29. *See also* self: as experimental
experimental writing: and characterization, 38–39, 54–56, 122–26; as feminine, 5–6; as poetry, 132, 135–36

Farganis, Sondra, 13
Felski, Rita, 6
Ferguson, Kathy, 9
Ferrer, Daniel, 178n. 52
Few Green Leaves, A (Pym), 89, 112–14
Finlayson, Iain, 88–89
Flax, Jane, 159
Fleishman, Avrom, 30
Forster, E. M., 1, 20, 58, 142
Foucault, Michel, 11, 97, 115, 170n. 25
Fox-Genovese, Elizabeth, 19
Freud, Sigmund, 4, 39
Friedman, Ellen, 5
Friedman, Susan, 5
Frye, Joanne S., 27
Fuchs, Miriam, 5

Georgianna, Linda, 18
Gilbert, Sandra, 4, 70
Gilligan, Carol, 8–9, 30, 32, 36, 37, 68, 71
Glass, James M., 186n. 2
Glass of Blessing, A (Pym), 92, 95–96
Glicksberg, Charles, 20
Goode, William, 13
gossip as discourse, 9, 13, 34, 35, 41; in Pym's fiction, 22, 78, 88; in Woolf's fiction, 34–36, 41–43, 55, 58, 69, 71–72, 74
Graff, Gerald, 159
Graham, J. W., 56
Graham, Robert, 79
Grant, Damian, 185n. 32
Green, Martin, 20
Greenway, William, 79
Griffin, Barbara, 77
Gubar, Susan, 4, 70

Hall, James A., 173n. 55
Handley, William, 40

Hawthorn, Jeremy, 13
Herrmann, Anne, 7, 26
Hilz, Starr Roxanne, 13
Hirsch, Marianne, 12, 175n. 31
Hitchcock, Peter, 7
Hite, Molly, 169n. 12
Homans, Margaret, 7–8, 13, 50
Hussey, Mark, 29
Hutcheon, Linda, 184n. 23

individual: as dialogic, 18–20; as experimental, 14, 15; as female, 20–22
individualism, 14, 16, 17–24; Woolf's critique of, 31–34
individuality, Shelley lacking, 66–67, 68
Irigaray, Luce, 5, 34, 151

Jackson, Tony, 54
Jacob's Room (Woolf), 27, 28, 38–47, 54, 80
Jameson, Fredric, 1, 129
Jane and Prudence (Pym), 78, 86–87, 92, 101–3
Janeway, Elizabeth, 171n. 35
Jardine, Alice, 5
Jeffreys, Sheila, 15, 97
Joyce, James, 1, 31, 38, 61, 78

Keats, John, 3, 17
Keble, John, 79, 87, 92–96, 98, 99, 100, 104
Kemp, Sandra, 73
Kennard, Jean, 86
Konkle, Lincoln, 153
Kristeva, Julia, 5

Lacan, Jacques, 4, 5, 7, 38; and Brooke-Rose, 122, 128, 130, 142
Larson, Edith, 79
Laurence, Patricia, 26
Lawrence, D. H., 1
Lawrence, Karen, 138
Lee, Judith, 73
Less Than Angels (Pym), 77, 79, 80, 83, 84, 85–86, 87, 88, 97–98, 100, 105–12
Levenson, Michael, 174n. 7, 186n. 2
Liddell, Robert, 84
Lidoff, Joan, 26
Lively, Penelope, 84
Loeffelholz, Mary, 167n. 3
London, Bette, 31

Index 203

Long, Robert, 78, 85, 182n. 43
Luchmann, Thomas, 14
Lyotard, Jean-François, 16, 30, 83, 125–26

MacPherson, C. B., 19
Malamud, Randy, 58
Marcus, Jane, 61, 177n. 49
Martin, David, 19
Martin, Richard, 133, 145
McGee, Patrick, 54, 73
McGowan, John, 159
Meese, Elizabeth A., 171n. 35
Mill, John Stuart, 21–22
Minow-Pinkney, Makiko, 5, 26, 47–48, 54
Moore, G. E., 32, 33
Mrs. Dalloway (Woolf), 20, 35, 47–49

Nandy, Ashis, 16, 77
Nardin, Jane, 84–85, 91
No Fond Return of Love (Pym), 84, 98–99, 104

O'Brien, Joan V., 186n. 3
Orlando (Woolf), 34–35, 74
Out (Brooke-Rose), 132, 133–36

Pater, Walter, 132
Pearce, Richard, 26
Pearsall Smith, Logan, 79, 80–81, 83, 84, 90
Phillips, Kathy, 61
Pickering, W. S. F., 91–92, 95
Pope, Alexander, 143, 185n. 32
Pound, Ezra, 125, 130
Prime of Miss Jean Brodie, The (Spark), 13, 85
Pym, Barbara, 2, 7, 22–23, 76–121, 117, 161. See also names of individual works

Quartet in Autumn (Pym), 77, 82–83, 84–85, 87–88, 93, 114–21

Rabinovitz, Rubin, 178n. 3
Richardson, Dorothy, 5
Robbe-Grillet, Alain, 134
Robinson, Lillian, 10, 17
Roche, Maurice, 131
Ronan, Marian, 186n. 3
Room of One's Own, A (Woolf), 10, 37, 67, 80, 129–30

Rosenbaum, S. P., 174n. 13
Rosenberg, Beth, 7, 169n. 15, 173n. 3
Rosenman, Ellen, 26
Rossen, Janice, 91

Said, Edward, 161
Sarraute, Natalie, 131
Schlack, Beverly, 66
Schwab, Gabriele, 5, 54
Scott, Bonnie Kime, 173n. 2
self, 1–3; as dialogic, 2–3, 10–12, 15–16; as experimental, 8–10, 13–14, 23–24; Foucault's concept of, 11, 97, 170n. 25; as simulation, 124–26, 145; as synonym for subject and subjectivity, 172–73n. 55; as unsuccessfully socialized, 14–15; Woolf's concept of, 28–32; Yeats's concept of, 58–61. *See also* individual; individualism
Showalter, Elaine, 8, 14, 84
Slack, Kenneth, 172n. 45
Smith, Robert, 180n. 23, 181n. 32
Snow, Lotus, 181n. 38
Sollers, Philippe, 131
Some Tame Gazelle (Pym), 85, 89, 99, 100–101
Spacks, Patricia Meyer, 9, 34–35, 36, 71–72, 88
Spark, Muriel, 13, 78
Spivak, Gayatri, 17–18
Stetz, Margaret Diane, 178n. 3, 179n. 9
subject. *See* self
subjectivity. *See* self
Such (Brooke-Rose), 127, 132, 133, 136–37
Sweet Dove Died, The (Pym), 104–5, 117
Sypher, Eileen, 55

Taussig, Hal, 186n. 3
Taylor, Charles, 172n. 43
Textermination (Brooke-Rose), 152, 155–57
Three Guineas (Woolf), 12, 15, 25
Thru (Brooke-Rose), 128, 131, 132, 142–43
To the Lighthouse (Woolf), 49–53, 85–86
Toulson, Shirley, 136
Trilling, Lionel, 3, 17–18, 179n. 20
Trivia (Pearsall Smith), 80–81, 90–91
trivia, 50, 76, 78, 79, 81, 85, 112, 114,

117, 161; and domesticity, 88–91, 105–7, 117–18; and religious discourse, 91–97, 98–99, 100, 107–9, 115
trivial, 2, 28, 46, 76, 94, 110, 114; as dialogic, 77–78, 79, 82–83, 90–91, 116; as feminine, 76, 80, 84, 88; Woolf's remarks on, 46

Unsuitable Attachment, An (Pym), 93, 96

Verbivore (Brooke-Rose), 123, 124, 128, 131, 152, 153–55
Vicinus, Martha, 15
Vogel, Lise, 171n. 40

Wallace, Miriam, 54
Warner, Eric, 55
Waugh, Patricia, 23, 38, 58

Waves, The (Woolf), 9, 33, 52, 53–75, 114, 123
Welch, Denton, 79
Weld, Annette, 178n. 3, 182n. 47
Wolff, Hans Walter, 171n. 43
Woolf, Virginia, 1, 2, 5, 7, 8, 9, 10, 12, 22, 25–75, 78, 80, 94, 129–30; on experiment, 12, 25, 28–29. *See also names of individual works*
Wyatt-Brown, Anne, 97
Wymard, Eleanor B., 180n. 23

Xorandor (Brooke-Rose), 126, 128, 152–53

Yaeger, Patricia, 7
Yeats, William Butler, 56, 58–61
Yonge, Charlotte, 79, 87, 93, 95, 96–97, 98, 109, 113
Young-Eisendrath, Polly, 173n. 55

Judy Little is a professor of English at Southern Illinois University at Carbondale. Her other publications include *Keats as a Narrative Poet: A Test of Invention* and *Comedy and the Woman Writer: Woolf, Spark, and Feminism*.